IMAGES
of America

CICERO

THE FIRST SUBURB WEST

IMAGES
of America

CICERO
THE FIRST SUBURB WEST

Betty Carlson Kay

ARCADIA
PUBLISHING

ISBN 978-0-7385-0786-6

Published by Arcadia Publishing
Charleston, South Carolina

Printed in the United States of America

Library of Congress Catalog Card Number: 00-107116

For all general information contact Arcadia Publishing at:
Telephone 843-853-2070
Fax 843-853-0044
E-mail sales@arcadiapublishing.com
For customer service and orders:
Toll-Free 1-888-313-2665

Visit us on the Internet at www.arcadiapublishing.com

Contents

ACKNOWLEDGMENTS

Thanks to all who went out of their way to provide information, photos, and support for me during the writing of this book: to the *Cicero Berwyn Life* Newspaper, who generously opened their picture files; to Karl J. Sup of the Eastland Memorial Society; to the Morton East Archives, Judy Vokac, Librarian; to the Cicero Public Library Staff; to the State Historical Library, Mary Michaels, Photo Curator; to John Binder of the Merry Gangsters Literary Society; and to Georgiana Becker of the Cicero Historical Society. Also, thanks go out to the following individuals: Michal Morganti Murphy, John Lulling, Ron Hainrihar, John Rokos, Bob Fuka, Lois Palmer Huth, Kay Erickson, Carol Gore, Lynne Carlson Sheaff, Linda Cowls, Dennis Walden, Joe Mantegna, John Husa, Stan Loula, and Mark Mourlas. The book's completion is due to your help.

INTRODUCTION

In 1957, Cicero celebrated its centennial with a parade and festivities. The celebrations that year honored the meeting held on June 25, 1857, at which the early settlers met and named the town they were forming Cicero, as suggested by Augustus Porter who formerly lived in the town of Cicero, New York. But the history of the area traces itself further back: to the Potowatami Indians; to the 1673 trek through the portage area by Jolliet and Marquette; even back to the glaciers that leveled the land and cut out the rivers and lakes.

Soon after Illinois became a state in 1818, activities were set into motion which opened the old Northwest Territory to astounding growth: the Erie Canal was built in 1825; the National Road opened from Cumberland, Maryland to Vandalia, Illinois; European immigration flooded the country with settlers looking for new opportunities in the west; and the Illinois and Michigan Canal opened in 1848. It looked as if the land just north of the IM canal would make an excellent place to farm, if only the lands were not quite so swampy!

When platted, the township area, later called Cicero, extended from Western Avenue to Harlem, and from North Avenue to Thirty-Ninth Street. (This explains why Western Avenue was so named). The earliest settlers chose to live and farm on the driest land, a ridge covered by oak trees. One settler, Joseph Kettlestrings, arrived in 1831 with his wife and three children, and when he opened a "bar" in a room attached to his house, he called it the Oak Ridge Tavern. James W. Scoville arrived in 1856, just at the time that settlers were clambering for the establishment of a governing body. Mr. Scoville was elected Town Assessor at the first meeting of the new town of Cicero, and Mr. Kettlestrings became the Overseer of the Poor.

Through a series of land annexations in the 19th century, the city of Chicago extended its boundaries to include much of Cicero's township. Then in 1901 a power play led to the split that created the present borders of Cicero, Berwyn, and Oak Park. Cicero, the first suburb west of Chicago, became an industrial hub, especially with the construction of Western Electric in 1903. These Hawthorne Works covered 203 acres of land and included 103 buildings. Needless to say, "The Western" employed thousands of workers who chose to reside in the area.

The town of Cicero filled mostly with hard-working Eastern Europeans, mainly of Slavic ethnicity. They prided themselves on living frugally and saving against the catastrophes they had endured in the old countries. The homes they built, the Savings and Loans they frequented, their bakeries and butcher shops, and the churches which they built and attended (with Masses said in their own languages) all lent an air of stability to this residential area.

But just as they came and brought their own old world customs and traditions to Cicero, now, a hundred years later, the town is filling with new customs and traditions as a largely Hispanic culture has moved in. How these changes have played out make for interesting history in "The First Suburb West."

One

The Portage

Louis Jolliet and Father Marquette breathed the late fall air, sweetened by wild asters, black-eyed Susans, and goldenrod. The Native Americans described their abundance by saying that three crops of grain could be harvested each year. The explorers appreciated such abundance, though they probably didn't appreciate the changes that huge glaciers had wrought millions of years before, leveling the land and digging out rivers and building up moraines. Now the men were just anxious to return home to Canada. To speed them on their way, the Indians took them on a shortcut through a muddy area between two rivers, shouldering the canoes for a few miles and doing battle with mosquitoes.

Jolliet watched with explorer's eyes as many miles were cut off the journey back to Lake Michigan. He studied the terrain carefully and wondered if a channel could be dug between the two rivers to join them. Jolliet could see increased trade developing as merchandise floated easily through the Great Lakes, down the Mississippi River, and into the Gulf of Mexico.

But Jolliet never returned to Illinois. His canoe overturned, his aides drowned, and his extensive notes and maps were all lost almost within sight of Montreal. As he recreated his notes from memory, he stressed the beautiful land of the Illinois valley and the possibilities at the Portage. Years later, the Illinois and Michigan Canal completed the dream of this far-sighted explorer and, as the state of Illinois opened to the world, the southern boundary of Cicero was formed.

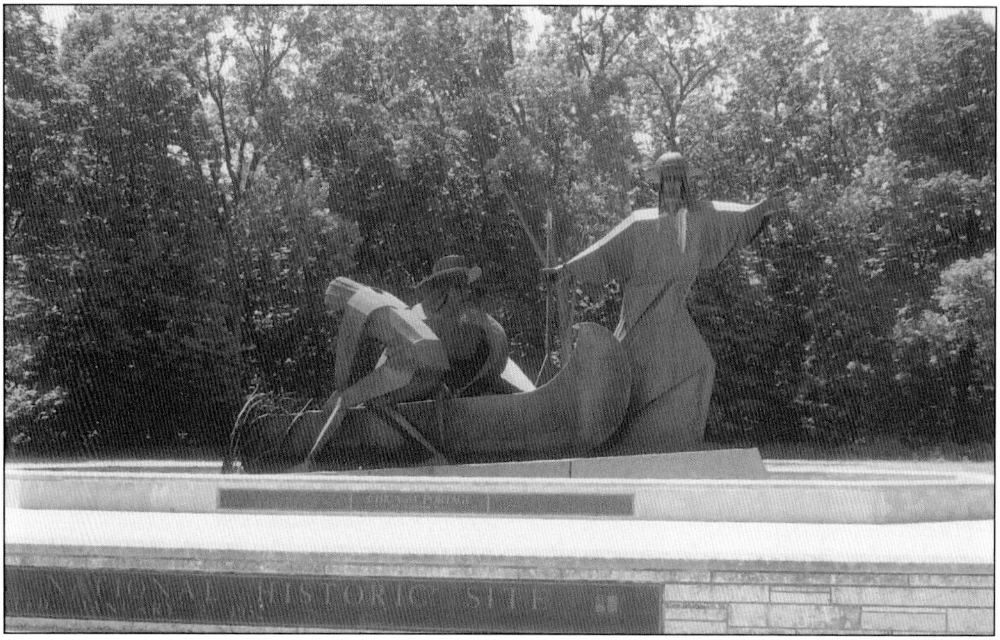

THE CHICAGO PORTAGE NATIONAL HISTORIC SITE. Designated on January 3, 1952, as a national historic site, the Portage Woods Forest Preserve is just north of the interchange of I-55 and Harlem Avenue. In 1989, this sculpture by Rebechini was erected. Louis Jolliet is directing the canoe through the reeds, probably anticipating the need to portage the canoe for the next few miles.

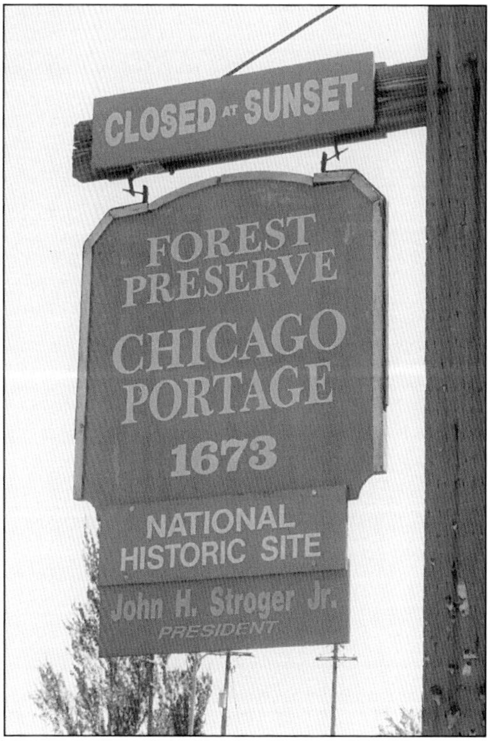

NATIONAL HISTORIC SITE SIGN AT PORTAGE WOODS. This sign on Harlem Avenue welcomes visitors to the site where in 1673, Louis Jolliet and Father Marquette portaged their canoes as a shortcut to Lake Michigan. The successful portage gave Jolliet the idea to dig a permanent cut through the swamp to allow easier passage of canoes and boats laden with trade. The Illinois and Michigan Canal was completed in 1848, thanks to Jolliet's foresight (and immigrant labor).

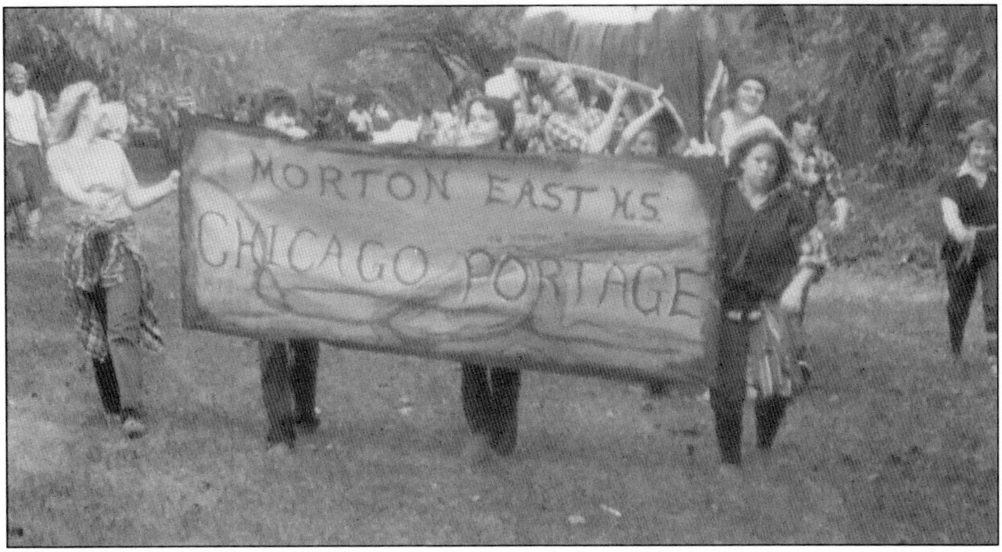

RE-ENACTING THE PORTAGE OF LOUIS JOLLIET AND FATHER MARQUETTE. Morton East students writing and editing the *PORTAGE* magazine (including local history and original poetry) were challenged to re-enact the portage undertaken so many years before by Jolliet and Marquette. Under the leadership of Mrs. A.J. Watson and Mrs. G.M. Cordulack, Morton East students braved the perils of a modern-day portage and made their own history. *PORTAGE* was conceived by John L. Leckel, Division Head, Language Arts. (Courtesy Morton Archives.)

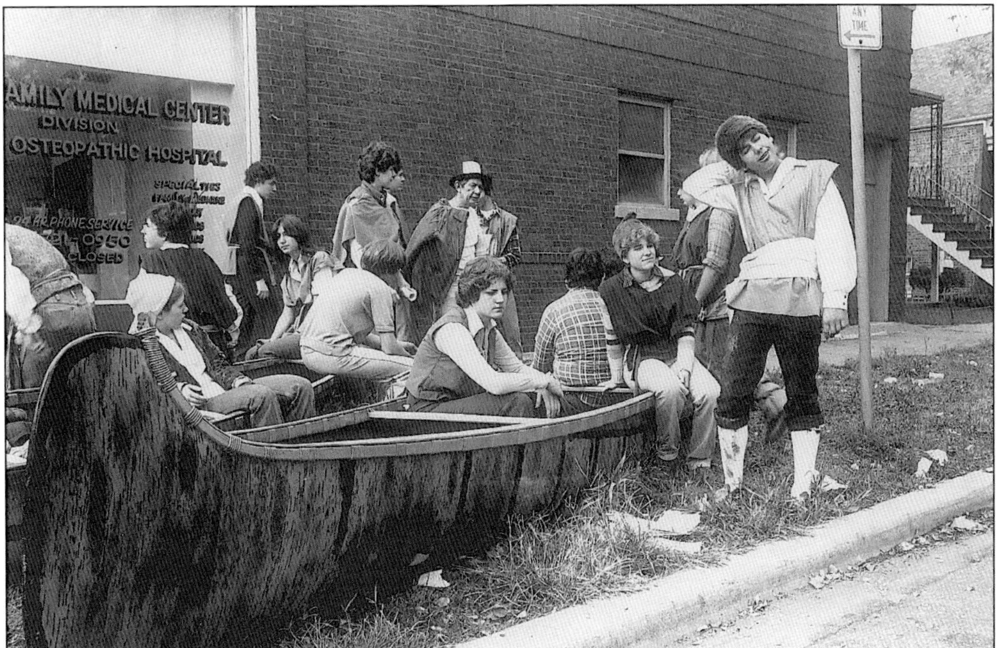

OCTOBER 17, 1977. "On October 17, 1977, 24 buckskin-clad 'voyageurs', along with a 20-foot canoe, set out to walk a nine mile route, from Thirty-first and Kedzie to the Portage Site on Forty-seventh and Harlem, that paralleled the actual route taken by explorers over three hundred years ago." (Don Kipper, *PORTAGE* '78; photo courtesy Mark Mourlas.)

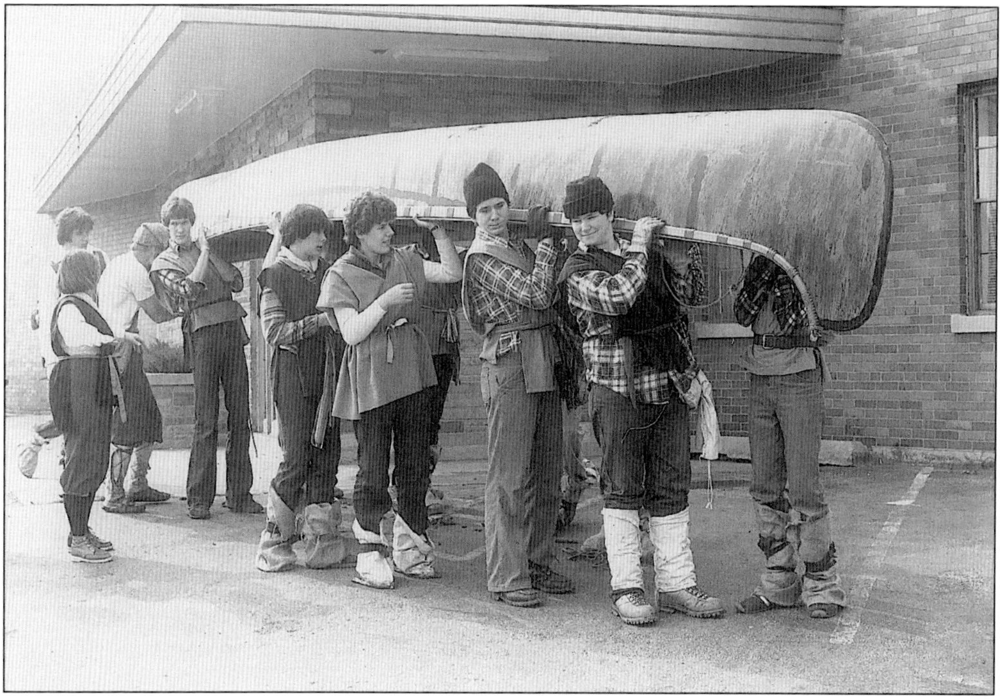

GETTING ORGANIZED. "The canoe was heavy and we had a difficult time, at first, organizing ourselves into two groups of people around the same height, so the weight of the canoe would be equally distributed. Once that problem was solved, the portage moved quickly and smoothly." (Don Kipper, *PORTAGE* '78; photo courtesy Mark Mourlas.)

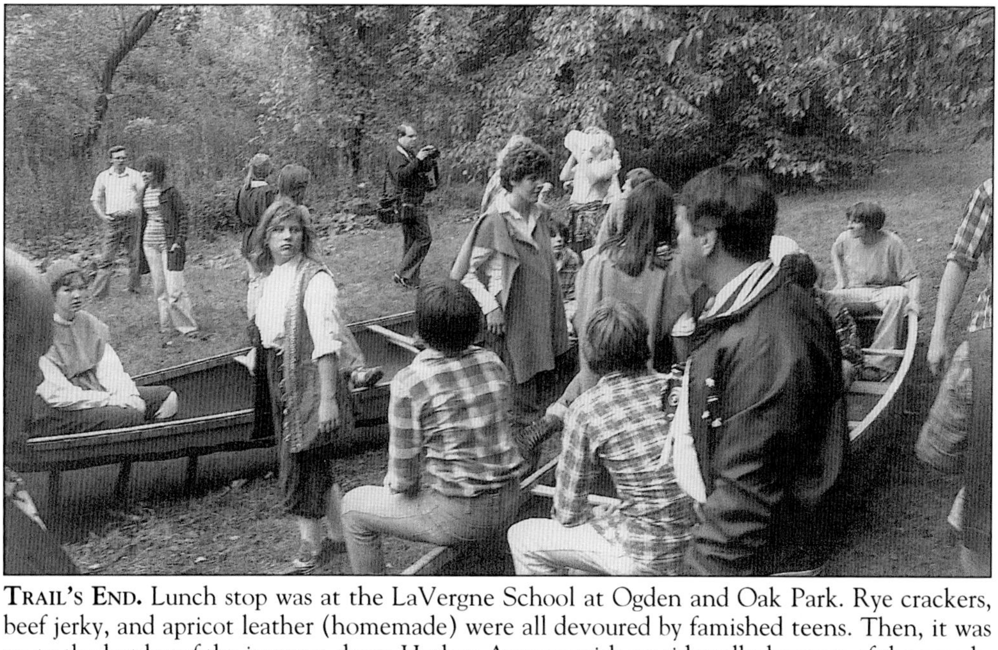

TRAIL'S END. Lunch stop was at the LaVergne School at Ogden and Oak Park. Rye crackers, beef jerky, and apricot leather (homemade) were all devoured by famished teens. Then, it was on to the last leg of the journey, down Harlem Avenue with no sidewalks because of the woods. Finally, the portagers arrived at their destination, the rock marker announcing the Chicago Portage. (Courtesy Mark Mourlas.)

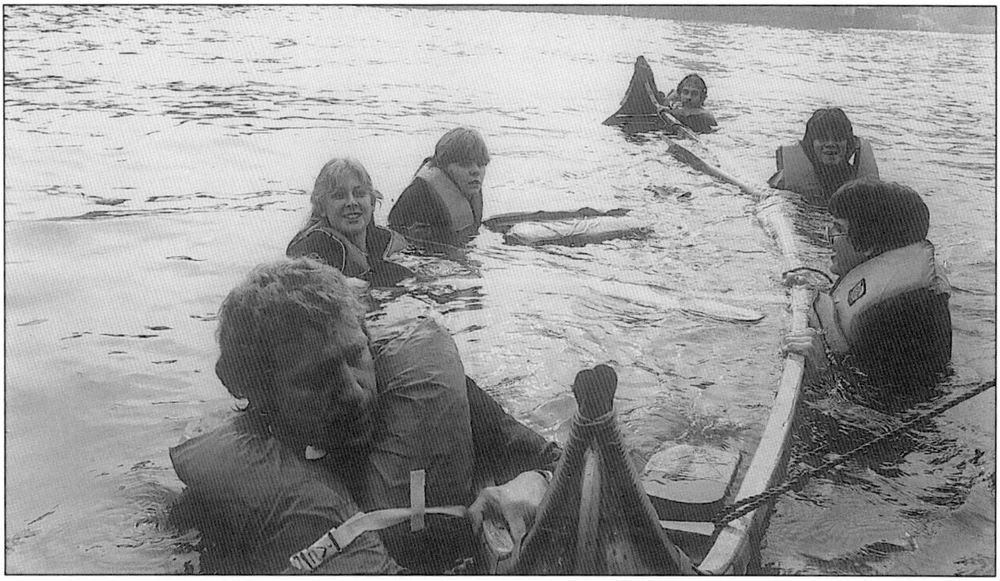

PORTAGE, 1979. The portage on October 18, 1979, differed from the earlier portage by adding a water leg to the trip and beginning at the Michigan Avenue Bridge. There the Morton East band and pompon girls stopped traffic as Harlan Mummert, the canoe expert, joined Mr. Swanson, Mr. Leitgeb, Mr. Serbick and eight students for the paddle down the river. Even an upset canoe didn't stop the hardy crew, who righted themselves and completed their mission. (Courtesy Mark Mourlas.)

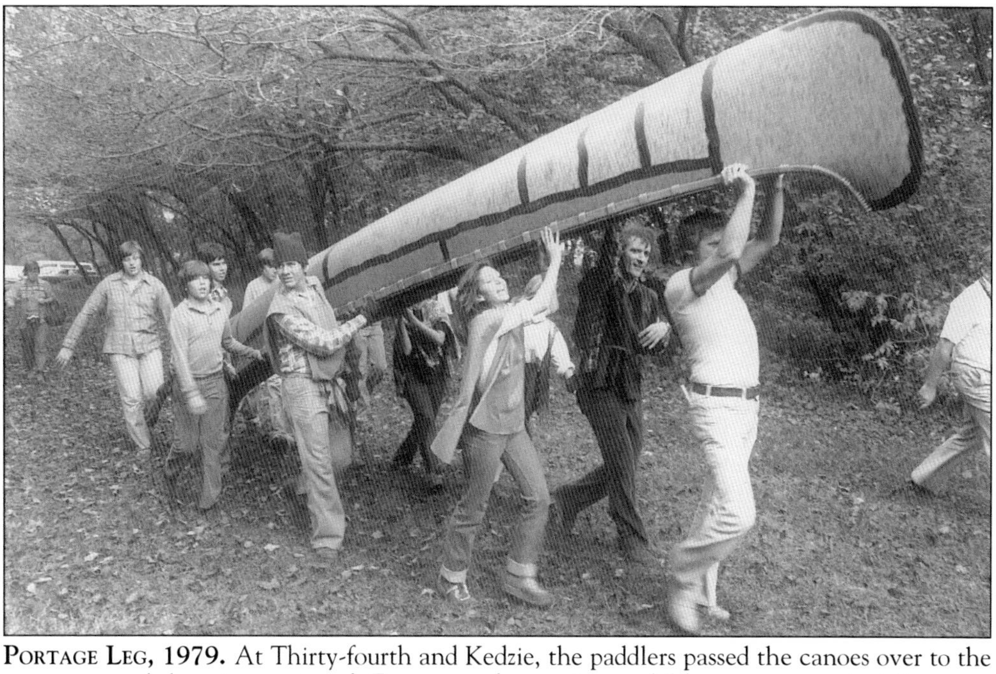

PORTAGE LEG, 1979. At Thirty-fourth and Kedzie, the paddlers passed the canoes over to the portagers, and the trip continued. Everyone who participated felt it was a worthwhile event, drawing attention to the importance of the Chicago Portage. It must have succeeded, as the wonderful sculpture of Marquette and Jolliet was erected in 1989, drawing increased public attention to the area. (Courtesy Mark Mourlas.)

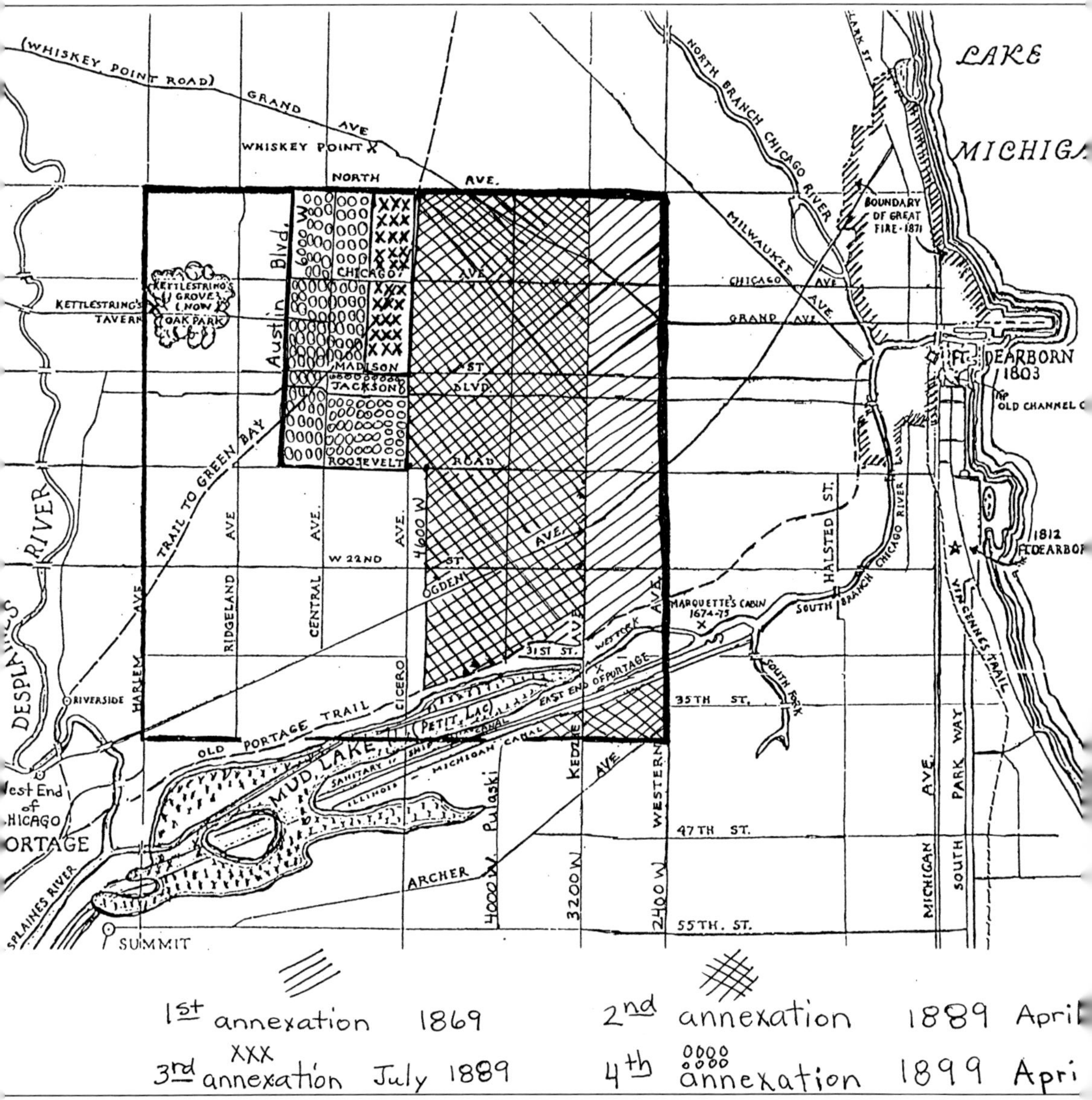

Annexation Map. Through a series of annexations beginning in 1869, the city of Chicago, working with the State Legislature, changed the size and shape of Cicero. Cicero used to extend to Western Avenue, which explains why Western Avenue is no longer on the western edge of Chicago! The second annexation, in 1889, was the largest. By the third annexation, also in 1889, and the fourth in 1899, the area once called Cicero Township had been markedly reduced in size.

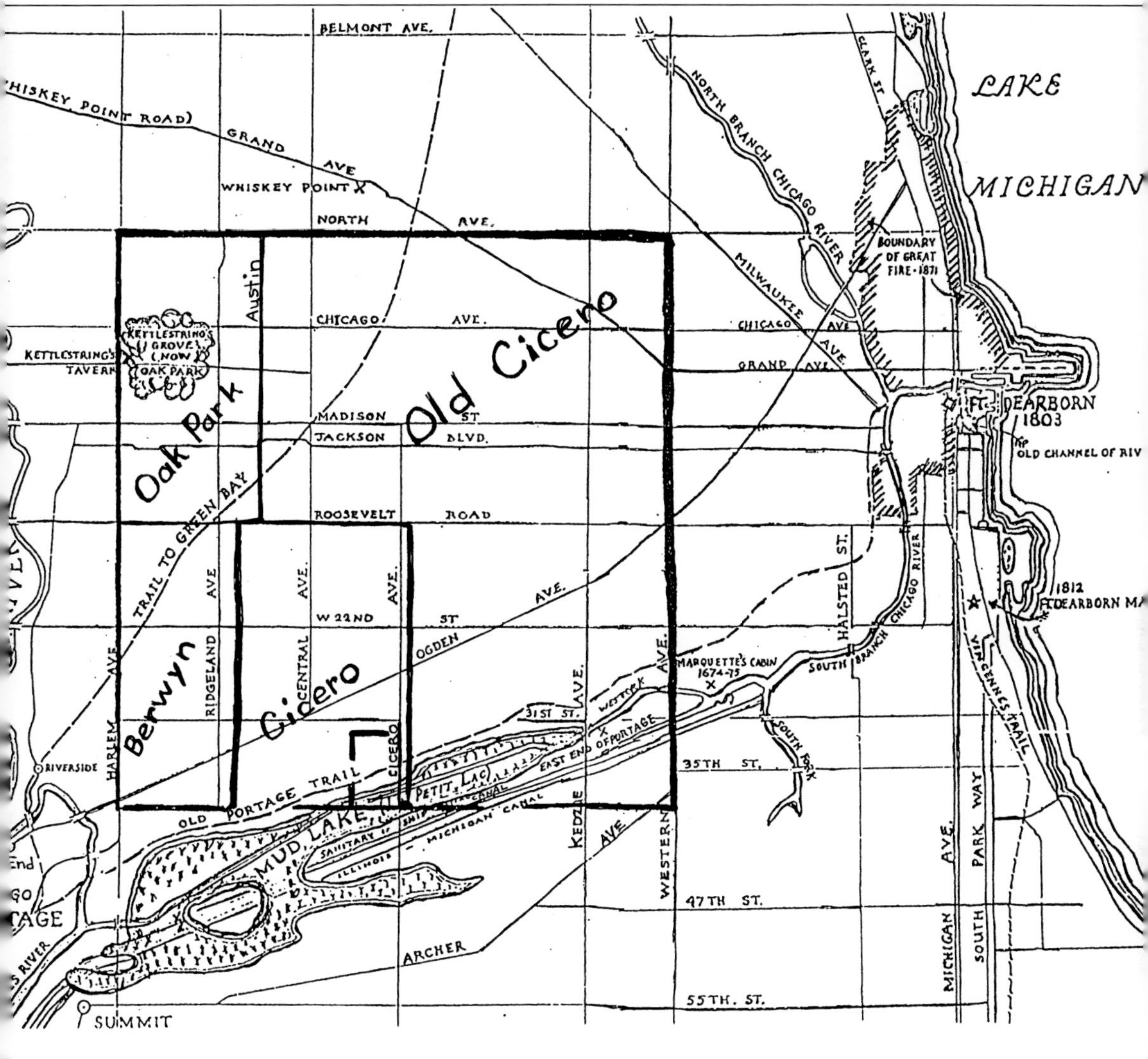

Current Boundaries. In 1901, a political power play took place with the upshot that Cicero, Berwyn, and Oak Park each became their own little town or village. The huge expanse once known as Cicero Township was thus further reduced to its present size. The shared names of the Founding Fathers, such as Kettlestrings and Scoville, played large roles in their common history prior to 1901. It seems strange, yet technically true, that Ernest Hemingway was born in what used to be Cicero!

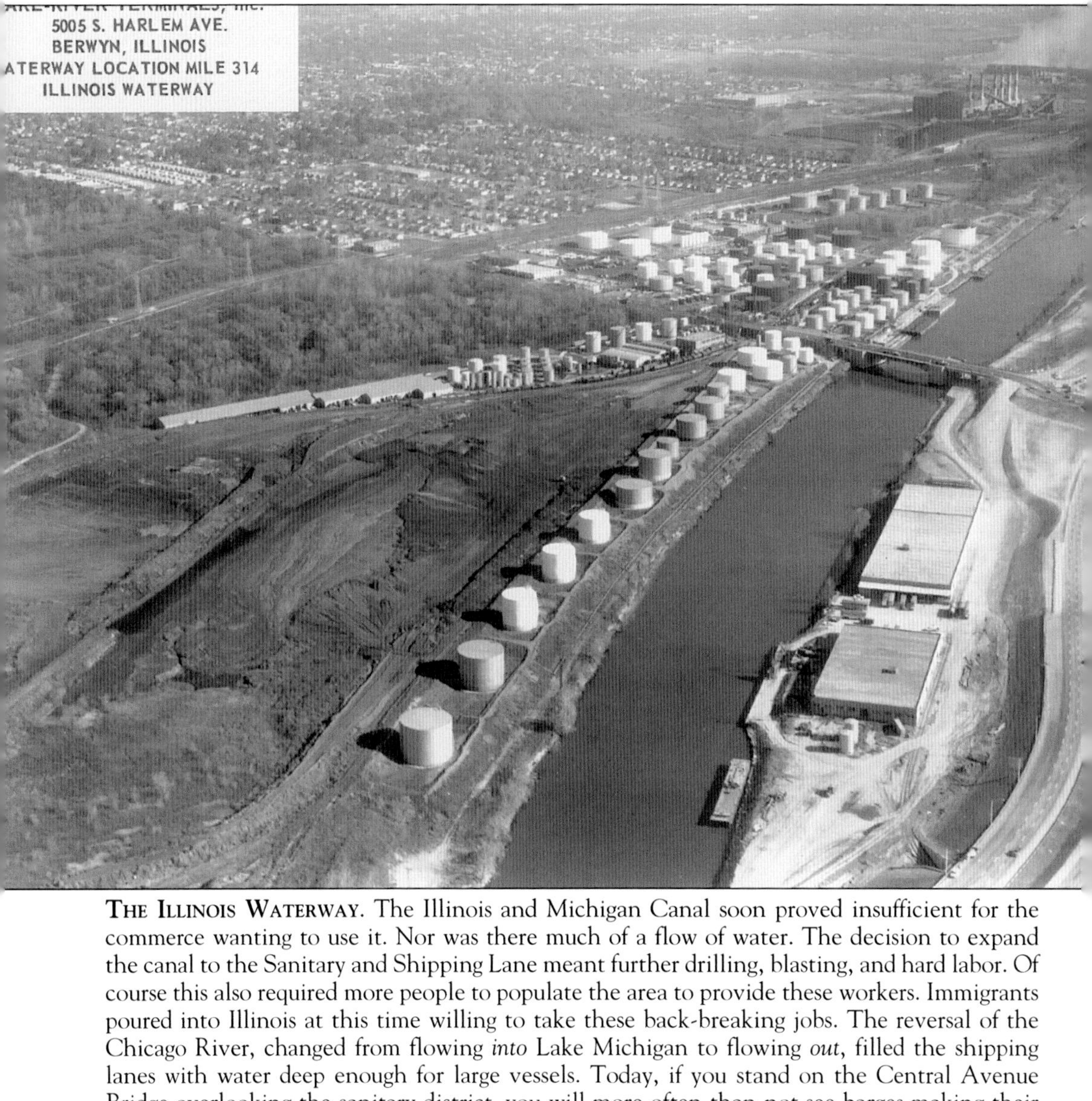

THE ILLINOIS WATERWAY. The Illinois and Michigan Canal soon proved insufficient for the commerce wanting to use it. Nor was there much of a flow of water. The decision to expand the canal to the Sanitary and Shipping Lane meant further drilling, blasting, and hard labor. Of course this also required more people to populate the area to provide these workers. Immigrants poured into Illinois at this time willing to take these back-breaking jobs. The reversal of the Chicago River, changed from flowing *into* Lake Michigan to flowing *out*, filled the shipping lanes with water deep enough for large vessels. Today, if you stand on the Central Avenue Bridge overlooking the sanitary district, you will more often than not see barges making their way up the lane. The old Mud Lake on the southern boundary of Cicero has become a huge corridor including the shipping lanes, train tracks, and highways. Jolliet would be amazed to see the results of his 1673 vision. (Courtesy *Life* Newspaper.)

Two

Western Electric, Hawthorne Works

As with so many other inventions, more than one person raced to invent the telephone at about the same time. Elisha Gray and Alexander Graham Bell both made patent claims on the telephone on February 14, 1876. The United States Patent Office issued the patent to Bell because his application came in a few hours before Gray's. Although Western Electric had started making telephones under Professor Gray's patent claims (the company had originally been organized in 1869 as Gray and Barton,) Bell's victory in the ensuing litigation over patent rights did not prove fatal to the fledgling company. The switchboards made by Western Electric were superior to others no matter whose telephone won the patent!

The Hawthorne Works in Cicero had the distinction of being the largest unit of the nationwide Western Electric facilities, principally producing phones, wire, and cable. Built on 203 acres of land, and comprised of 103 buildings, the Hawthorne Works was its own town within a town. It had its own athletic field, gymnasium, band shell, social clubs, company store, and railroad station. It pioneered personnel relations with comprehensive health plans including sickness, accident, and death benefits, as well as paid vacations, pensions, and savings opportunities.

When the huge six-story main building grew antiquated, the town of Cicero sighed deeply as the structure was torn down. "The buildings are old and the technology has changed. It breaks my heart, but I expected this for a long time," said a longtime Western Electric employee. The corner of Cicero and Cermak is now a shopping mall, with some architectural details reminiscent of Western Electric.

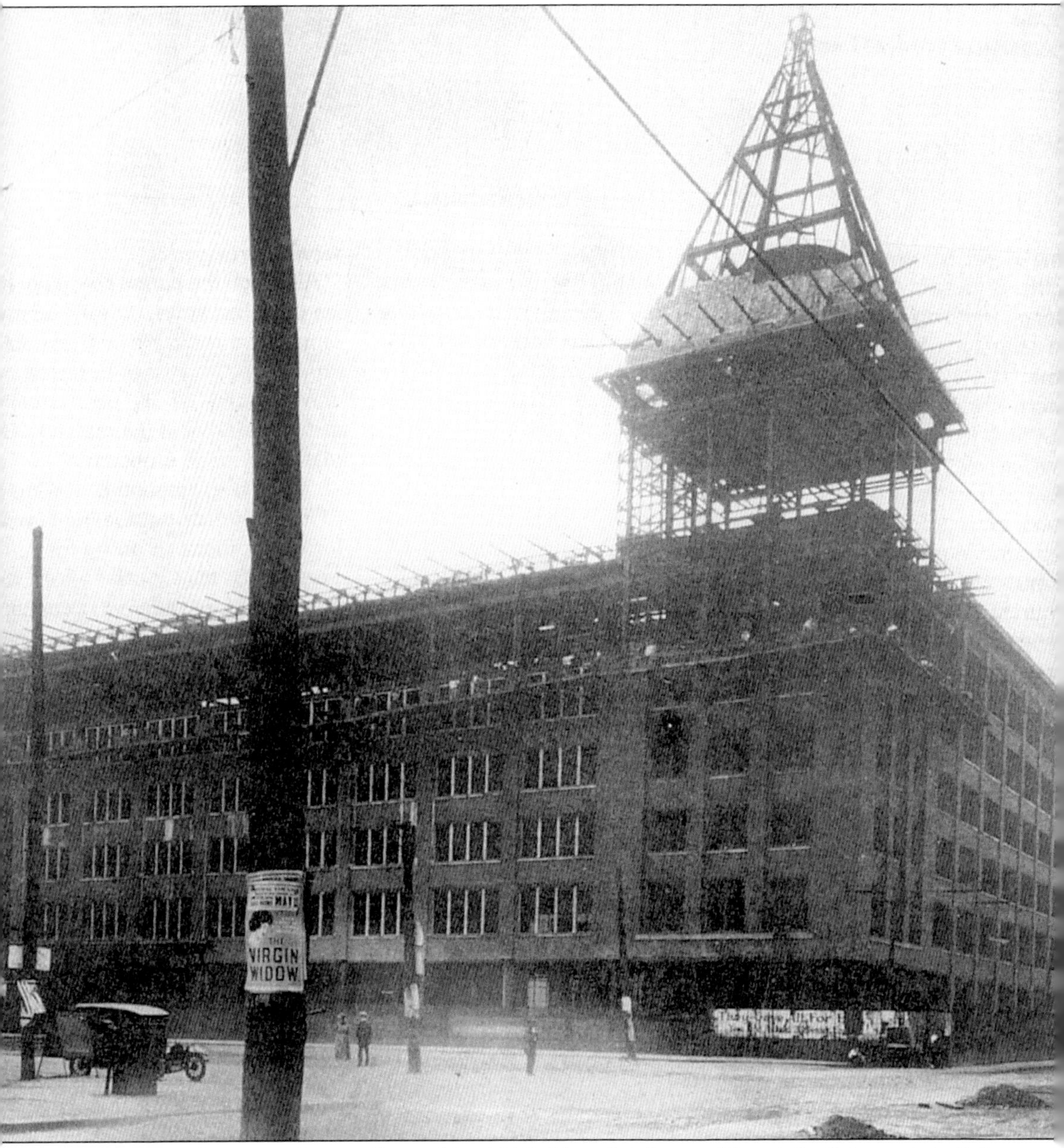

WESTERN ELECTRIC TOWER GOING UP, 1919. Though Western Electric built its main building on the corner of Cicero Avenue and Cermak Road in 1903, the tower that defined the plant was not erected until 1919. It stood over 183 feet high, and overlooked most everything else in Cicero. It was a landmark of pride as well as orientation. The architect, Charles Prchal, began the challenging project in 1918. The tower was so well planned and constructed that when the time came to tear down The Western, the tower did not fall with the building. The tower stood with solitary pride until it was toppled with explosives. Executive offices were located in the tower, as well as meeting rooms and a dining room.

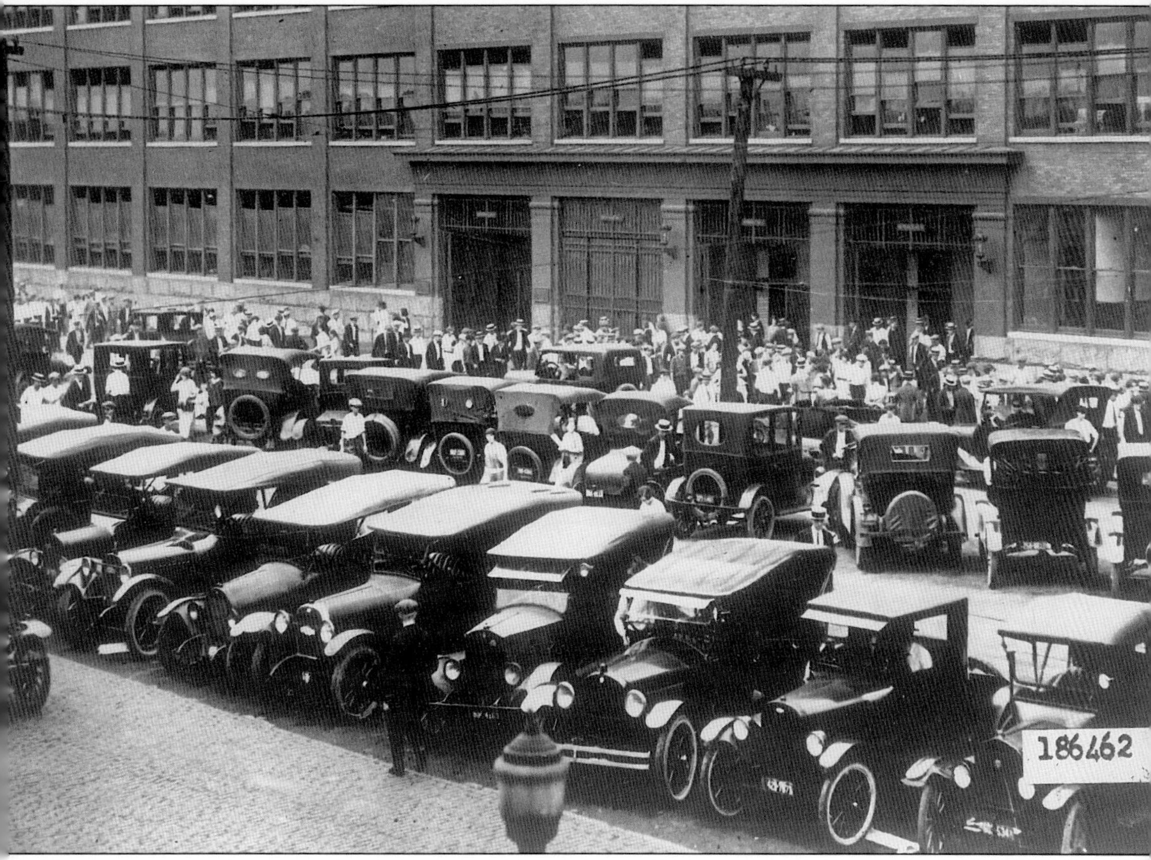

The Parking Lot Around Western Electric. The streets surrounding Western Electric resembled a parking lot during the day. Streetcar lines and autos filled Cermak Road. When the five o'clock whistle blew, everyone in the neighborhood knew the time. People then poured out of The Western, hopped in their autos, took the streetcar, or walked home. In later years, as automobile traffic increased, brick side streets (like Twenty-Second Place) became a favorite shortcut after work, thus avoiding the traffic lights on Cermak Road. Many a "middle-of-the-street" softball game was slowed by the often-repeated cry, "Car!" (Courtesy Harris Erickson Collection.)

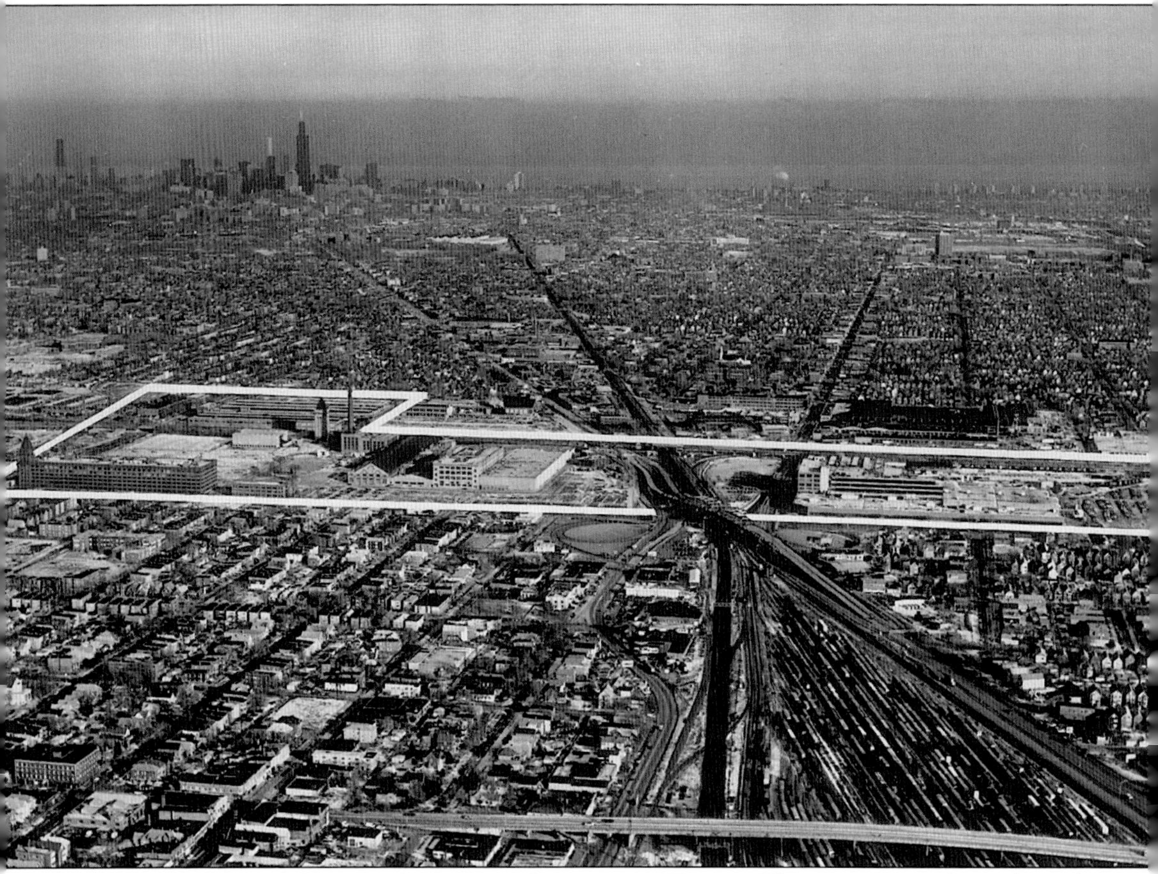

THE EXTENT OF WESTERN ELECTRIC, HAWTHORNE WORKS. This interesting photo from the collection of the *Life* Newspaper, shows the extent of the plant. The white line extends from Cermak Road on the north, past Thirty-First Street on the south, and crosses the Burlington Northern rail lines. Notice that part of the plant is in Chicago, on the other side of the dividing viaduct. The plant was strategically placed to take advantage of the trains heading to and from Chicago, and streetcars on both Twenty-Second Street and Cicero Avenue. The plant covered over two hundred acres and had over one hundred buildings, in this city within a city. The growth of the town of Cicero parallels the growth of The Western and other industry on the northeast end. (Courtesy *Life* Newspaper.)

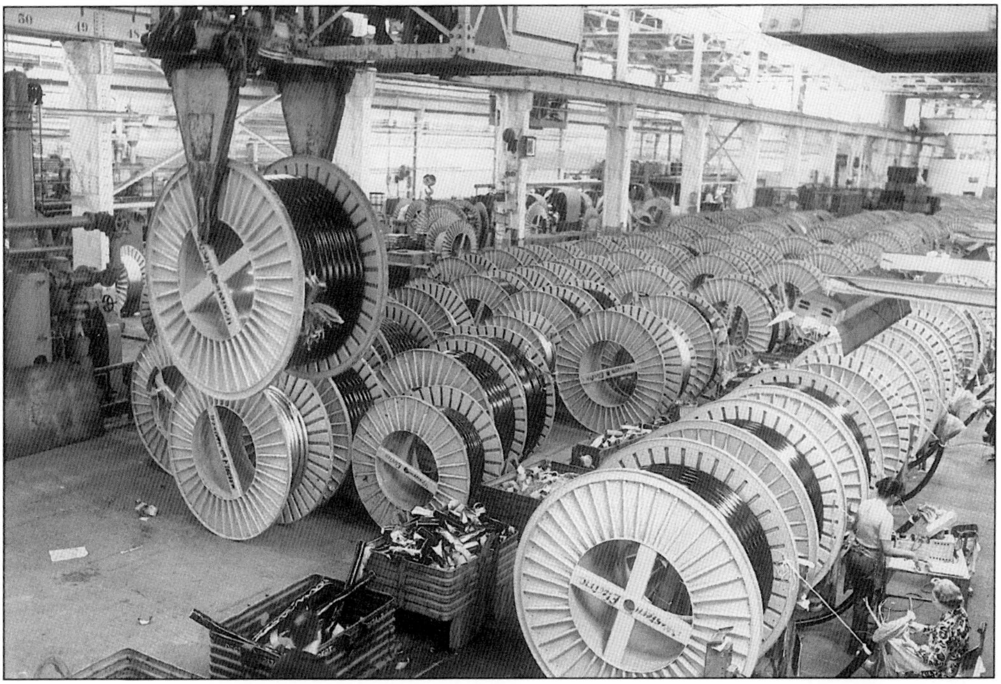

HAWTHORNE'S CABLE PLANT. Hawthorne's pulp insulated cable plant was one of the largest such plants in the world. Cable on these giant reels was buzz-tested (lower right) prior to being shipped to telephone companies. (Courtesy *Life* Newspaper.)

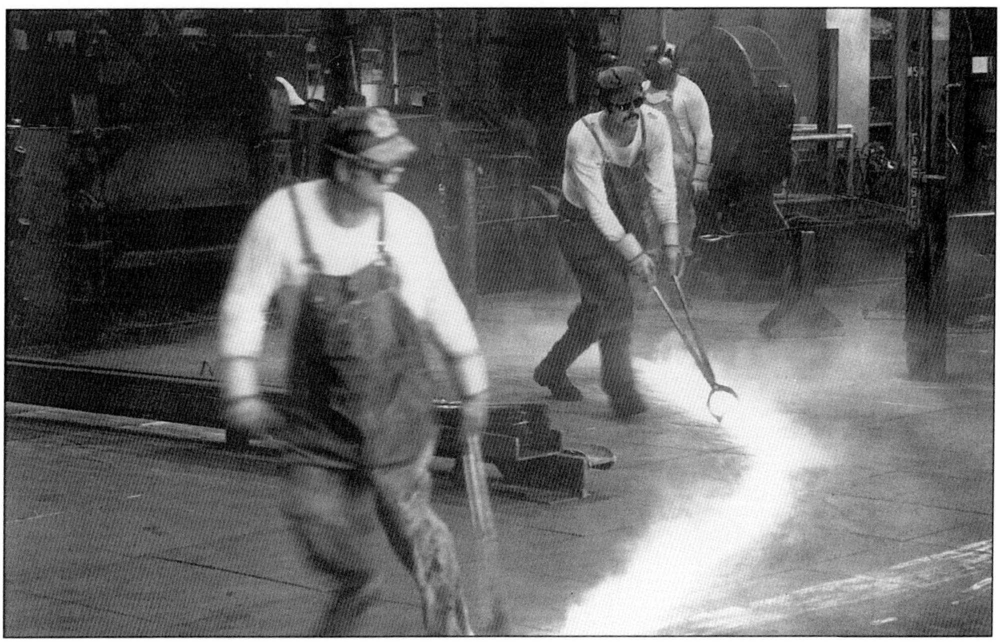

THE HOT ROLLING PROCESS. These men are engaged in the hot rolling process, making a ferrous magnetic alloy. Western Electric's Hawthorne Metals Mill was the only metals mill in the Bell System. This alloy was sent to other facilities where it was used to make magnets for telephone handset receivers. (Courtesy *Life* Newspaper.)

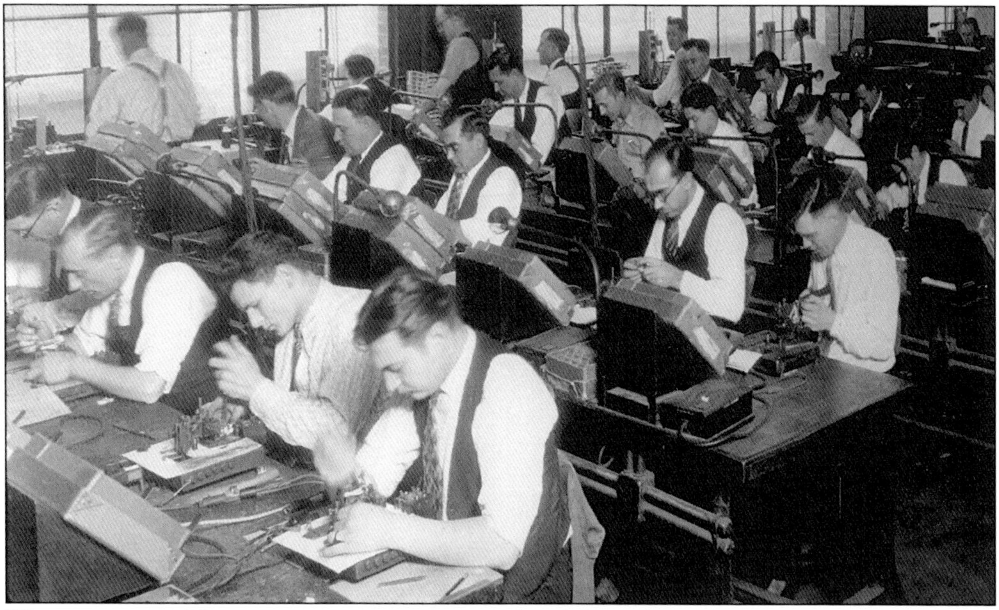

Working in the Hawthorne Works. Dress codes of the early 1900s meant that even workers doing an assembly line job came to work in shirts and ties, and often, vests. In the 1920s, Hawthorne began what they called Illumination Studies to determine if lighting affected workers' output. It was found that varying the lighting didn't change production levels much, but other innovative programs, such as job trading, *did* increase production. Coffee breaks were introduced, as rest periods were found to be beneficial also. (Courtesy Western Electric Museum in Morton East.)

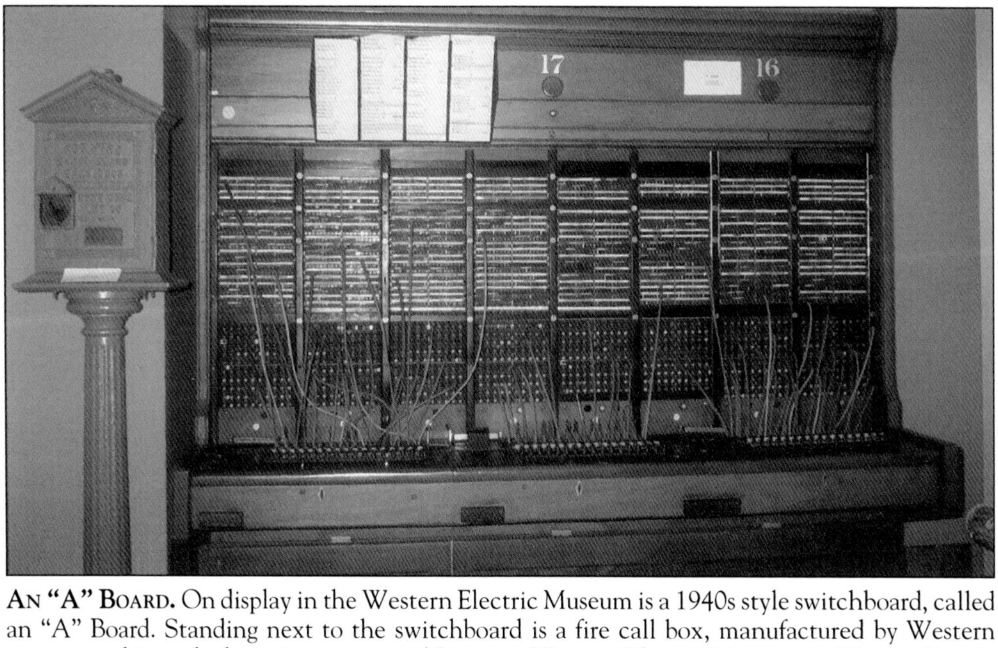

An "A" Board. On display in the Western Electric Museum is a 1940s style switchboard, called an "A" Board. Standing next to the switchboard is a fire call box, manufactured by Western prior to making telephone instruments. (Courtesy Western Electric Museum in Morton East.)

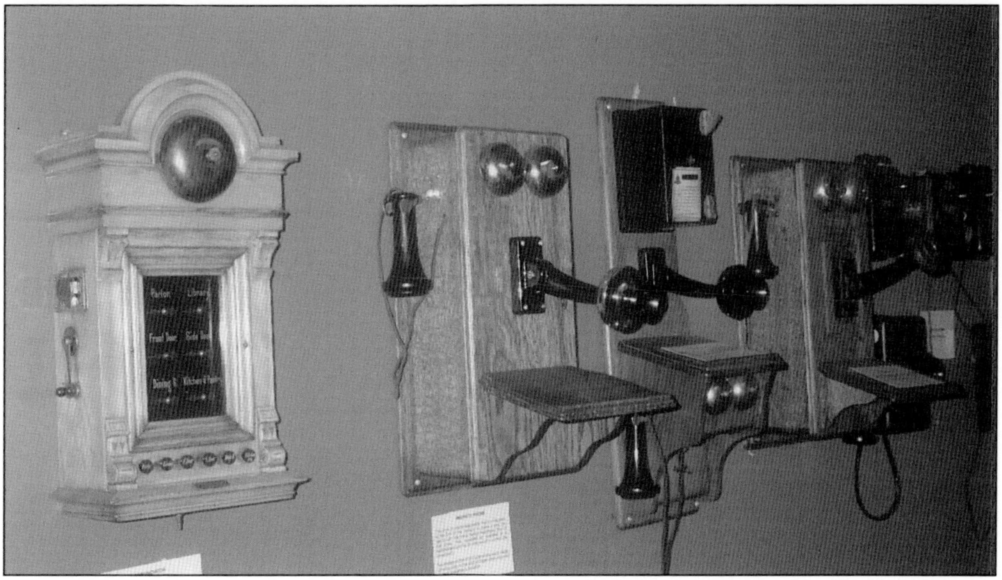

Old Telephones. Also on display at the museum are old telephones. The first is an Annunciator, made from 1884–1925. Next is a Magneto Phone, followed by an Oak Wall Phone, and another Magneto phone. (Courtesy Western Electric Museum in Morton East.)

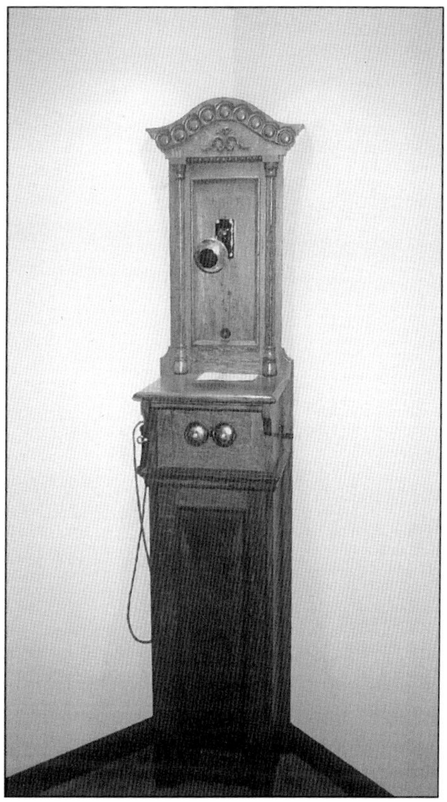

An Early Toll Phone. This early toll phone was rescued from destruction when it was found amongst trash destined to be hauled away. These days, the charming, freestanding telephone is on display in the Western Electric Museum. (Courtesy Western Electric Museum in Morton East.)

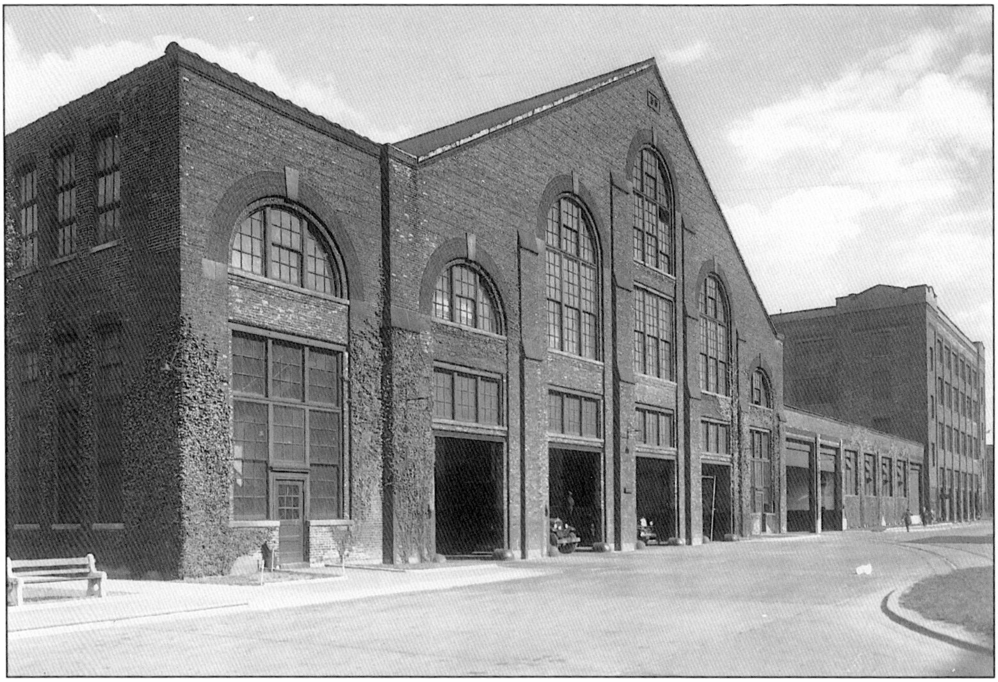

The Hawthorne Works "Garages." Still standing today in the year 2000 are the huge garages constructed to house Western Electric's manufacturing supplies and products, their own fire station, and their fleet of vehicles. Hawthorne had its own water reservoir and tower as well as an independent electric supply. (Courtesy Harris Erickson Collection.)

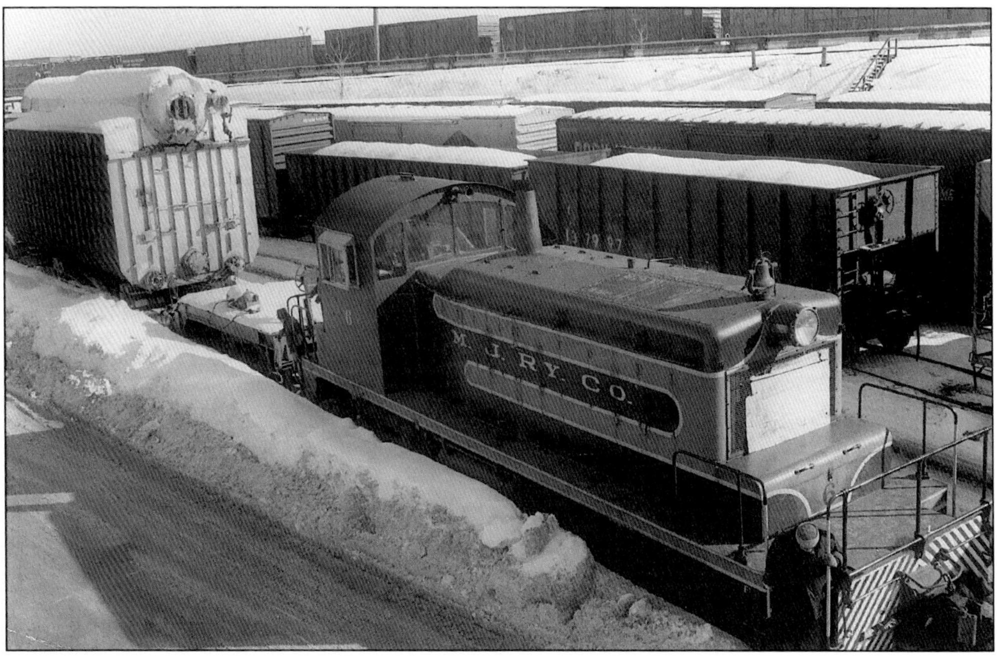

The MJ Railway. The Manufacturers Junction Railway was originally established to haul materials to build the Hawthorne plant. Then, it stayed on to move heavy freight cars, flatbeds, and tank cars onto the grounds and up to the many loading docks. (Courtesy *Life* Newspaper.)

HISTORICAL PRODUCTS DISPLAY, 1978. To celebrate 75 years of Western Electric's Hawthorne Works, an Historical Products Display was conceived. An Open House was held as part of the celebrations. Here, Florence Hybl demonstrates a 1924 vintage washing machine. Western Electric also made stoves, sewing machines, and a wide range of products before specializing in the manufacture of telephones. (Courtesy of *Life* Newspaper.)

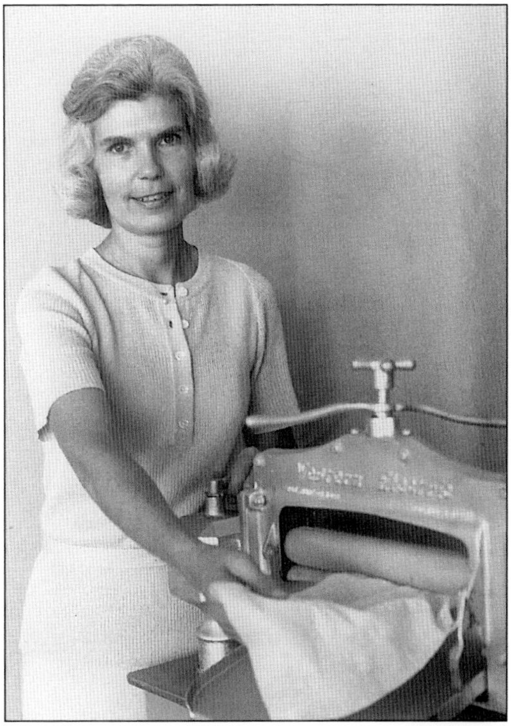

INSIDE THE WESTERN. This part of The Western is virtually unrecognizable by those who didn't work there. The campus inside the confines of the red brick fortress contained recreational space, as well as the second tower back by the power plant. It truly was a city within a city. An outdoor band shell provided musical entertainment in the warm weather. (Courtesy Harris Erickson Collection.)

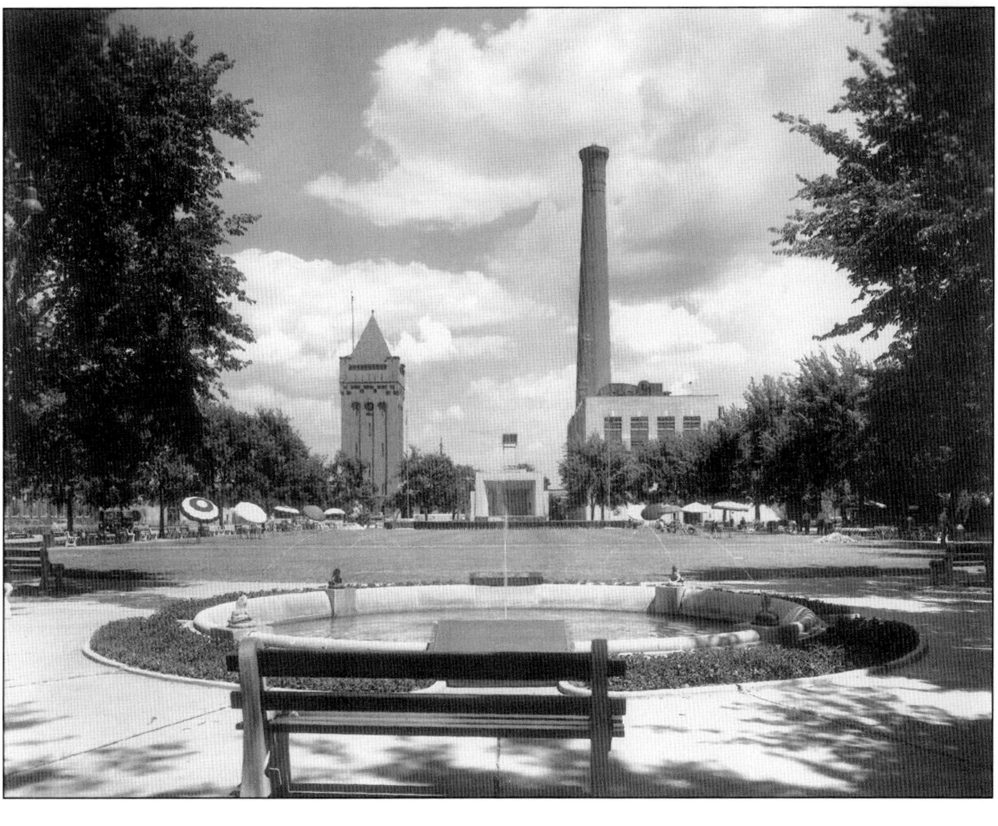

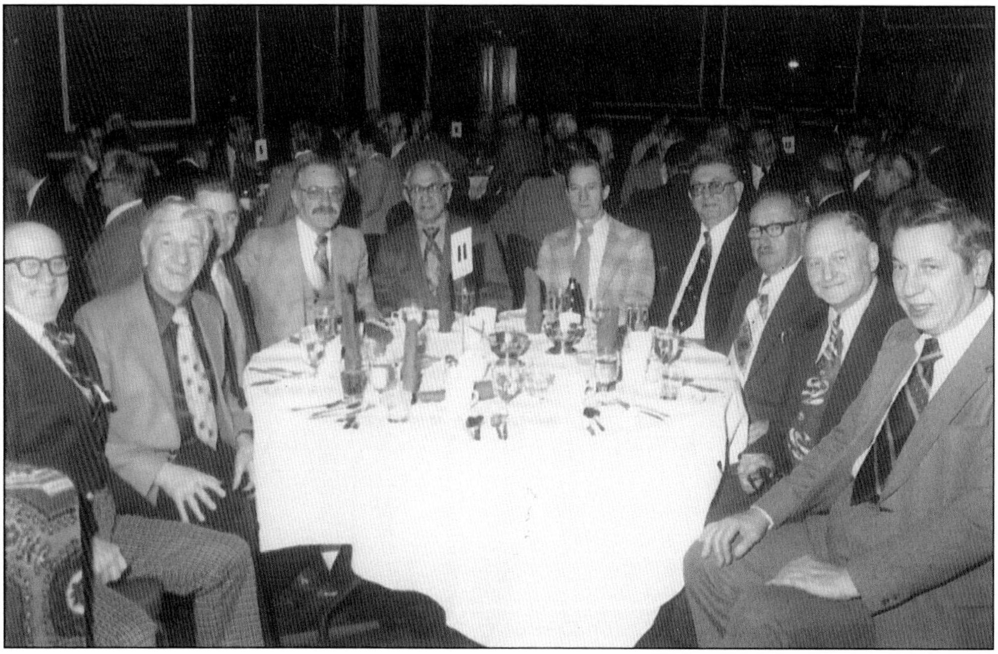

DINNER WITH LOCAL 1864. Chester Lasko (seated on the far right) was president of the Local 1864, representing the workers at Western Electric. Labor and management usually worked together to solve their grievances. On the far left is Frank Imber, followed by Harris Erickson, Treasurer of the local union. Harris Erickson retired in 1983 after working 41 years for Western Electric. (Courtesy Harris Erickson Collection.)

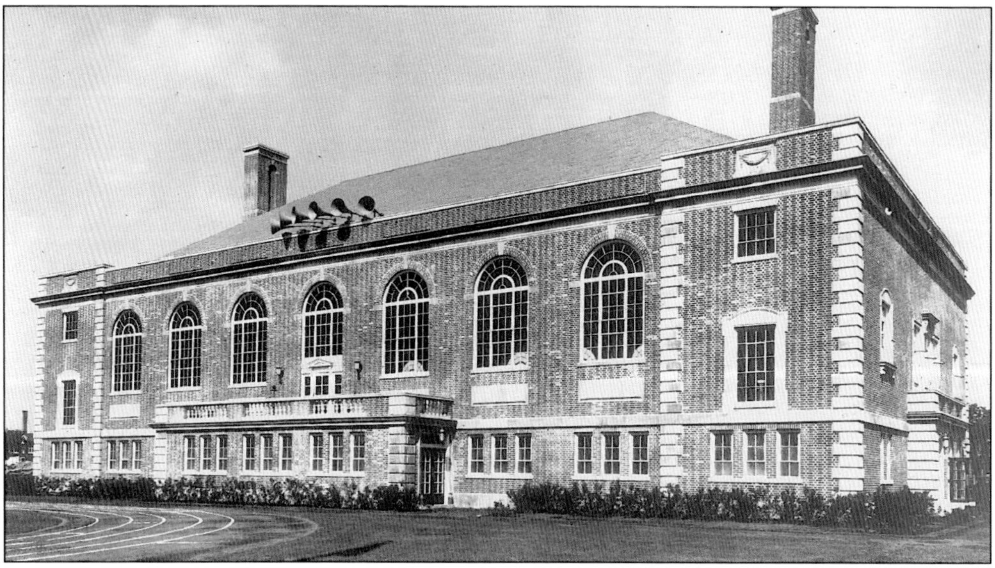

THE ALBRIGHT GYMNASIUM. Western Electric provided for its workers in many ways. Management was alert for safety issues, provided monetary benefits, and saw to the health of employees. Nurses and doctors were ever-present in the hospital, where annual employee physicals were administered free of charge. The workers were encouraged to make use of the nearby gymnasium and track, as were the Cicero Grade School gym classes. (Courtesy Harris Erickson Collection.)

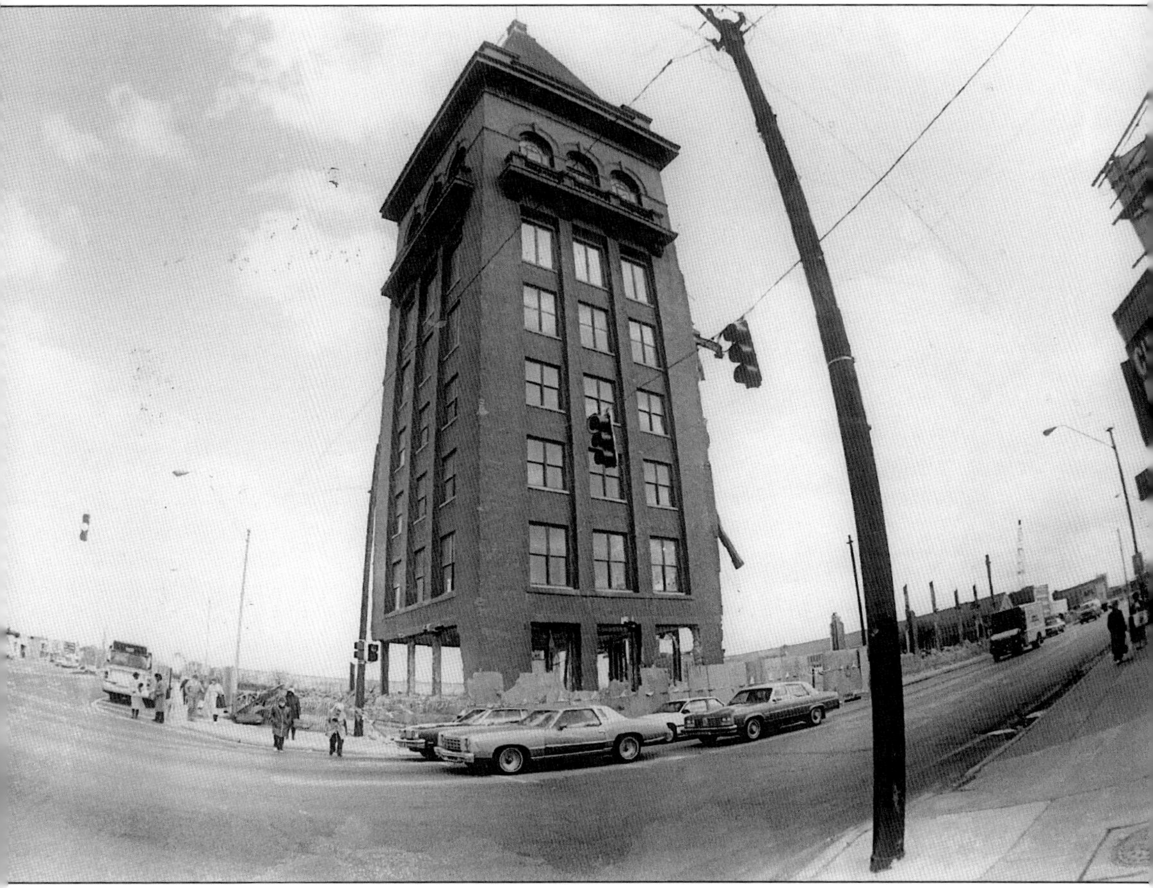

Standing Alone. However great The Western was in its heyday, in time it became hopelessly outdated. The six-story structure just wasn't adaptable to the needs of the 20th century world of technology, and plans were made to tear it down. One of the last things to go was the landmark tower at Cermak and Cicero. Though believed to be incapable of standing on its own, here it did just that, amidst the rubble of the rest of the plant. Finally, the tower itself was detonated and crumbled to the ground. (Courtesy *Life* Newspaper.)

GOING...

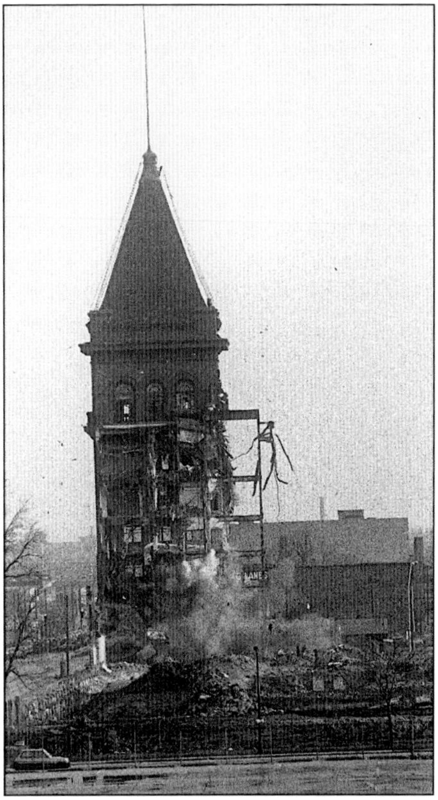

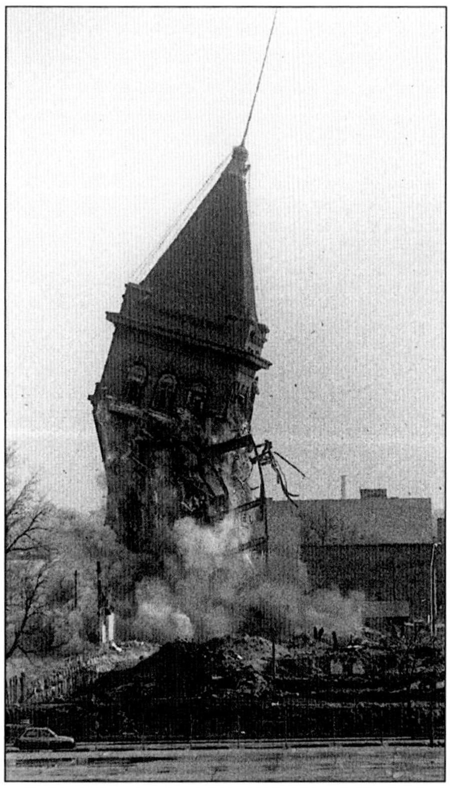

GOING...

GOING…

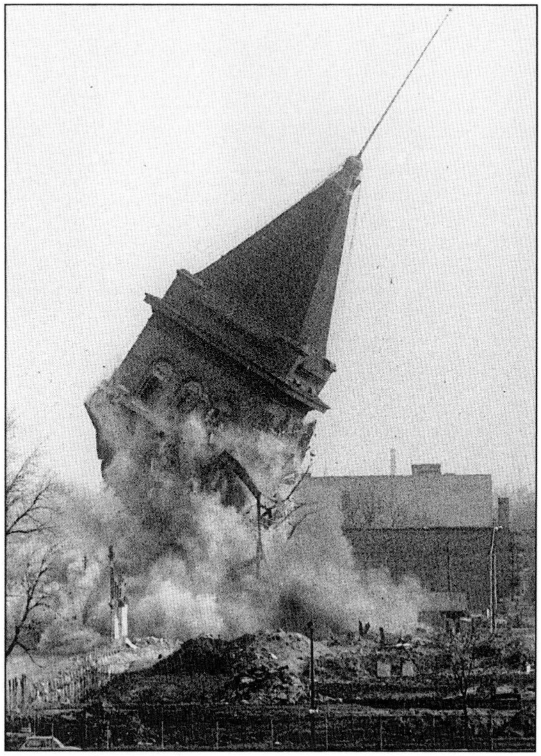

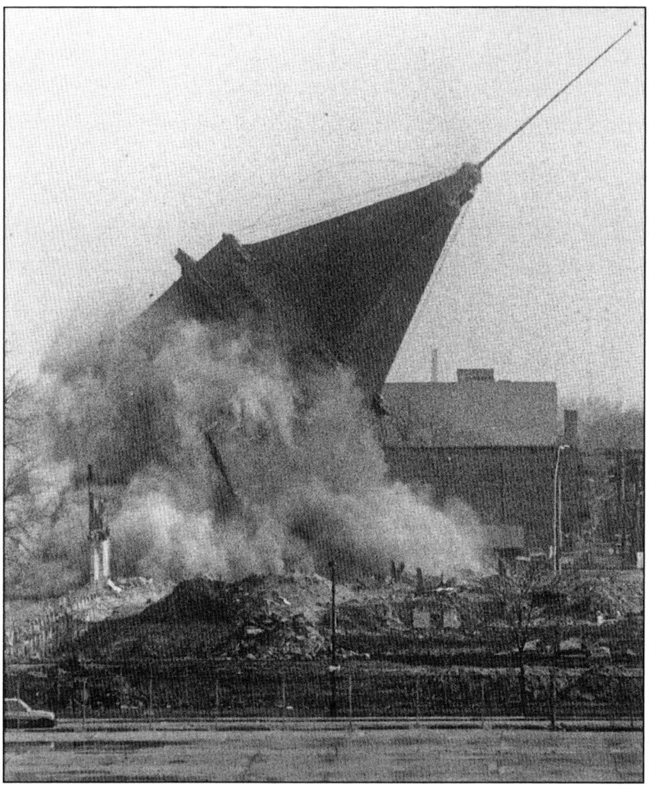

GONE.
(All photos on pages 28 and 29 courtesy *Life* Newspaper.)

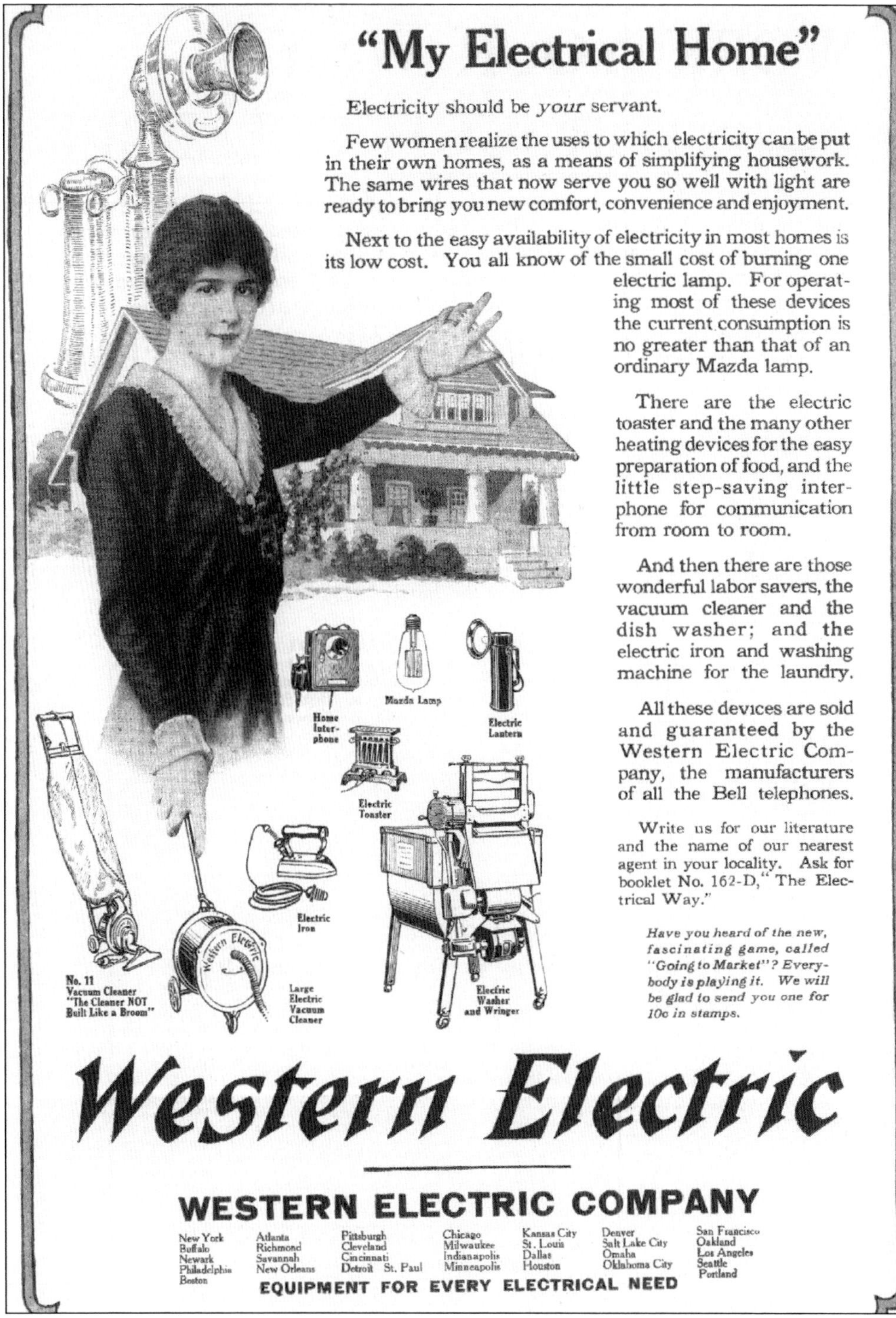

1915 ADVERTISEMENT. In 1915, Western Electric made a variety of appliances, including toasters, washing machines, dish washers, vacuum cleaners, and even an inter-room telephone. This ad for the all-electric home declares that not only is electricity readily available, but also that it is inexpensive. (Courtesy Karl J. Sup.)

Three

THE *EASTLAND*

Cicero's location played an unusual role in the *Eastland* tragedy. No, the ship didn't sink in Cicero. But the people on board the *Eastland* in the Chicago River that fateful July day were mostly workers from the Western Electric plant in Cicero, and by day's end, hardly a family in Cicero was untouched by the event.

July 24th, 1915, dawned full of anticipation. A full day's outing! A trip across Lake Michigan! A parade and picnic with banners and games and hoopla! Best of all, for the mostly young adults, the chance to be with sweethearts or meet a dreamed-of sweetheart.

Even boarding the *Eastland* was a gala affair with friends calling out to each other to hurry below decks where a band was already playing. The gentle leaning of the ship was just part of the fun until about 7:25 a.m., when the listing went too far, and the hilarity turned into terror. Those on deck stood a chance if they could swim and if a non-swimmer didn't drag them down into the muddy water. Those below deck soon found that 20 feet of water is as deadly as 2,000 feet.

Many homes and churches in Cicero were hung with black crepe in the next few days. Several whole families were wiped out. For many, the family breadwinner was no longer present to support the older and younger generations. Life changed drastically. And the hopes of many newly immigrated citizens were drowned with the young people that day.

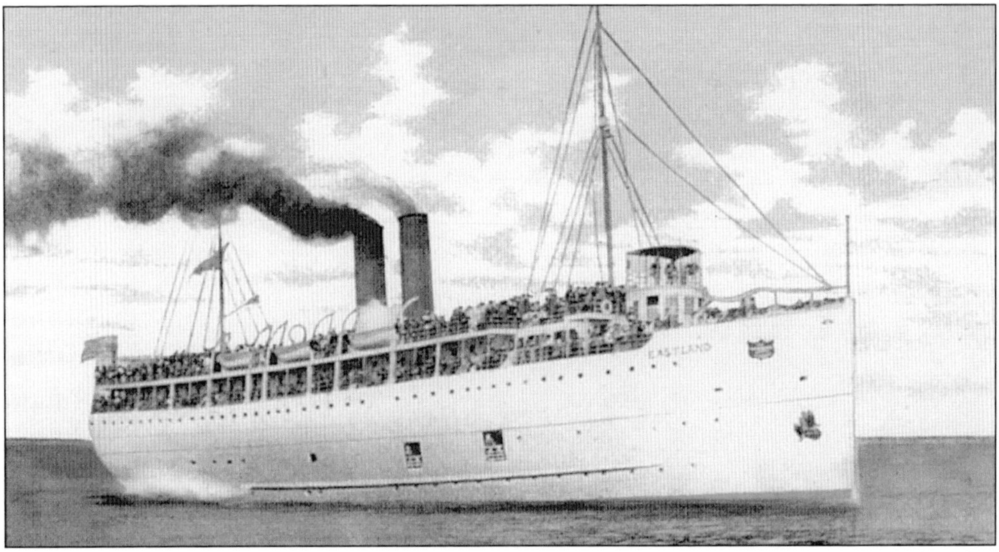

SS *Eastland*. The SS *Eastland* was built in 1903, the only passenger ship built by the Jenks Ship Building Company. Later, to increase her speed, some machinery was relocated, and a new draft system and air-conditioning system were added, leading the ship to be chronically top-heavy. Adding more lifeboats, required after the 1912 *Titanic* disaster, made her dangerously unsteady.

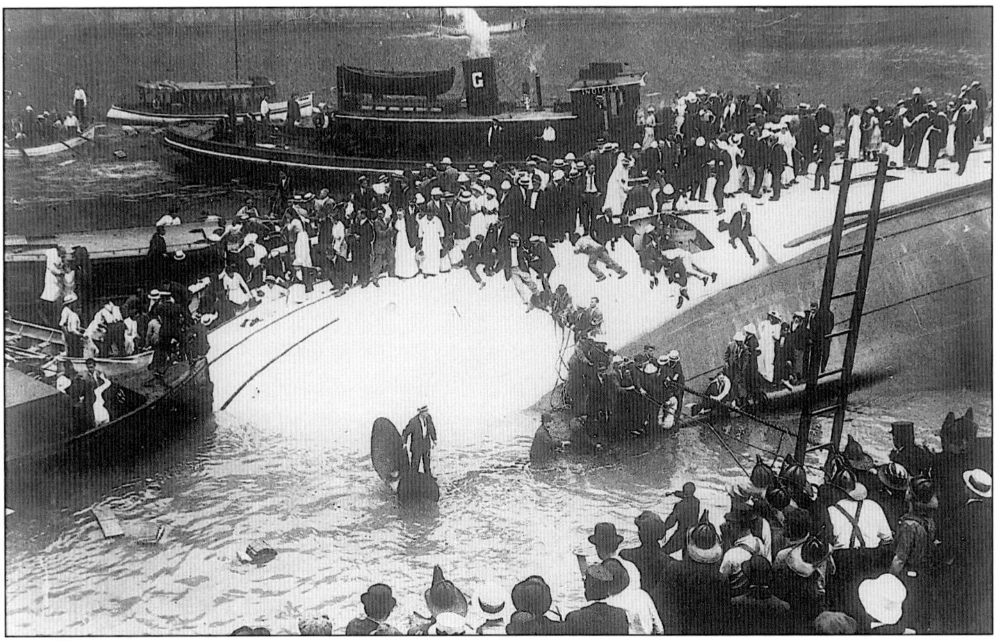

The Picnic That Didn't Take Place. Western Electric workers had enjoyed company picnic excursions to Michigan City for several years. The year 1915 would see the biggest crowd ever, nine *thousand* people planning to spend a happy day crossing Lake Michigan, picnicking, and returning home tired, yet rested, after a fun-filled day off work. The *Eastland* was to be the first ship leaving that morning. It was filled to capacity when disaster struck the top-heavy ship. Some on deck were able to jump or swim to safety when the ship rolled on its side. Those caught below deck were doomed. (Courtesy Illinois State Historical Library.)

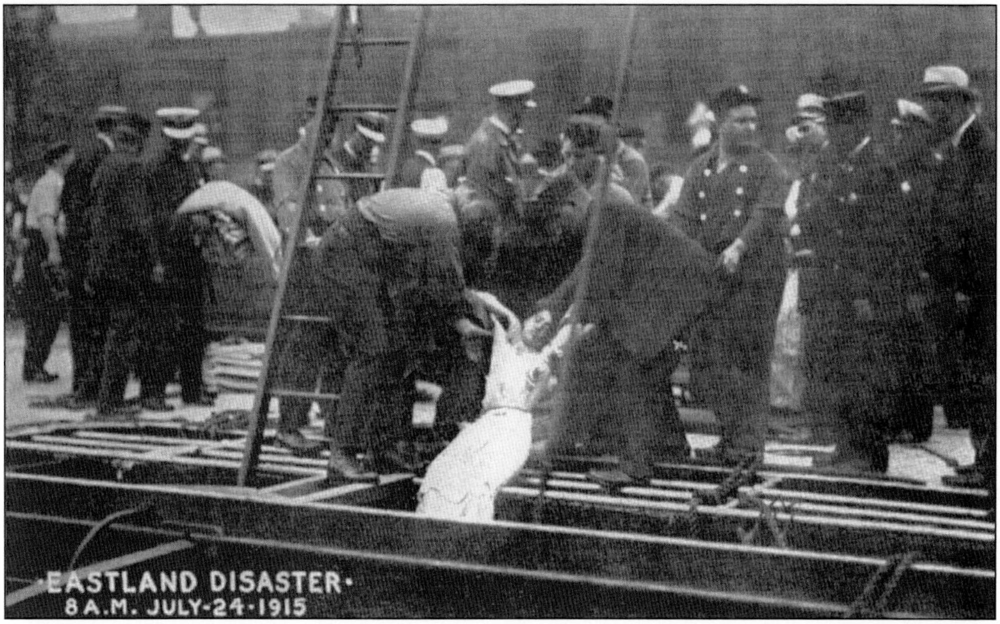

The White Picnic Dress. Picnic attire for ladies was a long white cotton dress; cool, yet modest. Here, a young lady's body is pulled from the side of the ship. Little did she know that her picnic dress might also become her burial dress. (Courtesy Karl J. Sup.)

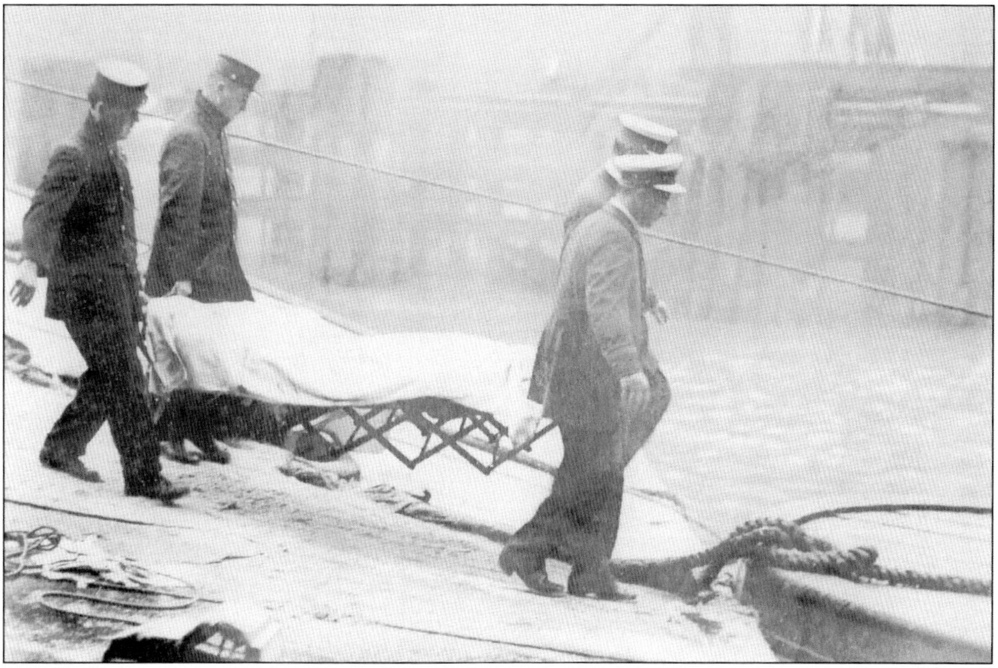

Stretcher Bearers. These men are carrying a victim on a stretcher onto the deck of the tug *Kenosha*. This image clearly shows the slope of the hull and the subsequent necessity of spreading ashes on it to increase traction. During the course of the rescue it had begun to rain, further complicating an already chaotic scene. (Courtesy Karl J. Sup.)

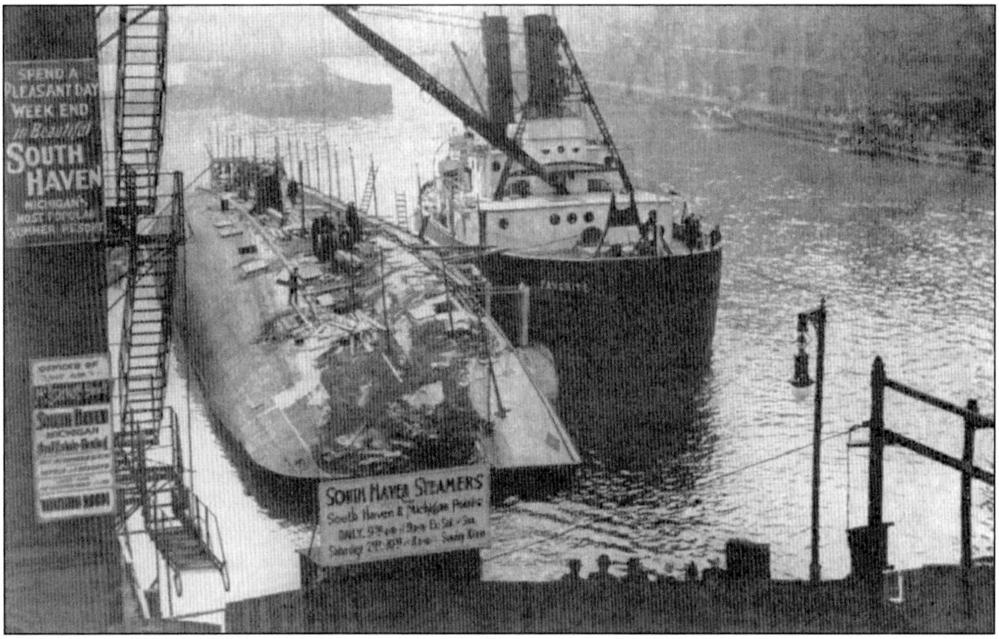

"Spend a Pleasant Day..." Sign. The large sign painted on the building near the *Eastland* wreck boldly advertises "Spend a Pleasant Day or Weekend in Beautiful South Haven, Michigan's Most Beautiful Summer Resort." It is ironic, because when the picture was taken, the *Eastland* was resting on her side in about 20 feet of water, and 844 passengers had lost their lives. Their pleasant day had a tragic ending. A salvage ship, the *Favorite*, has pulled up along side. (Courtesy Karl J. Sup.)

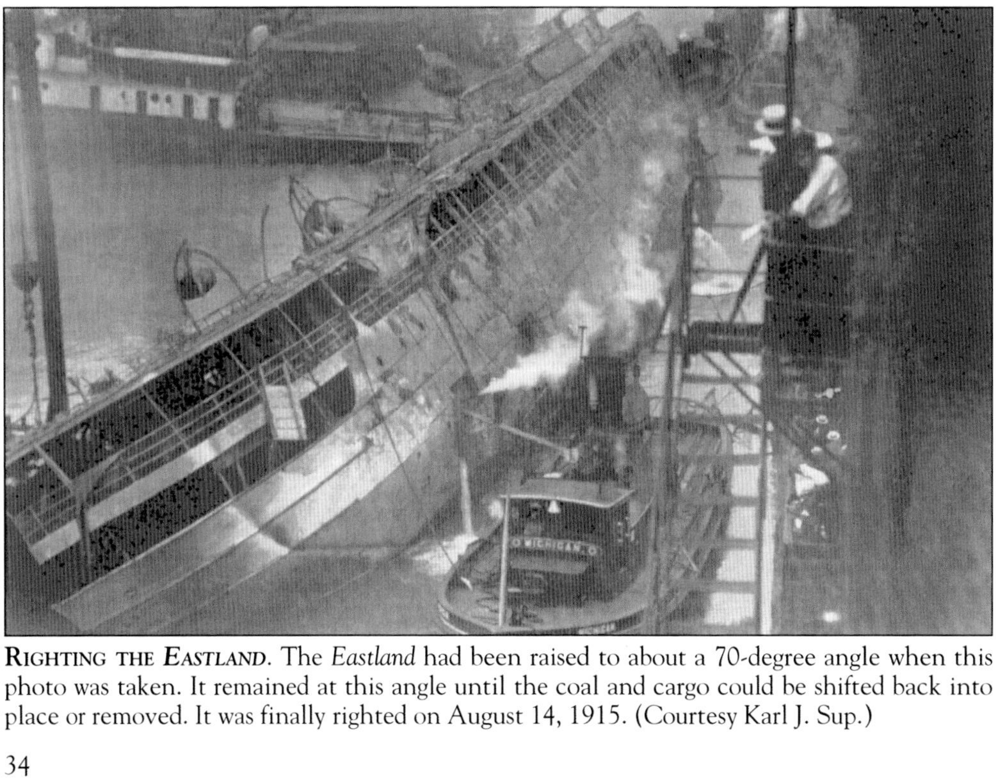

Righting the *Eastland*. The *Eastland* had been raised to about a 70-degree angle when this photo was taken. It remained at this angle until the coal and cargo could be shifted back into place or removed. It was finally righted on August 14, 1915. (Courtesy Karl J. Sup.)

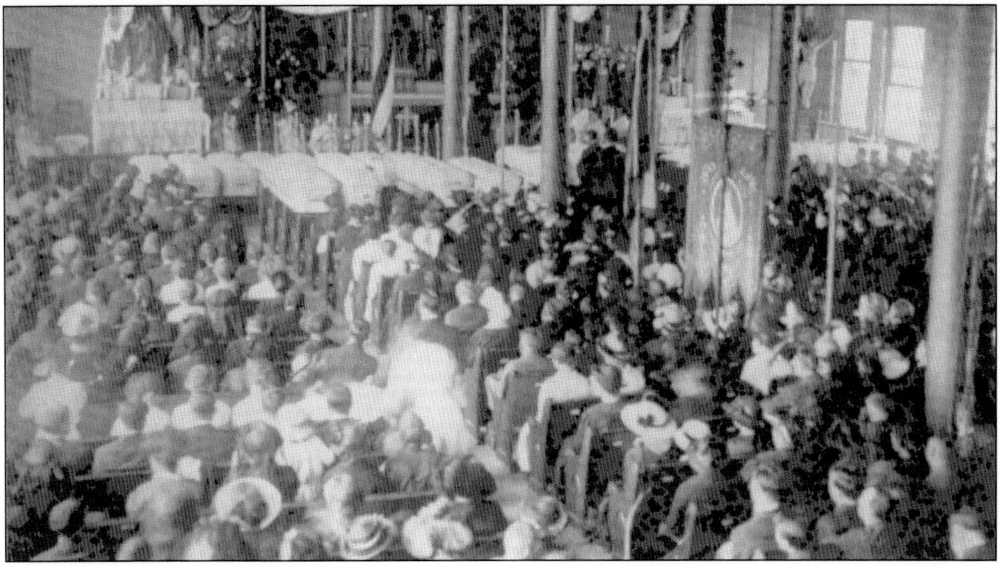

THE 29 CASKET FUNERAL AT ST. MARY'S OF CZESTOCHOWA. The town of Cicero was overwhelmed in the days following the event. Hearses were in short supply, as were cars in general, and Western Electric made their fleet of vehicles available to those in need. Churches were forced to double up on services. In fact, St. Mary's of Czestochowa, near the plant, held a Mass for 29 people. Mary Queen of Heaven held a service for 13 in an unfinished facility. (Courtesy Karl J. Sup.)

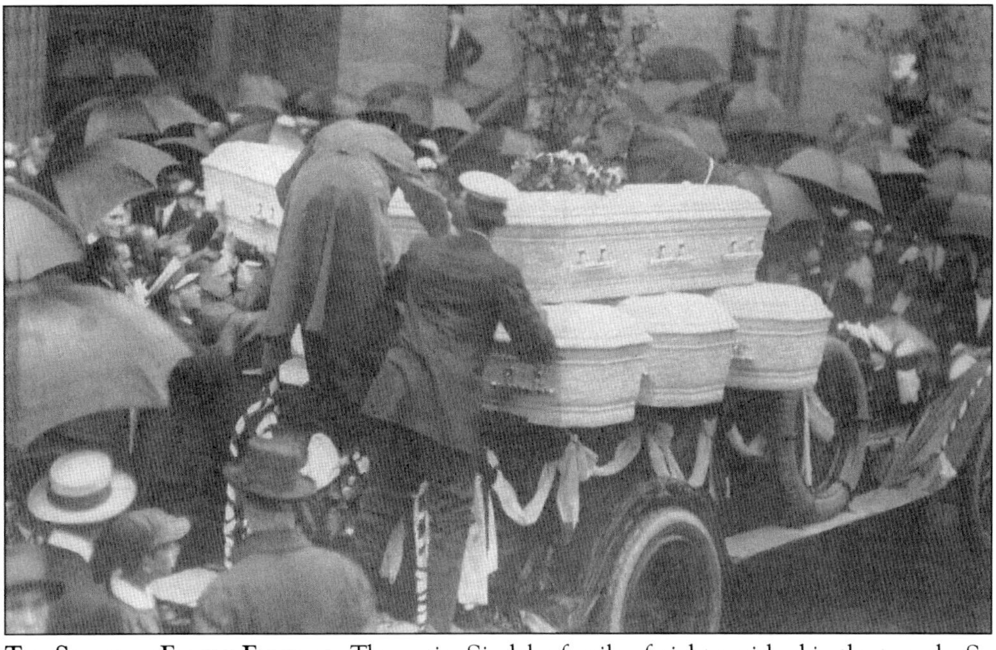

THE SINDELAR FAMILY FUNERAL. The entire Sindelar family of eight perished in the tragedy. So many funerals were held on Wednesday, July 28, Chicago's official day of mourning, that Marshall Field and Company allowed 39 of its largest auto trucks to be used as hearses, as seen here. Homes draped with black crepe were a common sight on the streets of Cicero. One person recalled that on at least one Cicero street, every house had a black drape. (Courtesy Karl J. Sup.)

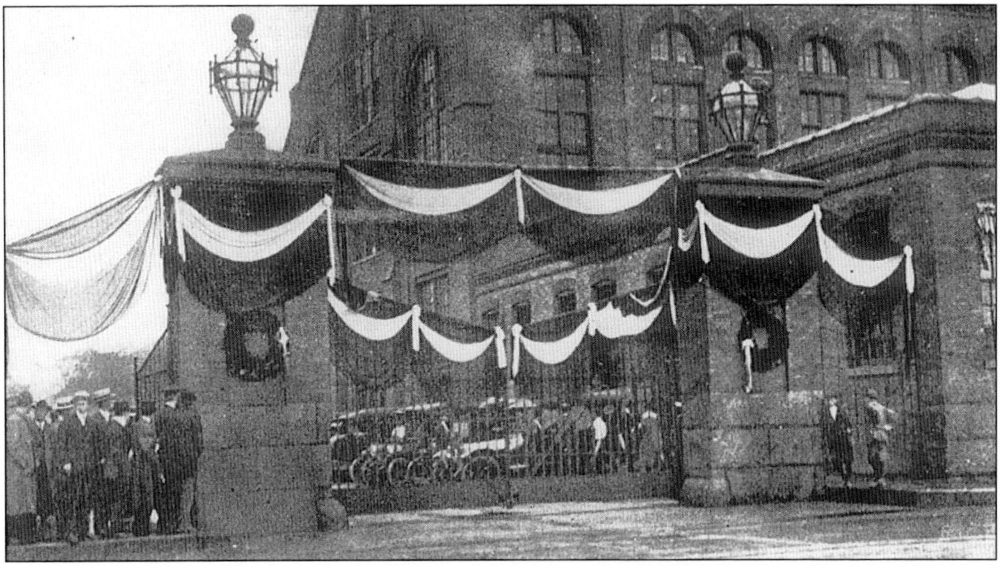

The Hawthorne Gates Draped in Mourning. Aid began arriving on the chaotic scene immediately after the *Eastland* turned over on her side. Strangers helped as they could, and underwater divers were called into action. The Hawthorne Works were closed for several days, and workers volunteered their time and vehicles to get help to the families in need. The Western reopened on Thursday the 29th, and on one bench where 22 women had worked, only two had survived.

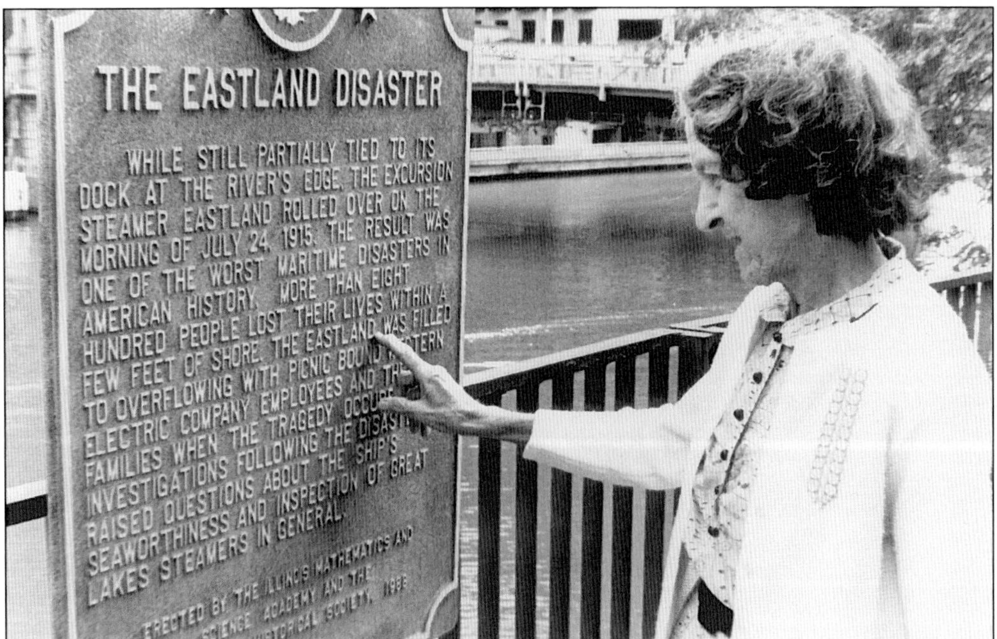

Libby Klucina Hruby, Survivor. In July of 1990, The Historical Society of Cicero held a wreath-laying ceremony at the site of the *Eastland* disaster. The plaque had been placed at the site by students of the Illinois Math and Science Academy, and the Illinois State Historical Society in 1988. Pictured here reading the plaque is Libby Klucina Hruby, who survived the disaster at the age of ten. (Courtesy *Life* Newspaper.)

Four

THE CAPONE ERA

A combination of several factors lead Al Capone to make his headquarters in Cicero during the years of Prohibition. First, Cicero's location grabbed the attention of "Big Al" and his men when Chicago elected a Democratic mayor intent on ridding the city of organized crime. "The First Suburb West" was just barely outside Chicago, but was safely out of the reach of her police jurisdiction. Second, Mayor Klenha of Cicero and many of her police officers could be easily bought and controlled by the "mafia." Third, Cicero had many speakeasies that already got their beer from breweries run by the Capone-Torrio organization, so it felt like home.

Al Capone made The Hawthorne Hotel his headquarters while in Cicero, from 1924 through 1931. Taking virtual control of Cicero in 1924 was an easy matter. Simple brute force on election day was all that was needed. Voters were harassed while waiting in line to mark their ballots and told for whom to vote. If they seemed uncooperative, the ballot was ripped from their hands and marked for them. Democratic poll watchers were beat up, tied up, and even locked in basements until the day ended.

So many intimidating black sedans were driving around town that election day, that the one filled with undercover policemen from Chicago went unnoticed until the detectives jumped out and opened fire on the trio standing on the Cicero Avenue corner "influencing" voters. Frank Capone soon lay dead, but Al still successfully controlled the election. The stranglehold on Cicero lasted for years before "Scarface" went to prison for tax evasion. But the reputation for corruption in Cicero lingered.

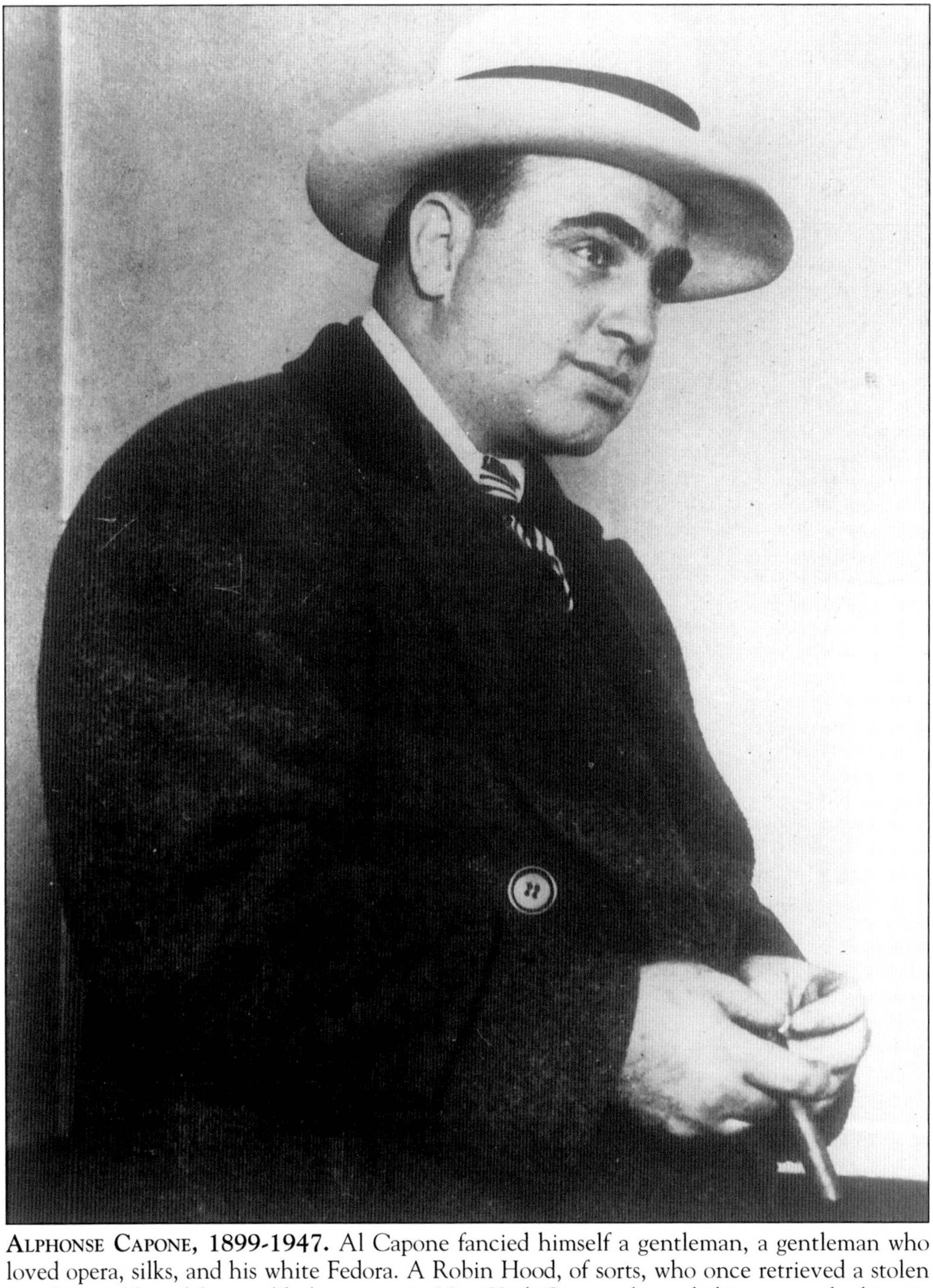

Alphonse Capone, 1899-1947. Al Capone fancied himself a gentleman, a gentleman who loved opera, silks, and his white Fedora. A Robin Hood, of sorts, who once retrieved a stolen wooden washboard for an elderly woman in New York City, and paraded its return, basking in the hero-worship. He called everyone a friend; he was loving and generous with his family; and he started soup kitchens during the Depression, all the while masterminding the most violent series of crimes imaginable during Prohibition. Capone had arrived in Chicago at the age of 19, and was head of the mafia before he was 25. By the time he was 31, he was in jail and losing power fast. (Courtesy Illinois State Historical Library.)

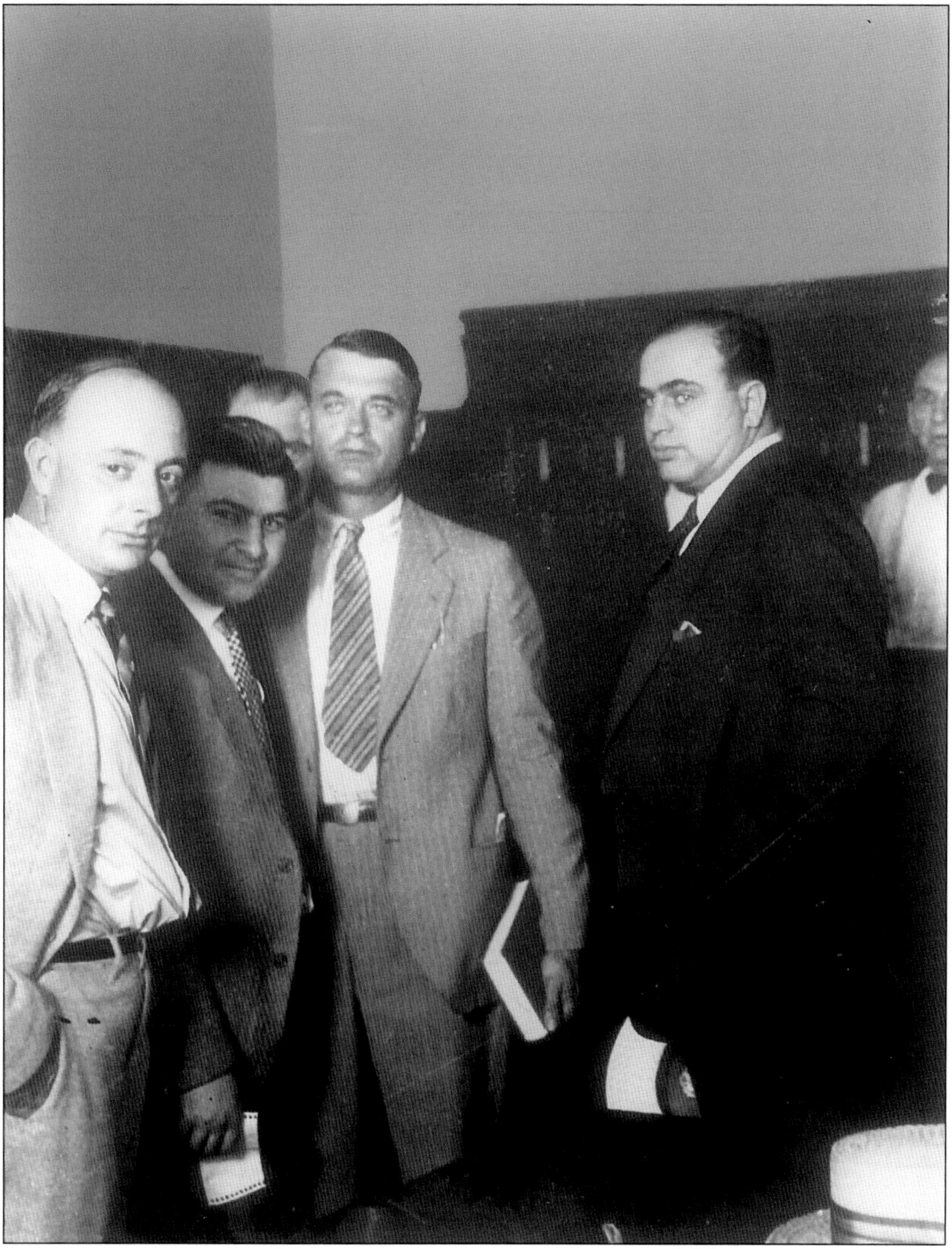

SCARFACE. Al Capone was born and raised in New York City in a loving family who had emigrated from Naples, Italy. He was kicked out of school after hitting a teacher, spent some time with the Five Points Gang of Manhattan, and tried his hand at legitimate jobs, including bartending at the Harvard Inn. There he made a pass at a pretty girl, whose brother, Frank Galluccio, defended her honor with a knife. Thirty stitches later, Capone had two scars on the left side of his face, which he usually tried to hide. Al didn't care for the nickname Scarface, much preferring "Snorky," slang for stylish. (Courtesy Illinois State Historical Library.)

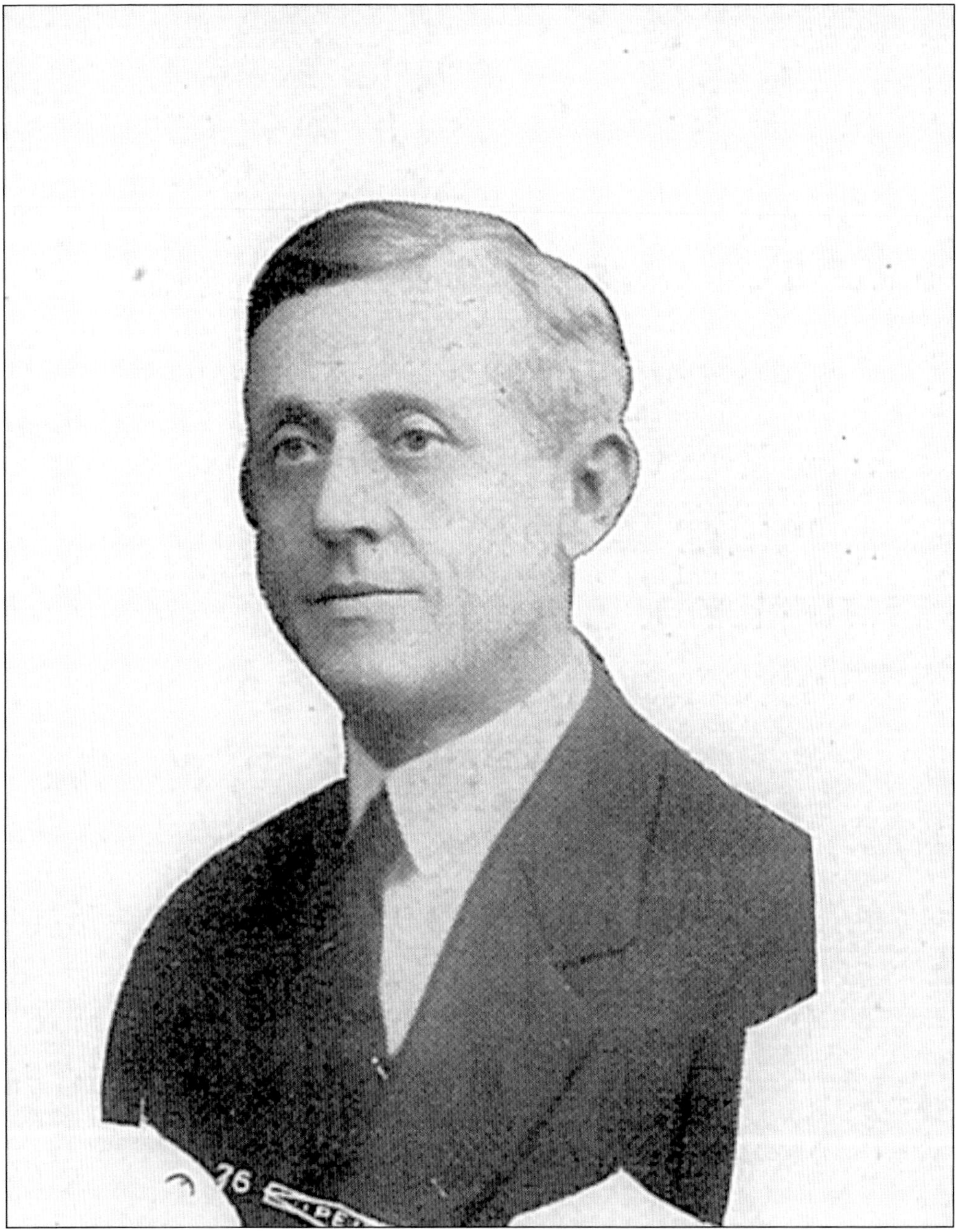

MAYOR KLENHA OF CICERO. When a Democratic mayor was elected in Chicago bent on getting rid of the mafia, the easiest place for Capone to set up his headquarters was in the first suburb west, namely, Cicero. Capone had already received a friendly reception there, so he vigorously (and violently) helped re-elect the Republican Mayor Joseph Klenha in 1924. Then Mayor Klenha seemed to have a change of heart, and mentioned cleaning up the town of Cicero, too. This would not do, as his election had been paid for dearly by Al, whose own brother was killed on a Cicero corner. After beating Klenha up on the steps of Cicero City Hall, the Mayor co-operated, and Capone showed him respect. In fact, Al cut him in on the action to such a degree that Mayor Klenha eventually was named in a federal indictment!

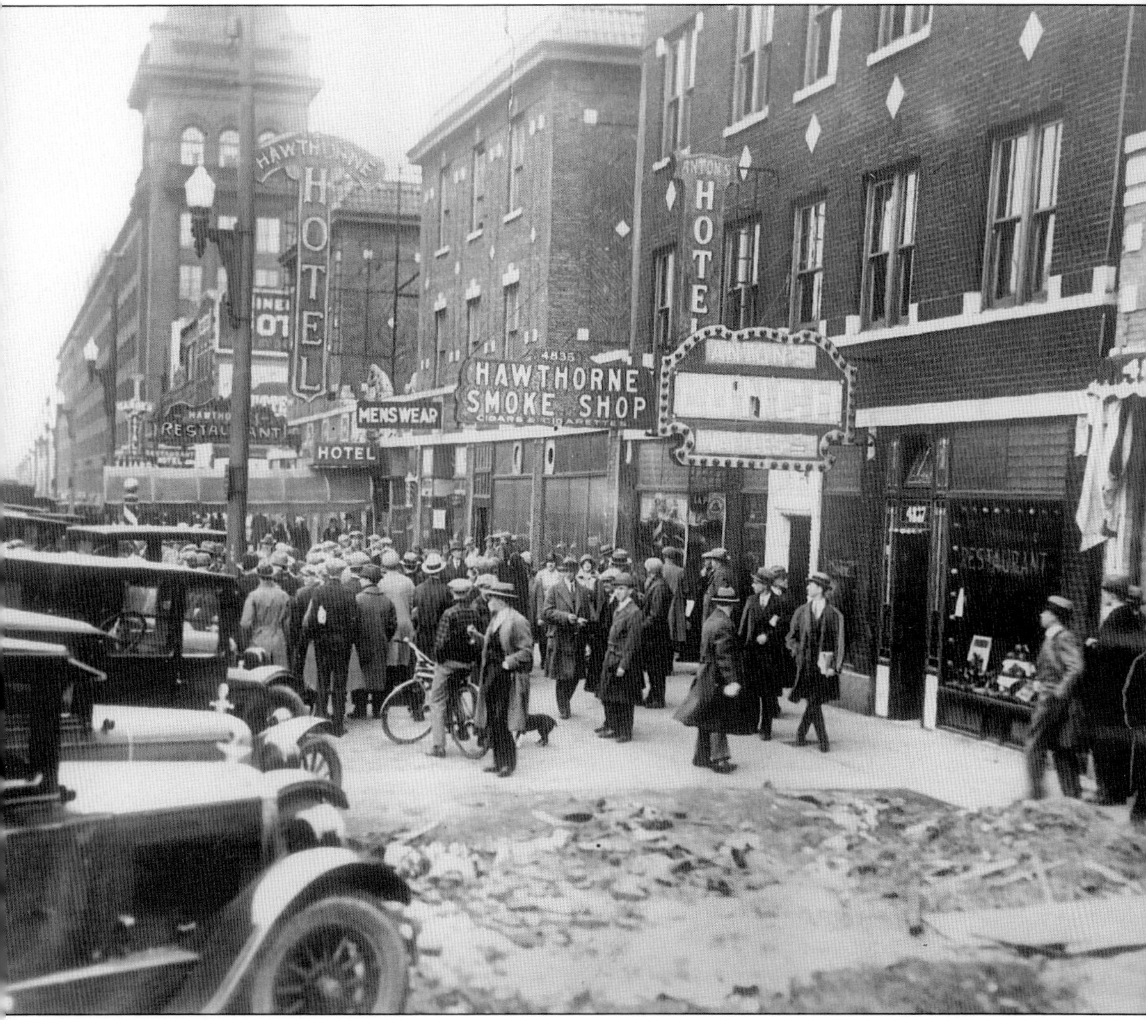

THE HAWTHORNE HOTEL AND SMOKE SHOP, 1926. The Hawthorne Restaurant, on the corner of Cicero and Twenty-Second Street, was the scene of an ambush that almost ended Capone's career on September 20, 1926. Al and his bodyguard, Frank Rio, sat drinking coffee at a table "away from the window, facing the door." First, a sedan shooting blanks drove by, creating curiosity. As Capone stepped toward the door to see what was going on, Rio tackled him and knocked him to the floor. Rio understood that the real attack was still coming. A procession of ten sedans slowly rolled down the block as men began firing their machine guns starting at the Anton Hotel, and continuing until they got to the corner. Windows, plates, and chunks of paneling all showered down. Thousands of bullets were shot that day, all waist and chest high. Finally, one gunman knelt in the restaurant doorway and emptied a hundred-round drum before swaggering away. "If you smell gun powder, you're in Cicero," became an oft-repeated phrase. (Courtesy John Binder.)

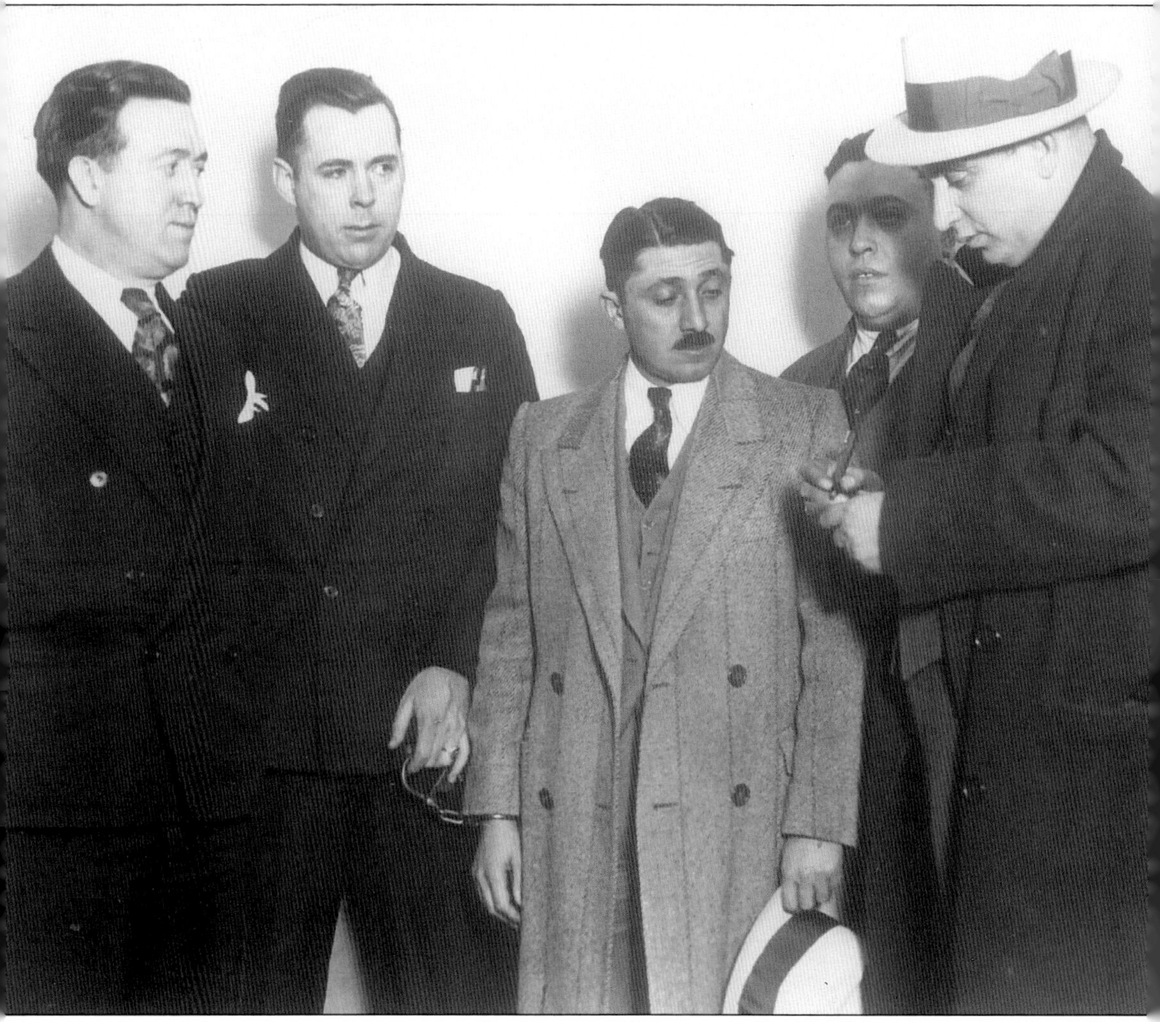

Frank Nitti, Capone's Eventual Successor. Al Capone's "business" (he often called himself an antique dealer) employed 400 people and involved over 160 gambling joints and 123 saloons in Cicero alone. This was a world that dealt in cash. But what do you do with that much cash on a daily basis? You have to trust someone, and Al trusted Frank Nitti, a small man with slicked-down hair parted in the middle. Frank Nitti oversaw the gambling operation and skimmed off his share of the profits. He often took cash to Cicero banks and exchanged the bundles for cashier's checks. The banks cooperated and left little paper trail. But dogged tax men eventually found Nitti's signature on a check, opening the door for tax evasion charges. In 1943, when all looked hopeless, Nitti chose to end his life on the railroad tracks in Riverside rather than join Capone in jail. (Courtesy Illinois State Historical Library.)

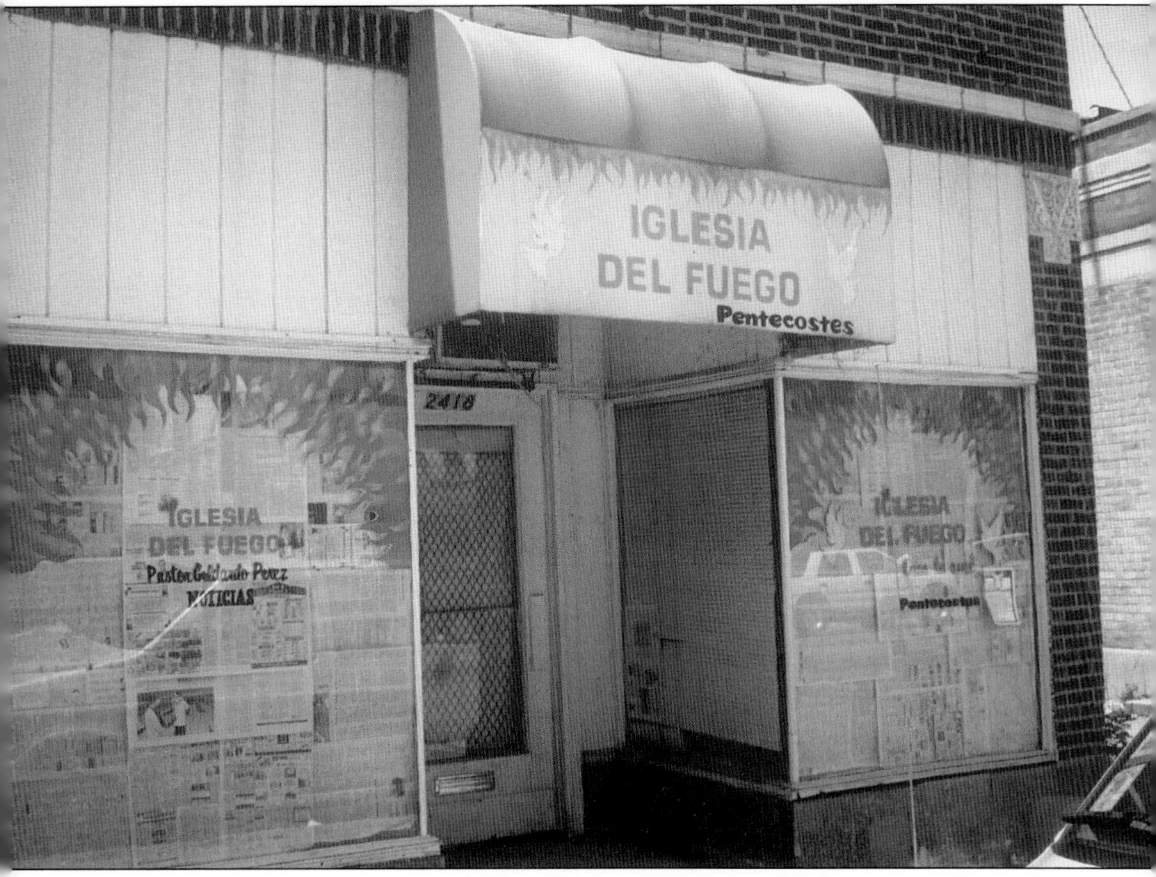

THE OLD *CICERO TRIBUNE* OFFICE ON FIFTY-SECOND. Not many dared to oppose Capone's violent tactics and lived to tell about it. One such person was Robert St. John, a reporter who opened his own newspaper, The *Cicero Tribune*, in 1922, at 2418 S. Fifty-Second Avenue (now Laramie). He verbally attacked Capone and the corrupt administration of Cicero. He endlessly reported on the brothels and racketeering. One morning, while crossing the street to his office, St. John was attacked by Ralph Capone and two others, who beat him unconscious. Upon leaving the hospital, St. John was told that his bills had been paid by a hefty man with a scar on his left cheek. That same man had also managed to buy off St. John's business partners, and he essentially now owned the paper. St. John left the office that day, never to return.

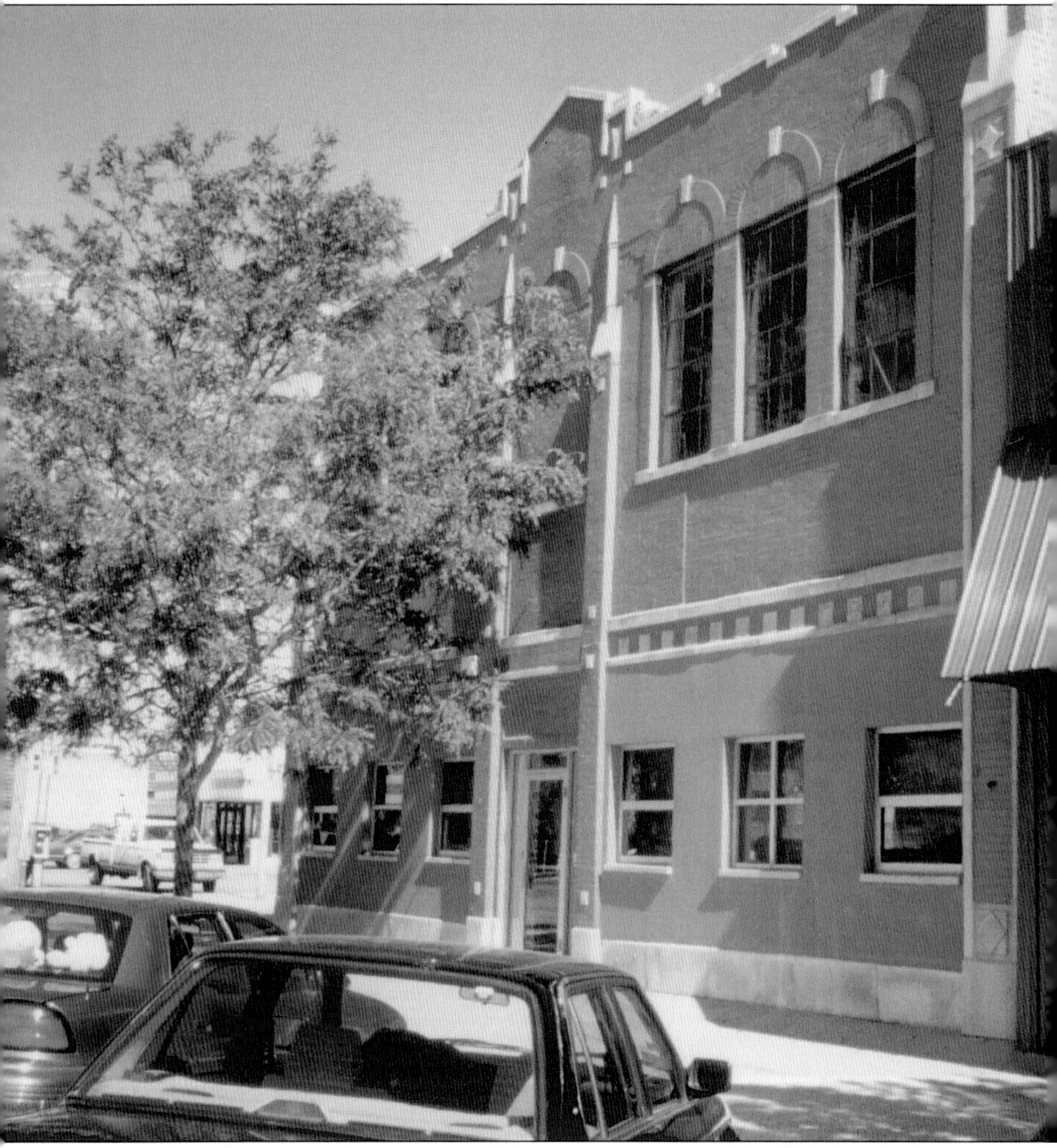

Reputed to Be the Cotton Club, Owned by Ralph Capone. Al Capone was a family man. He supported his relatives financially, while never talking "business" with the ladies. His younger sister, Mafalda, named after an Italian princess, married John Maritote on December 14, 1930. Their huge wedding needed a church large enough and with a willingness to allow an outsider to use the facility during the Advent season. St. Mary's of Czestochowa, just off Cicero Avenue at Thirtieth Place, fit the bill. Guests entered through a canopy that extended to the curb. Flowers overflowed the altar and the aisles. Afterwards, a party was held at Ralph Capone's Cotton Club, and featured a wedding cake in the shape of a yacht, nine feet long and four feet high, with "Honolulu" in icing on its prow. Al, however, missed the fun. He was safely tucked away in Florida, avoiding a warrant for his arrest.

Five

Morton East High School and College

The community of Cicero recognized the need for education. In fact, education was seen then, as it is now, as the key to improving oneself and one's situation. Cicero forefathers and foremothers also believed that quality education would help the town prosper. In 1894, the first high school students met on the second floor of an old red brick building on Ogden Avenue, called Clyde High School. In less than ten years, the student body outgrew the first building and moved to a new building at Austin and Twenty-Fifth Street. Over the years, new buildings replaced old ones that were destroyed by fire, or simply outgrown.

In 1926, Chodl Auditorium was built and has graced Cicero with its presence and landmark status. Morton alums have fond memories of the many ways the auditorium was used in different years: as a study hall, a gymnasium, and as a theater. Fortunately, the auditorium has been lovingly renovated and is treated with the respect it deserves. The huge Hope Memorial Field House now occupies what used to be houses and a parking lot on the east side of Fifty-Ninth Court. An Olympic-sized pool replaced the basement pool where the boys' gym classes swam without suits, and the girls shared suits that had more holes than fabric. A second-story crosswalk makes it easy to get to the gym in any weather.

The brass is still polished, the walls are newly painted, and the old building has stood up well considering the thousands who have walked her floors and leaned on her lockers. The hallways actually seem quieter today than they did in the '60s, but the laughter remains, and the sound of Spanish being spoken is a recent addition. There's important work being done today, just as in yesteryear.

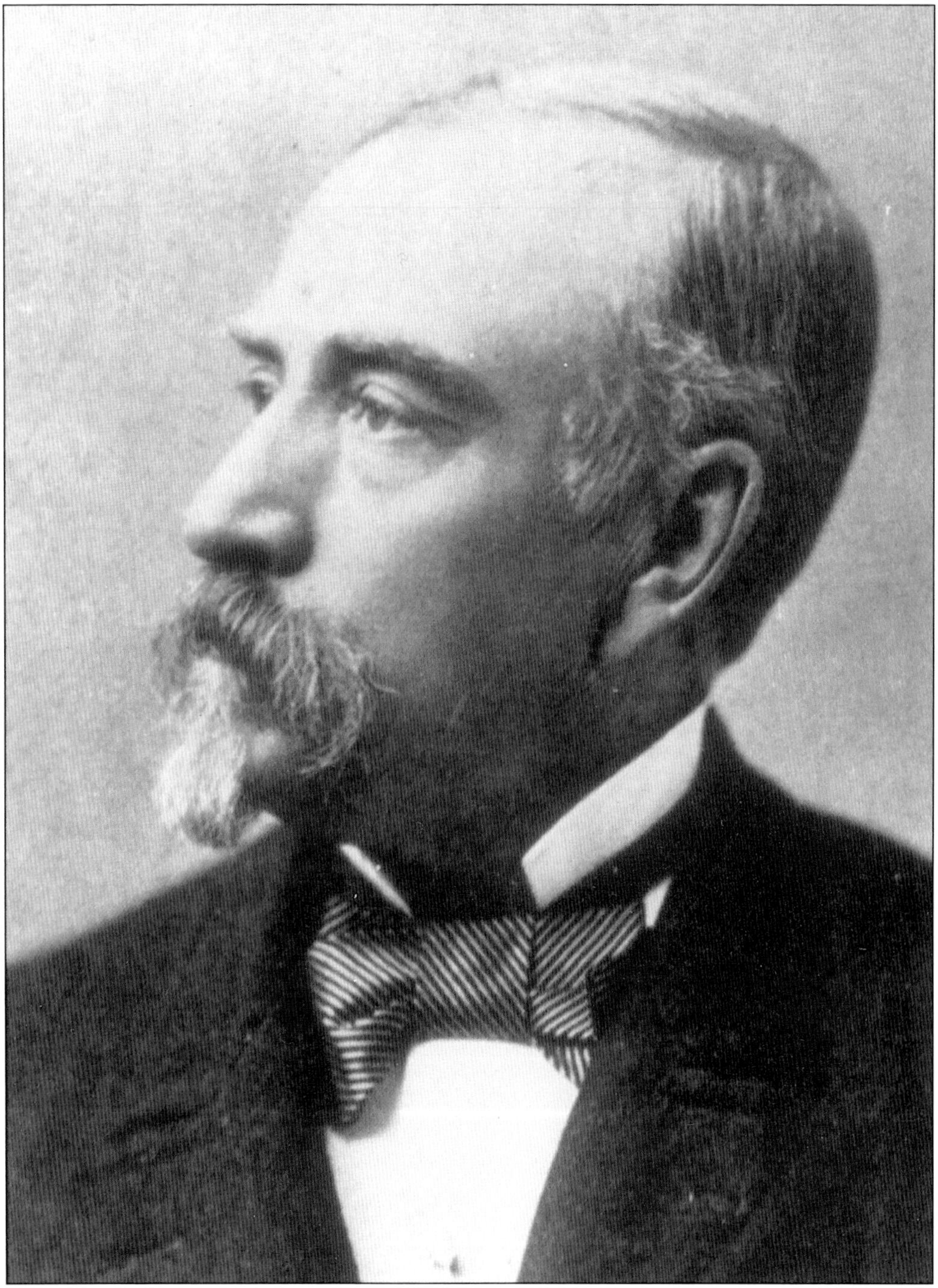

JULIUS STERLING MORTON, 1832–1902. J. Sterling Morton was a political leader and nature lover who established the United States' observance of Arbor Day. He was Secretary of Agriculture in President Grover Cleveland's cabinet. The Morton Park area and Morton High Schools were named after this important Nebraskan, due to his friendship with a prominent fur trader and grain dealer named Portus Baxter Weare, who resided in Cicero and encouraged the town's development. (Courtesy Morton Archives.)

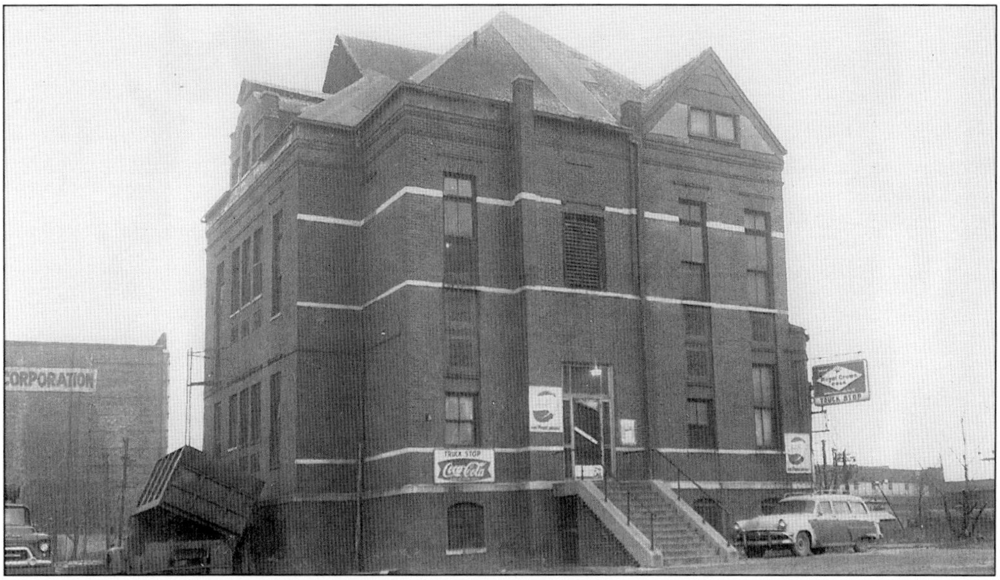

THE CLYDE TOWNSHIP HIGH SCHOOL. In 1889, eight young people comprised the first freshman class on the second floor of the "little red schoolhouse" at Ogden and Fifty-Ninth Avenue. Annie Hall, Marybelle Moore, Lulu MacDonald, Margaret Hancock, Edith Roome, Guy Bennett, Ed Moore, and Thomas Hancock had graduated from the elementary school on the first floor in June. By 1899, when H. Victor Church became principal, there were 44 students, necessitating a larger building. (Courtesy *Life* Newspaper.)

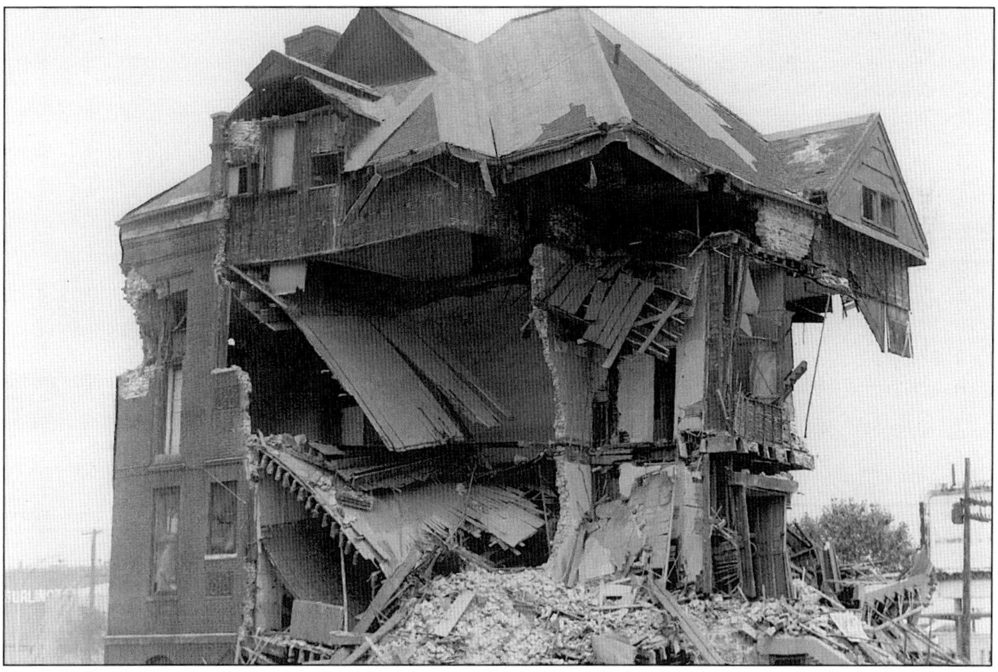

TEARING DOWN THE " LITTLE RED SCHOOLHOUSE." The old high school was later used as a truck stop before it was finally torn down to make way for new buildings on the lot. The population growth on the north side of the Chicago, Burlington, and Quincy tracks indicated the need for a new, large high school there. (Courtesy *Life* Newspaper.)

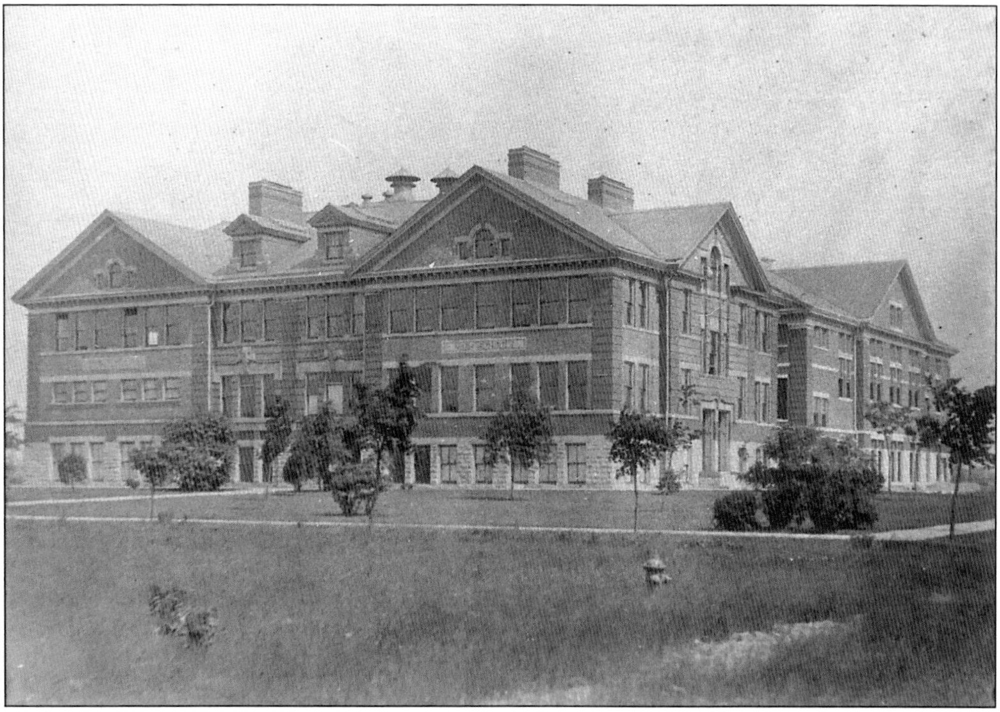

The New J. Sterling Morton High School. In 1903, a new high school was built on the site at Twenty-Fifth and Austin Boulevard. It was considered the epitome of school structures. The new facility included classrooms, an auditorium, a gymnasium, and physics and cooking laboratories. So rapidly was the community growing, however, that an addition was needed by 1908. (Courtesy *Life* Newspaper.)

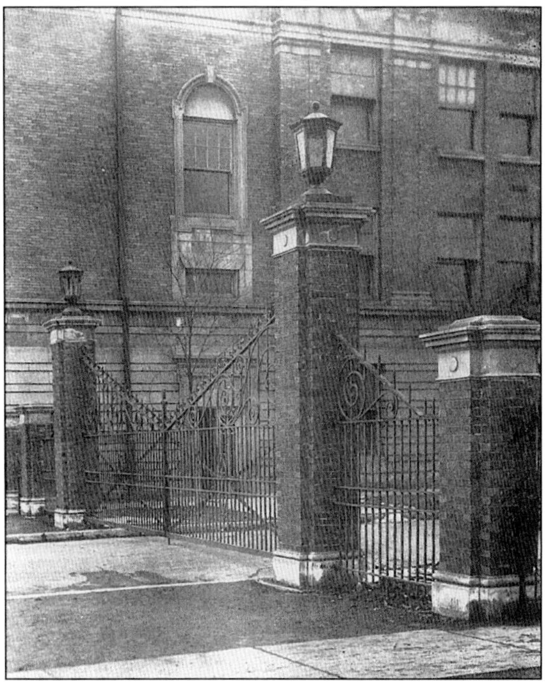

The Gateway to Education. Stepping inside the beautiful old gates at the Morton High School and Junior College facility was a step into the world of arts and culture as well as education. The often harsh, industrial noises of Cicero were muted in the halls of learning. The people of Cicero had little money or time for the pursuit of the finer things in life, but the opportunities offered at Morton filled lives with the beauty missing on the streets.

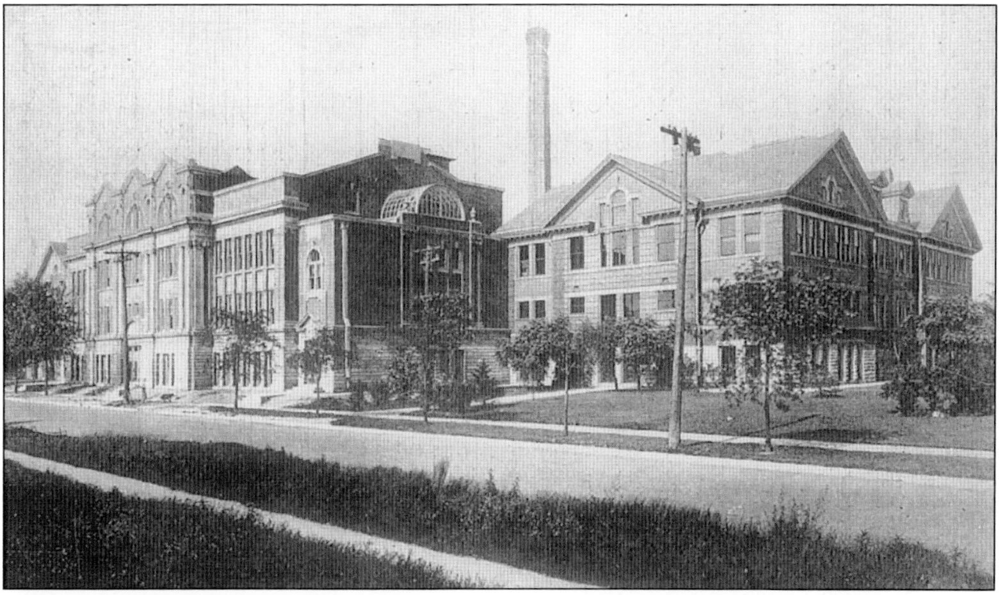

1923 Yearbook Photo of JSM. Additions to the high school were made in 1908 and 1923. Then, on December 29, 1924, fire totally destroyed the auditorium and gymnasium. The community leapt into action and built another addition including 30 more classrooms, a library, new laboratories, and cafeteria. But the best part of the addition was the new auditorium.

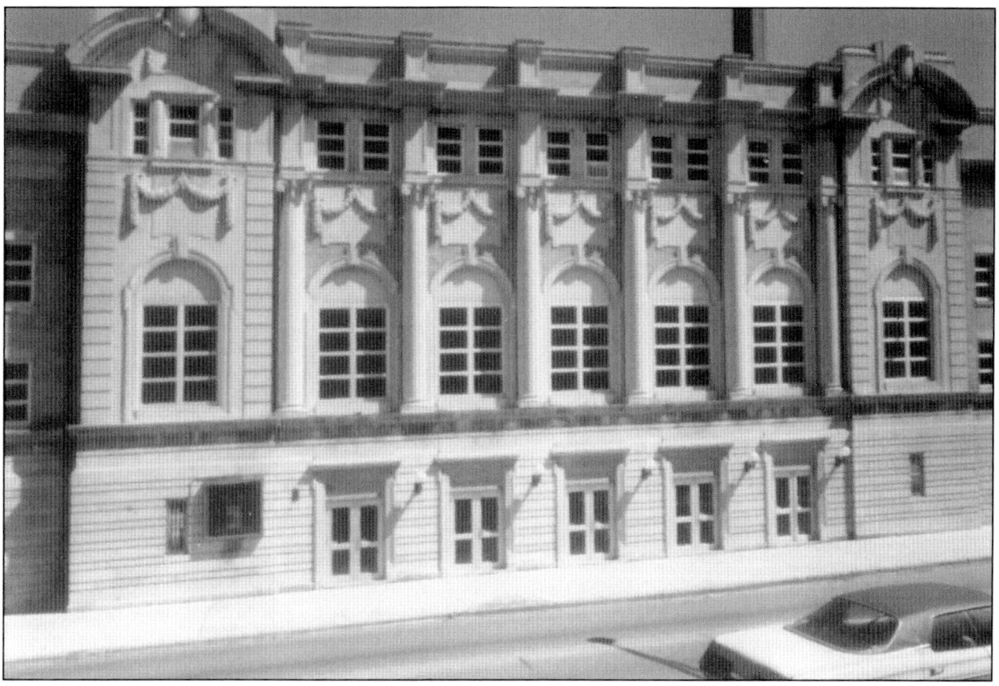

The Chodl Auditorium, 1928. "One of the finest school auditoriums in the world" was named after Edward W. Chodl, long-time president of the Board of Education. Over the years it was used as a study hall, a gym, and a basketball court (the seats were the most comfortable "bleachers" of any school.) Theater productions were held on the stage in the spring and fall when gym classes could be held outside. (Courtesy Morton Archives.)

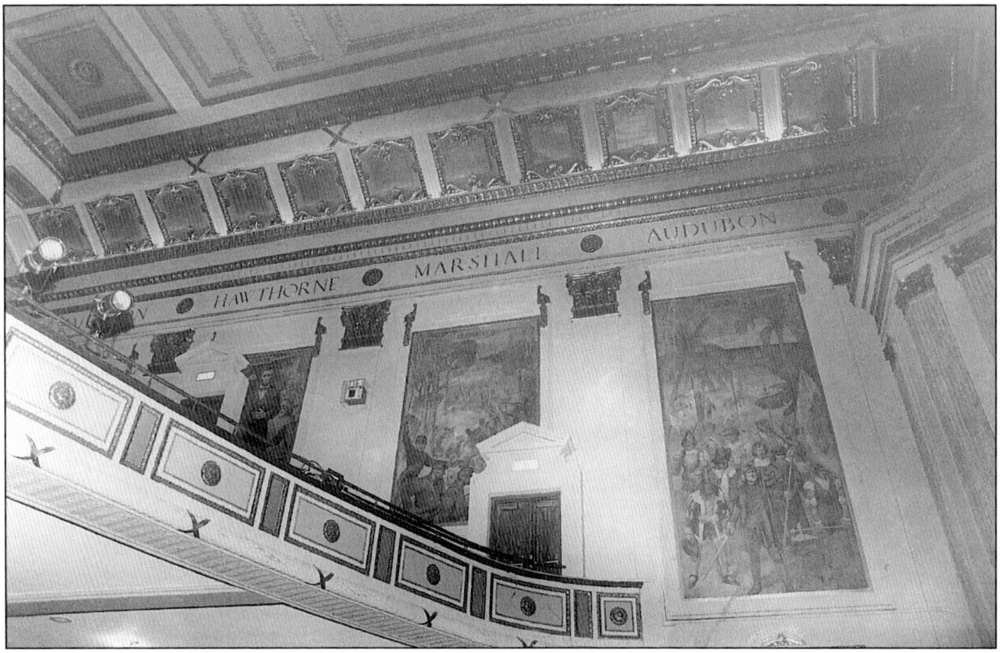

THE INTERIOR OF THE CHODL AUDITORIUM. Restoration in the 1980s returned the auditorium to its previous glory. The murals, painted by C.M. Fox of Marshall Fields' Art Design Studio, depict historical events such as "The Pilgrim's Landing," "Lincoln Giving the Gettysburg Address," "Fort Dearborn," "The Battle of Gettysburg," and "The Battle of Argonne." With a seating capacity of 2,800 the auditorium is used for community events as well as school productions. (Courtesy *Life* Newspaper.)

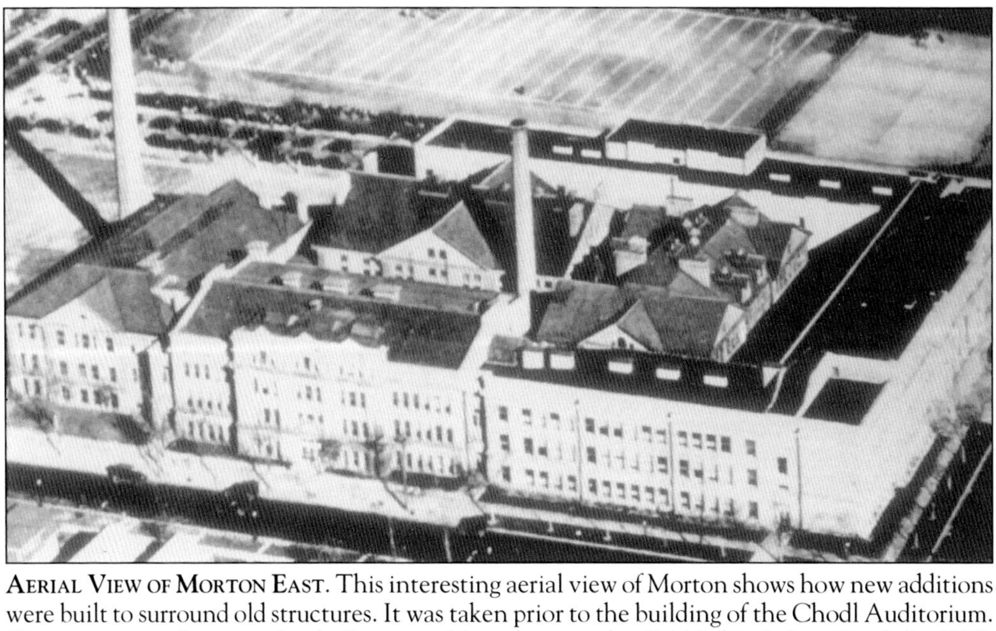

AERIAL VIEW OF MORTON EAST. This interesting aerial view of Morton shows how new additions were built to surround old structures. It was taken prior to the building of the Chodl Auditorium. Sharp eyes can also see a football game taking place on the field behind the school. In 1929, there were 4,700 students attending the high school, and counting the Junior College and other departments, the total was nearly 6,500 students. (Courtesy Morton Archives.)

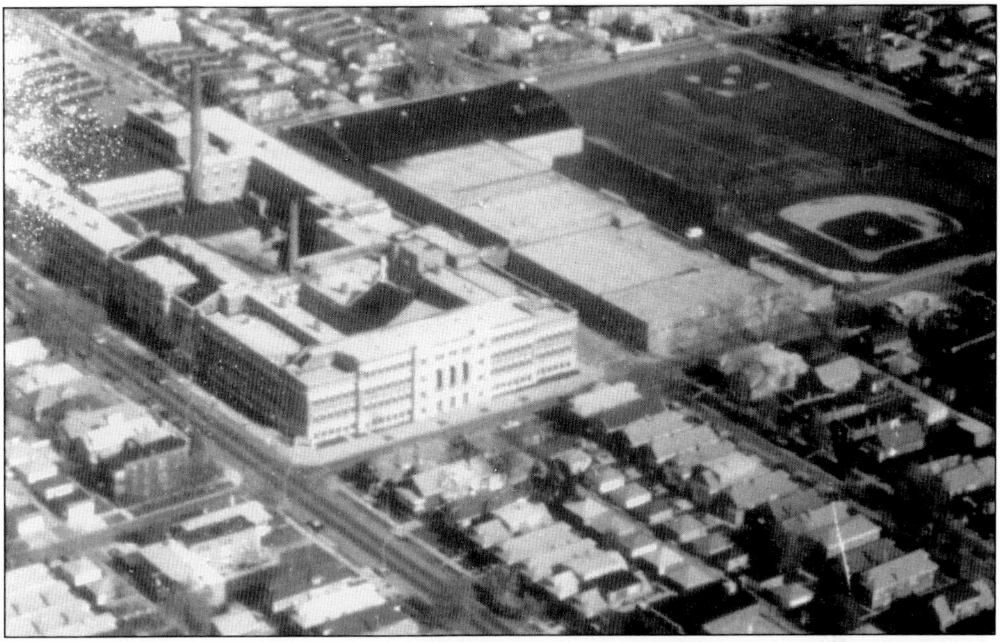

A Later Aerial View. This aerial view from the '70s shows the newest addition to Morton, the Dr. Joseph Ondrus Athletic Complex. It also shows that several interior buildings have been removed. (Courtesy Morton Archives.)

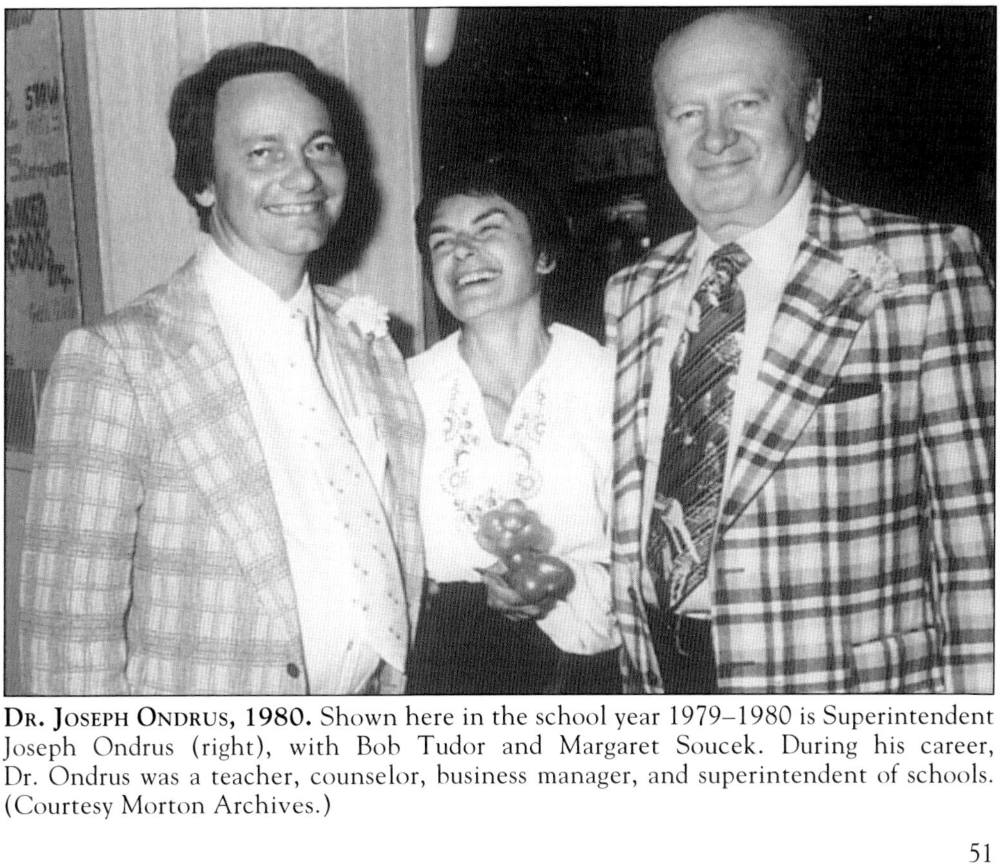

Dr. Joseph Ondrus, 1980. Shown here in the school year 1979–1980 is Superintendent Joseph Ondrus (right), with Bob Tudor and Margaret Soucek. During his career, Dr. Ondrus was a teacher, counselor, business manager, and superintendent of schools. (Courtesy Morton Archives.)

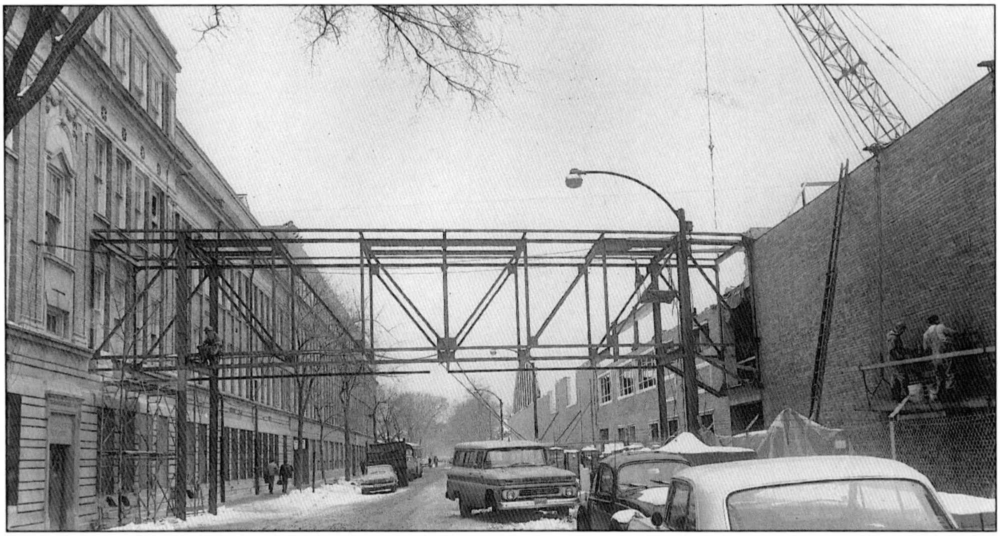

The Crosswalk Over Fifty-Ninth Court. When the new athletic complex was built in the late '60s, a second-floor crosswalk joined the two structures for ease in getting to and from classes in all kinds of weather. (Courtesy *Life* Newspaper.)

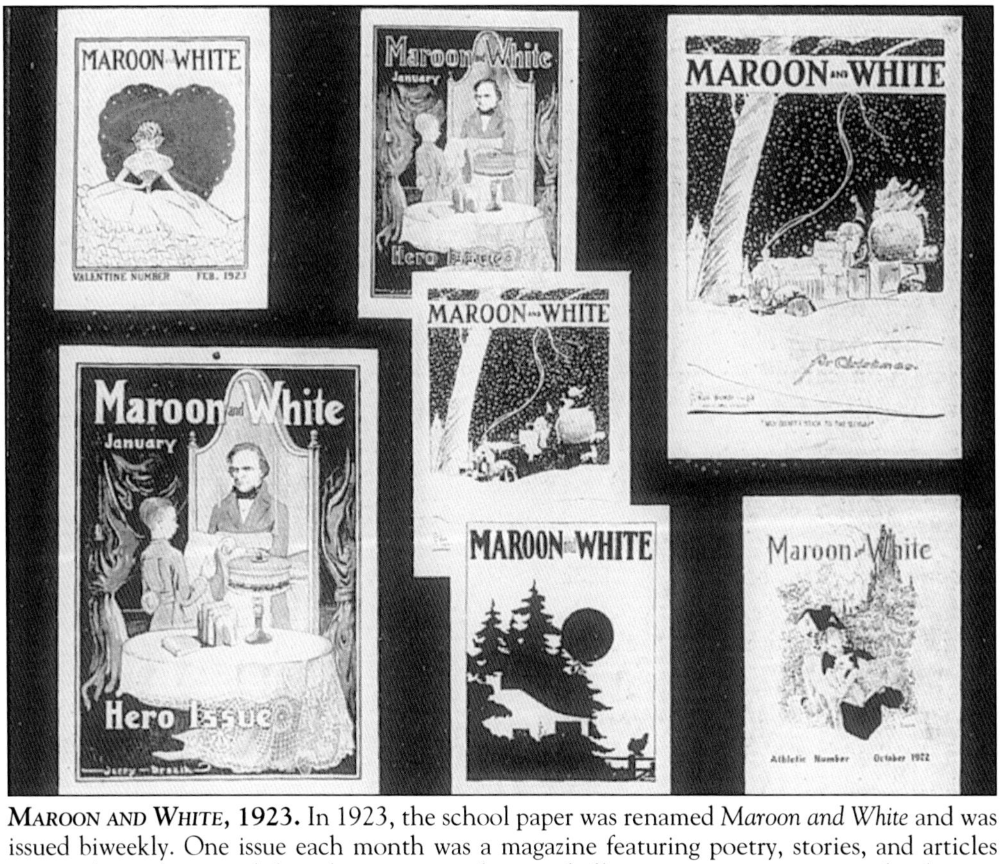

Maroon and White, 1923. In 1923, the school paper was renamed *Maroon and White* and was issued biweekly. One issue each month was a magazine featuring poetry, stories, and articles written by students, and the other was an eight-page bulletin containing current school news. The last issue of the year was a "Farewell Issue" which featured articles written by seniors.

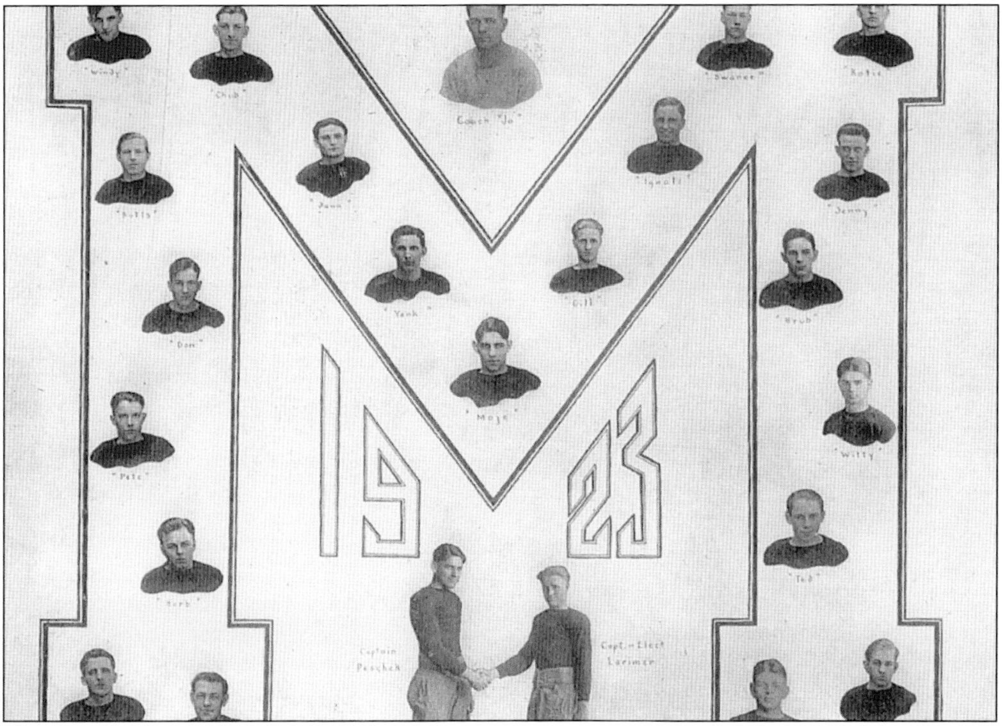

Football, Heavies, 1922–23. "In the fall of 1922, for the first time, Morton entered a football team in the suburban league, and although we did not win a championship, we started the ball rolling." This quote from the 1923 yearbook went on to say: " Larimer, quarterback, was the lightest man on the team, but what he lacked in weight, he made up for in speed. 'Gil's' head and legs got many a touchdown for Morton." Gil Larimer returned to Morton East as a much loved Social Science teacher and Student Council advisor.

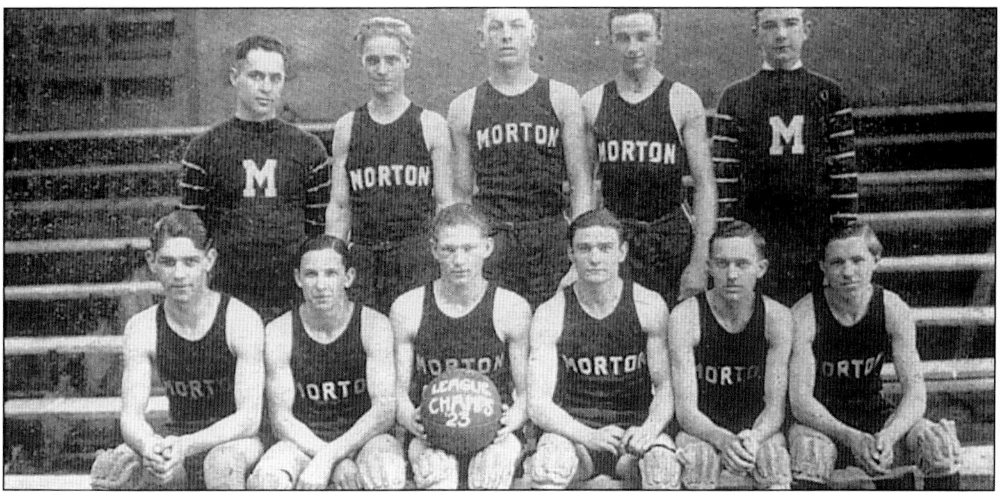

Heavyweight Basketball, 1923. "Before packed stands in the home gym, Coach Long's big five set Oak Park down firmly 34–28 in the closing game of the most successful season a Maroon and White quintet ever had seen. Morton's championship five won their games by perfect teamwork and coordination. They played clean, hard basketball and had only one man sent from the floor on personals all season."

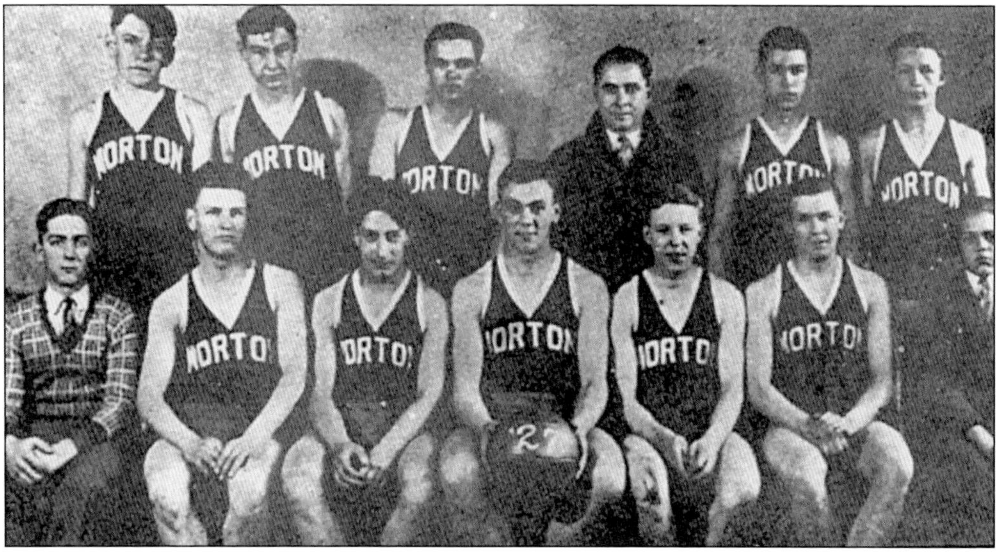

NATIONAL CHAMPIONSHIP BASKETBALL TEAM, 1927. In 1927, The Morton Longmen, under the direction of Coach H. Karl Long, brought honor to Illinois and glory to Morton by winning the National Basketball Tournament at the Bartlett Gym of the University of Chicago. The final score of the championship game against Kansas City was 18–16. The rules then were quite different from current rules.

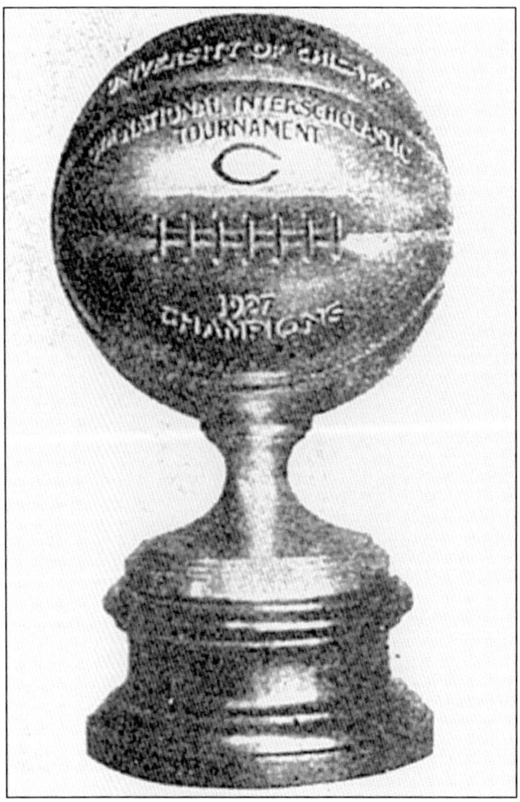

THE NATIONAL TROPHY. Winning the first-place trophy was a thrill for the whole team. There was a week-long celebration. School was let out, theaters showed free movies, and there was dancing in the streets. One team member, George Fencl, later became coach of the 1943 Mustangs, state baseball champions.

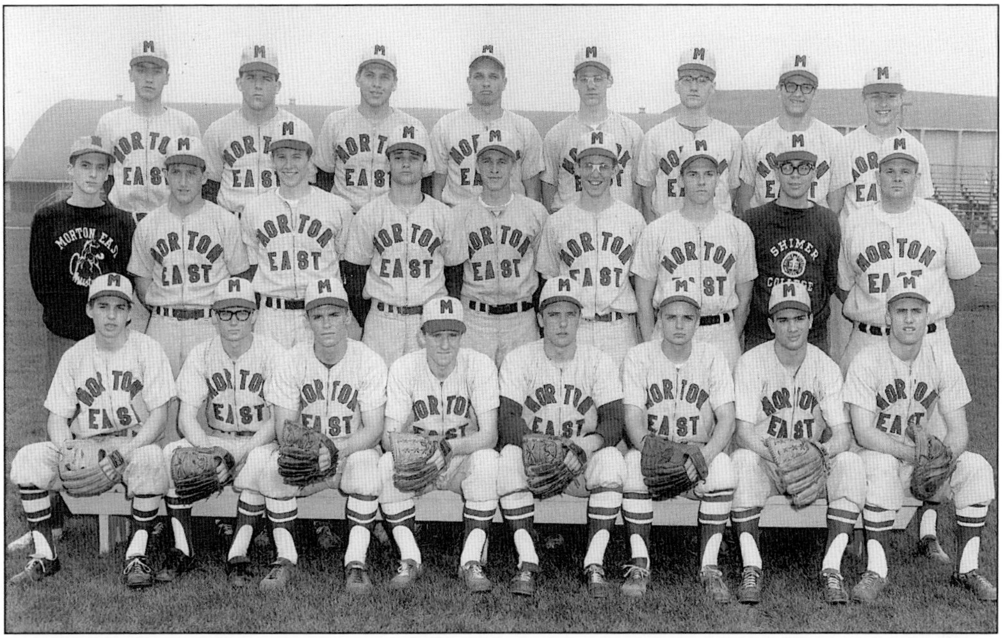

BASEBALL TEAM, 1965. When the basketball season ended each year, many went on to join the baseball team in the spring. Pictured here, from left to right, are: (front row) Steve Vanek, Jim Jackson, Bob Vashinko, George Vokac, Gary Vondrack, Phil Lewandowski, Bob Fenilli, and Russell Vandenburg; (middle row) Fred Halenar, Terry Reid, Ken Palmer, Ron Hainrihar, Bob Fuka, Glenn Sowa, John Draut, Al Jirkovsky, and Herb Salberg; (back row) Jack Funcik, Jim Mlady, Jim Peters, John Posen, Ken Brown, Marty Horgan, Jim Mack, and Bob Miller. (Courtesy Ron Hainrihar.)

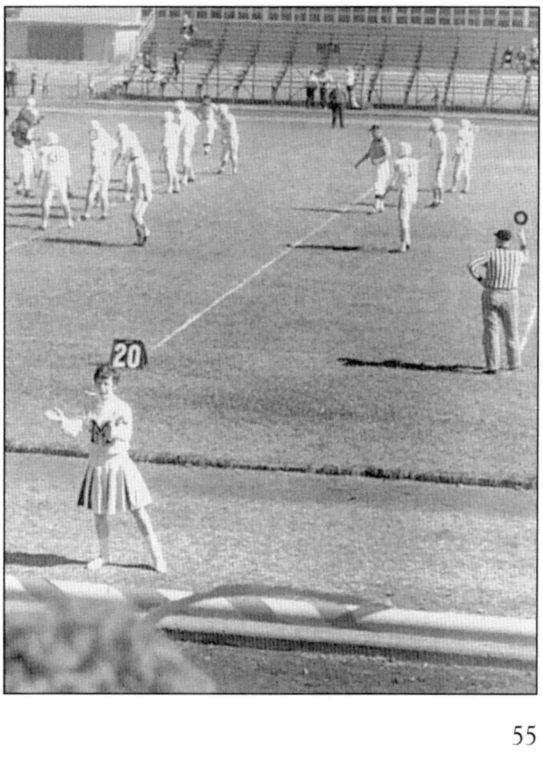

CHEERING FROM THE SIDELINES, 1960S. Michal Morganti (Murphy) leads the cheering fans from the sidelines of the football game played at Morton West. Michal was a gymnast famous for doing back flips across the field, or during basketball season, across the auditorium stage. Spectators counted as she flipped—sometimes 23 times! (Courtesy Michal Murphy.)

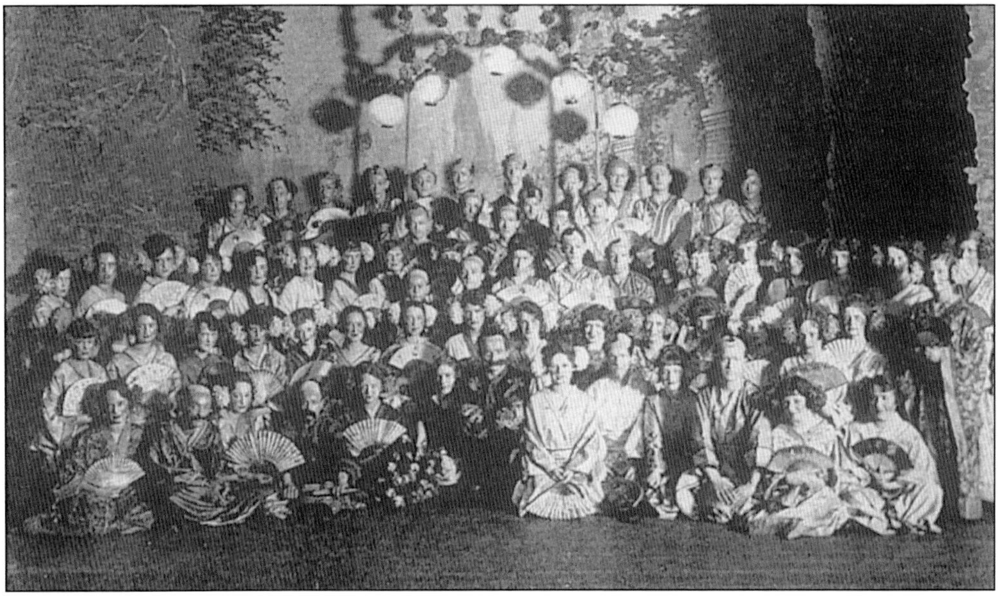

THE MIKADO, 1923. The second operetta ever performed at Morton was in 1923 under the direction of F.C. Gorman. That year the Mikado was played by William Kostka. Other "stars" included Kenneth Morton, George Reilly, Tom Weatherwax, William Rockett, Mary Louise Wright, Arline Cubbin, Marian Muir, and Olive Wistain. The tradition of fine productions continues at Morton. (Courtesy Morton Archives.)

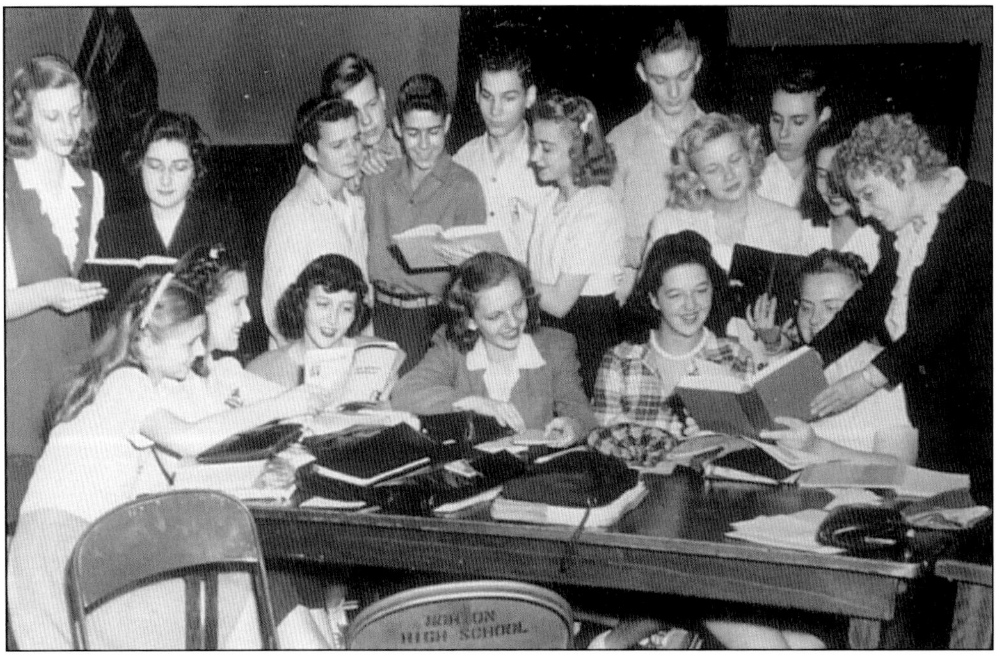

MISS COGGESHALL, THEATER TEACHER. A legend in her own time, Miss Coggeshall is seen here with a group of young people in the 1940s. She was a much loved theater teacher who received messages in later years from former students such as this one: "Dear Miss Coggeshall, To someone I shall never forget. Each part in each play under your direction will always hold a special place in my heart. 12-25-46." (Courtesy Morton Archives.)

John Kriza, Class of '36. A promising young star named John Kriza got his start at Morton in the '30s. In high school, he took part in many activities from Czech Club to swimming. But his greatest love was dancing, and in 1939 he made his debut with the Chicago Opera Ballet. In 1955, he joined the Corps de Ballet Theatre and worked his way through the ranks until he became the leading male dancer in 1955. (Courtesy Morton Archives.)

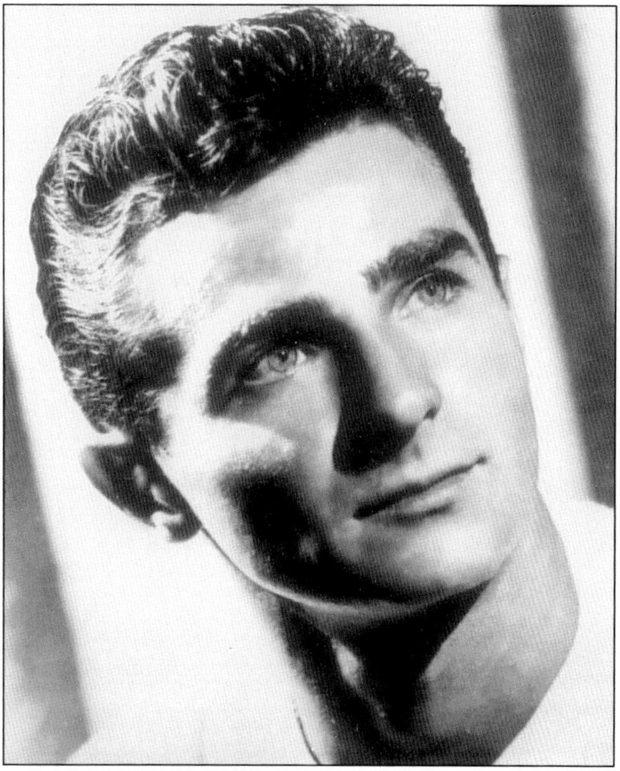

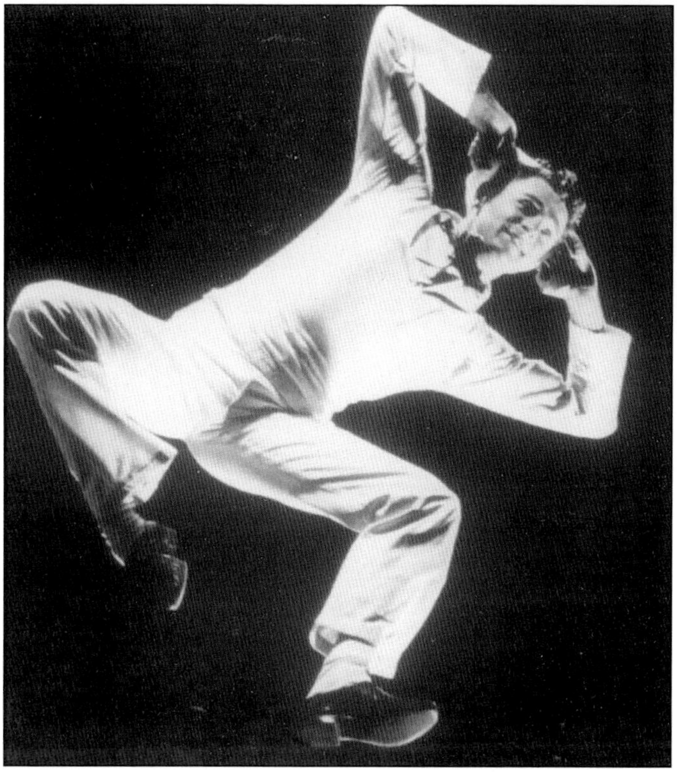

John Kriza on Broadway. John Kriza danced on Broadway in such musicals as the *Follies Bergeres* (1940) and *Panama Hattie* (1941). Before his accidental death in 1975 in Naples, Florida, John also danced classical roles in *Giselle*, *Swan Lake*, and *Les Sylphides*. (Courtesy Morton Archives.)

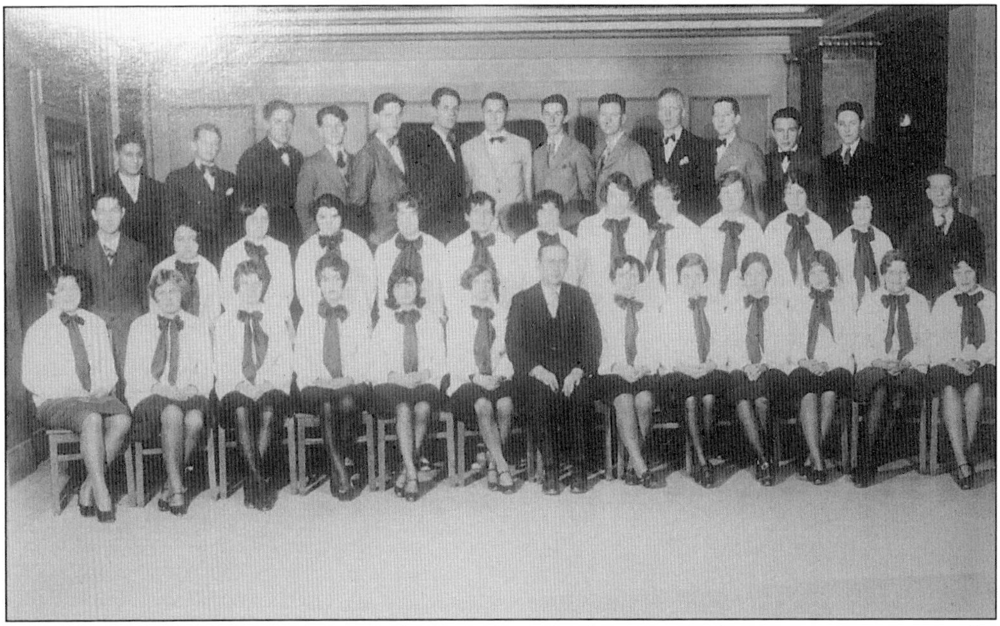

FIRST AEOLIAN CHOIR, 1928–29. The '20s saw the beginning of theater programs in the high school, and also the music program. Pictured here is the first Aeolian Choir, with Charles Haberman directing. (Courtesy Morton Archives.)

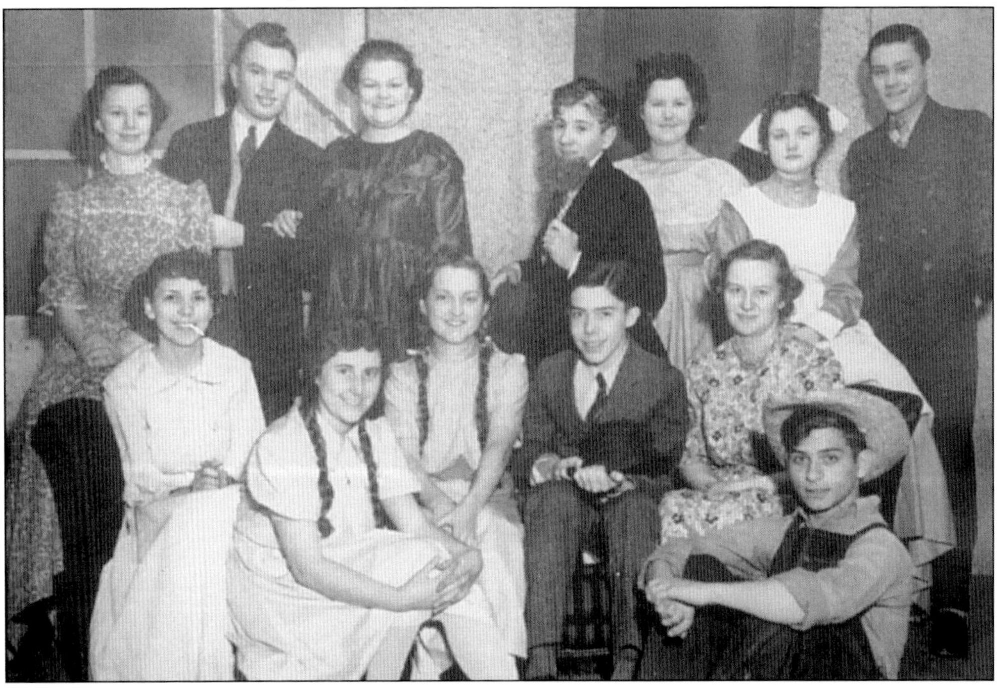

ANNE OF GREEN GABLES, 1939. The senior play in 1939 was *Anne of Green Gables*. Pictured here in the cast photo are, from left to right: (on floor) Francis Discipio; (seated) Marie Amrain, Gwendolyn Lamoreaux, Jane Fijal, Lawrence Johnson, and Evangeline Raevers; (top) Elaine Johnson, Raymond Michalec, Edna Vaculik, George Hejna, La Verne Trcka, Grace Michels, and Keith Smejkal. (Courtesy Morton Archives.)

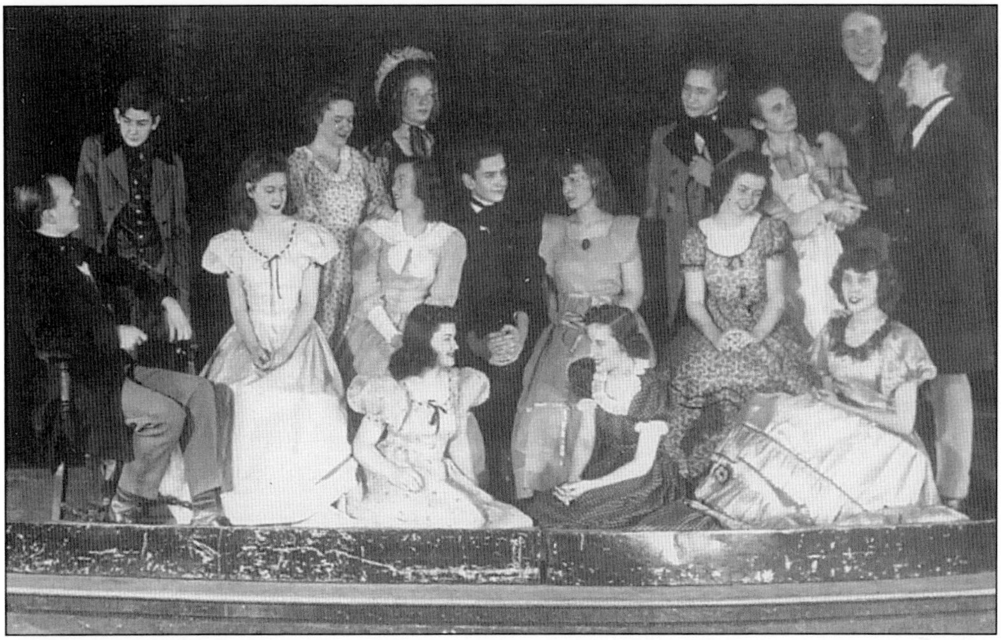

Honest Abe, 1942. The 1942 senior play was *Honest Abe*. Pictured from left to right are: (seated on floor) Pearl Mack and Margaret Launer; (seated on chairs) Fred Page, Rosemaire Datwyler, Phyllis Ashworth, Roger Tate, Jacqueline Kimbark, Hendrika Van Beekum, and Shirley Hrndka; (standing) George Koptic, Corinne Campbell, Barbara Hopp, Donald Barnes, Frank Pliml, Albert (Bud) Novotny, and Roy Janice. (Courtesy Morton Archives.)

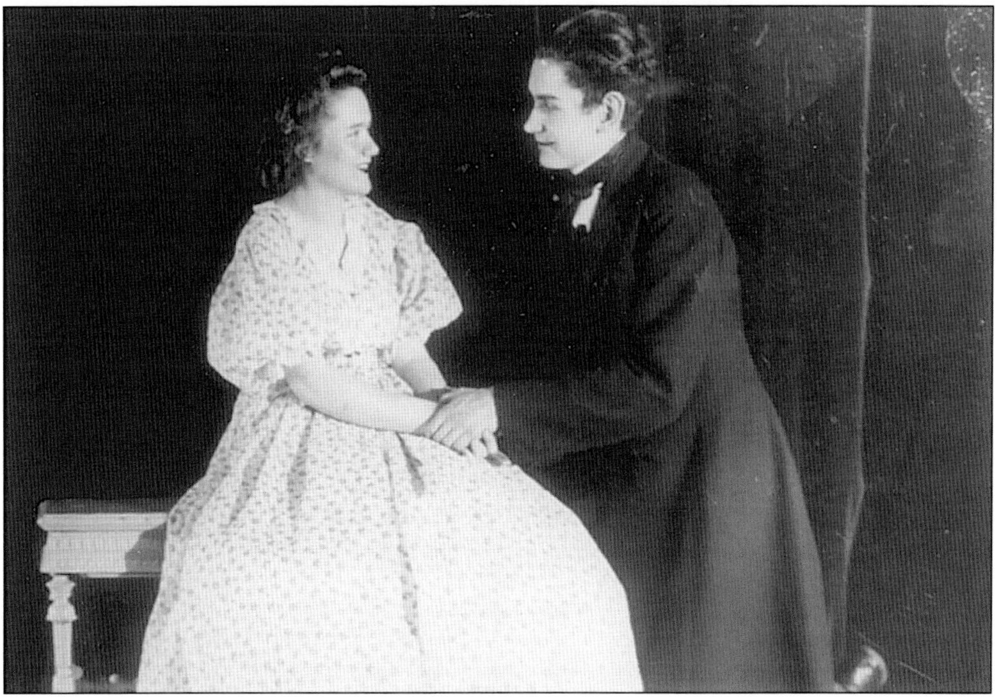

The Stars of *Honest Abe*. Corinne Campbell and Roger Tate starred as Mary Todd Lincoln and Abraham Lincoln in the play *Honest Abe* in 1942. (Courtesy Morton Archives.)

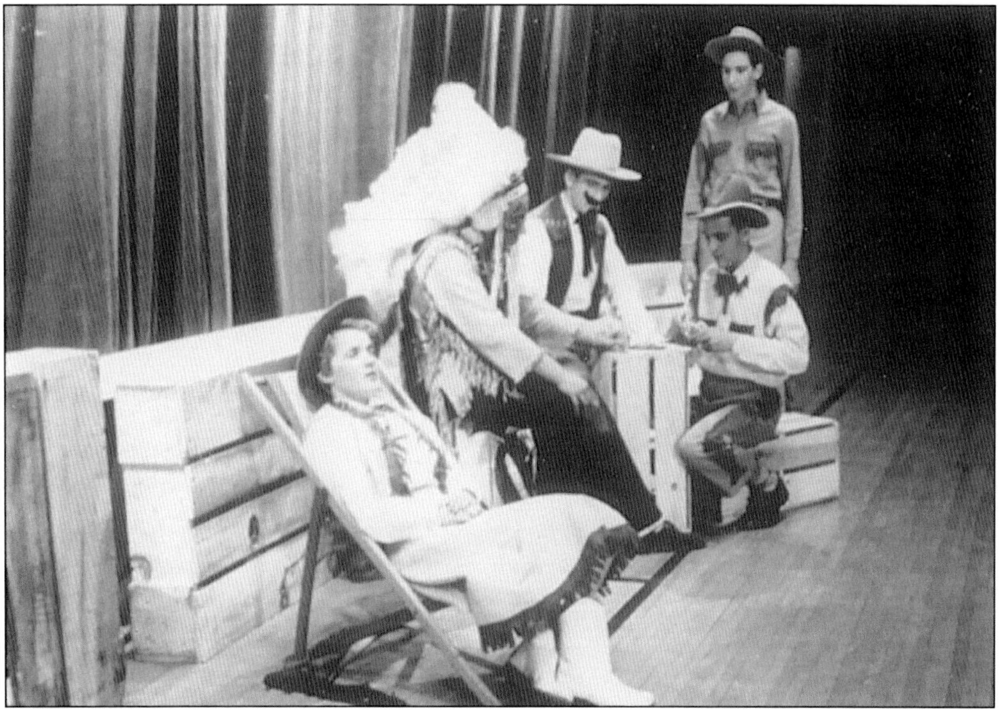

ANNIE GET YOUR GUN, 1956. In 1956, Robert Teeter directed *Annie Get Your Gun*, starring Shirley Kuhajek, Dennis Parichy, Larry Hale, Arnold Matthews (sitting) and Roy Johnson (standing.) (Courtesy Morton Archives.)

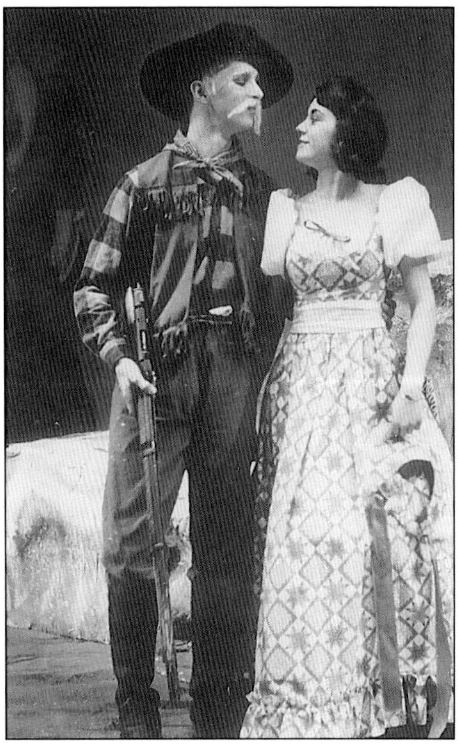

THE STARS OF ANNIE GET YOUR GUN. The play *Annie Get Your Gun* was double cast. "Annie" was played by Shirley Kuhajek and Brenda Bren, "Frank" was played by LaRoy Krizka and Stan Koutsky. Each performed the lead role at one of the two performances and alternated as a "walk on." (Courtesy Morton Archives.)

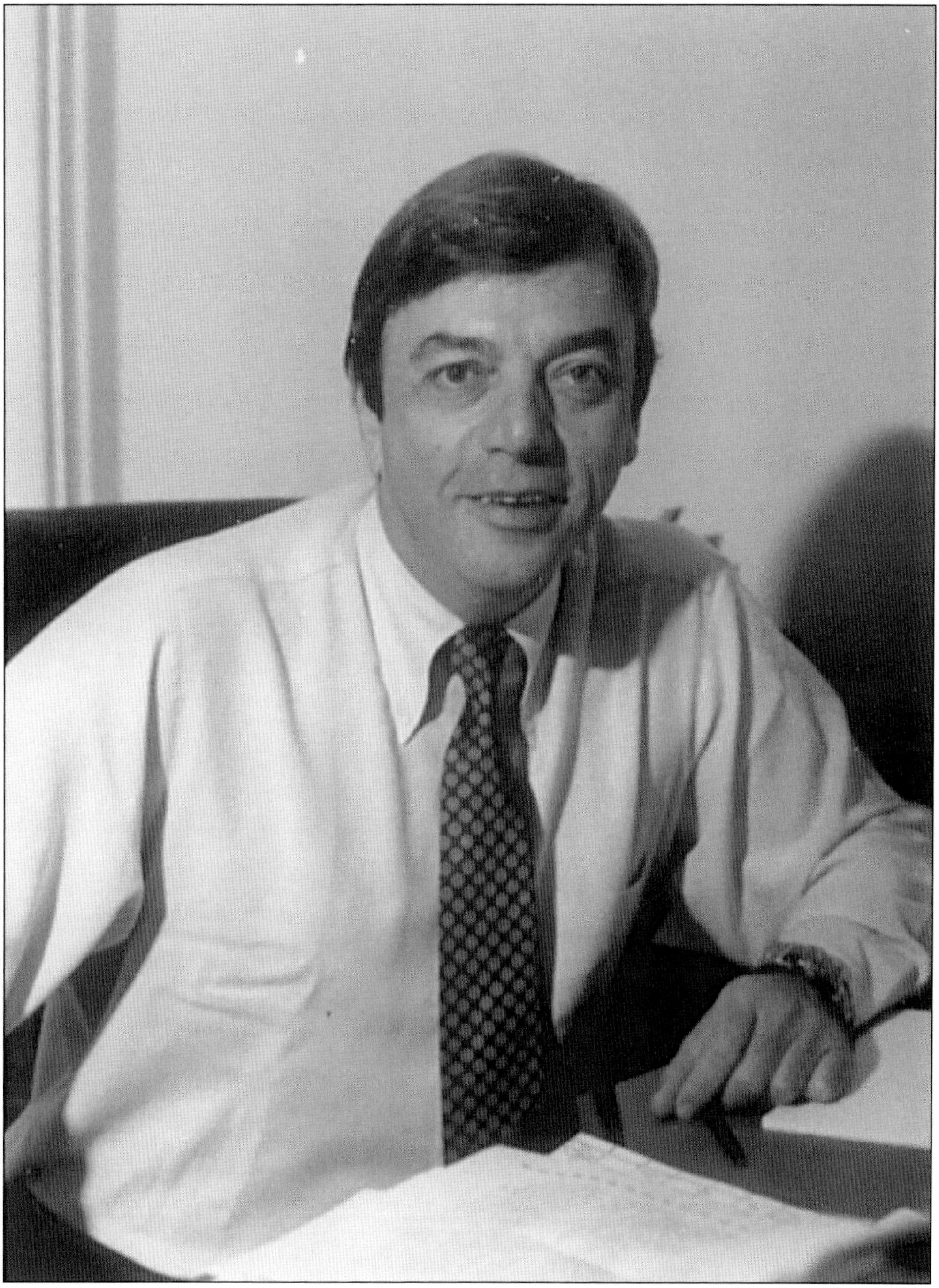

JACK LECKEL, DRAMA TEACHER. In the '60s, '70s, and '80s, Jack Leckel was an energetic, dynamic figure on the Morton East campus. Always ready to direct a play, or help out a student, Mr. Leckel impacted the lives of hundreds of Morton students and teachers. In an interview in 1999, Joe Mantegna recalled, "He didn't just work with the students who were interested in drama, he reached out to all the kids he felt had some talent. That's how he found me." (Courtesy Morton Archives.)

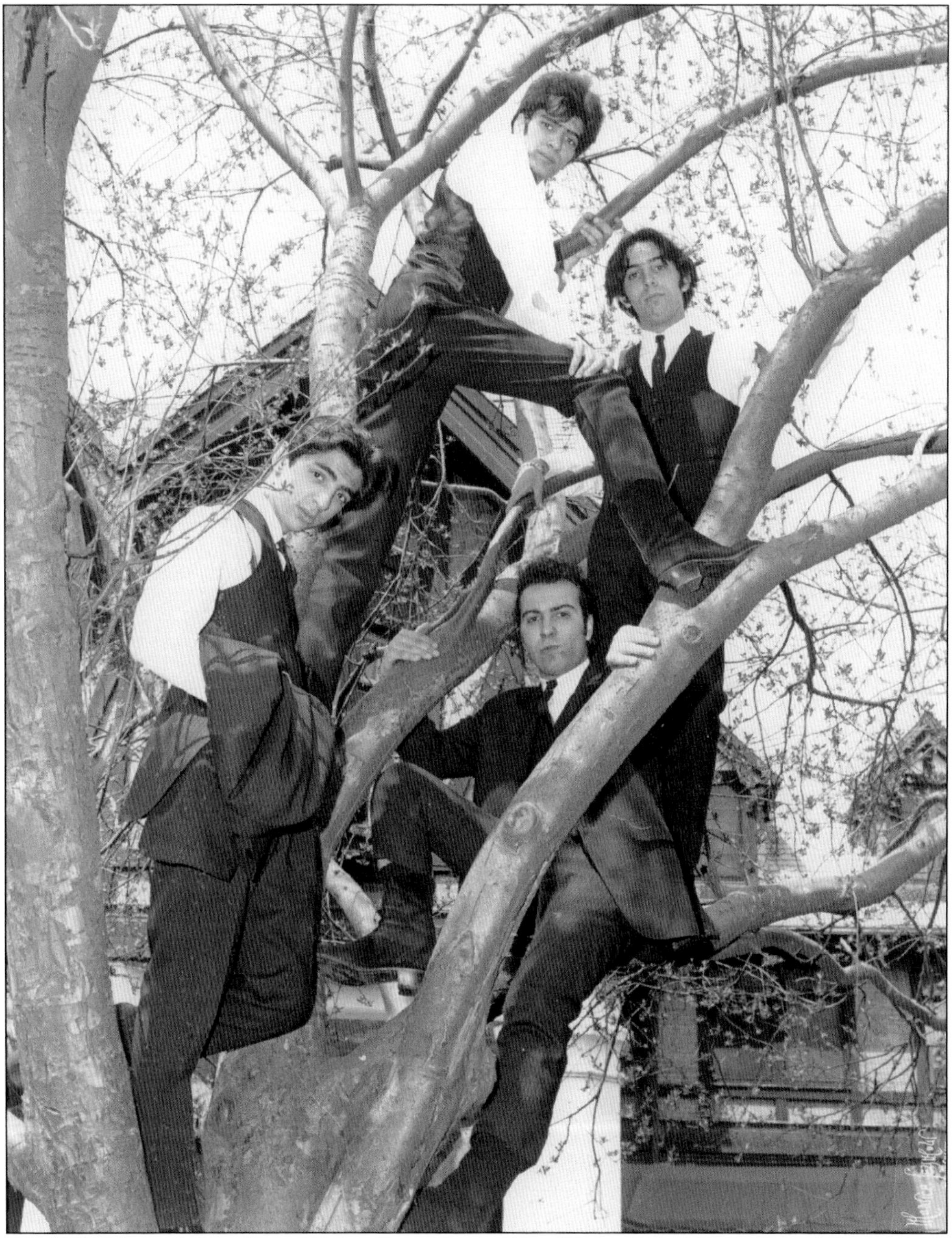

THE APOCRYPHALS. During his Morton years, Joe Mantegna played in a rock band called The Apocryphals. The band included, clockwise from the top: Tom Massari, Neal Sordelli, Chris Montagna, and Joe Mantegna. They had many gigs in and around Cicero, including playing warm-up for Neil Diamond on the night after Martin Luther King Jr. was shot in April, 1968. After a great concert, The Apocryphals went up onto Morton East's roof where they could see flames shooting from the fires burning on Madison Avenue. (Courtesy Linda Cowls, photographer Maurice Seymour.)

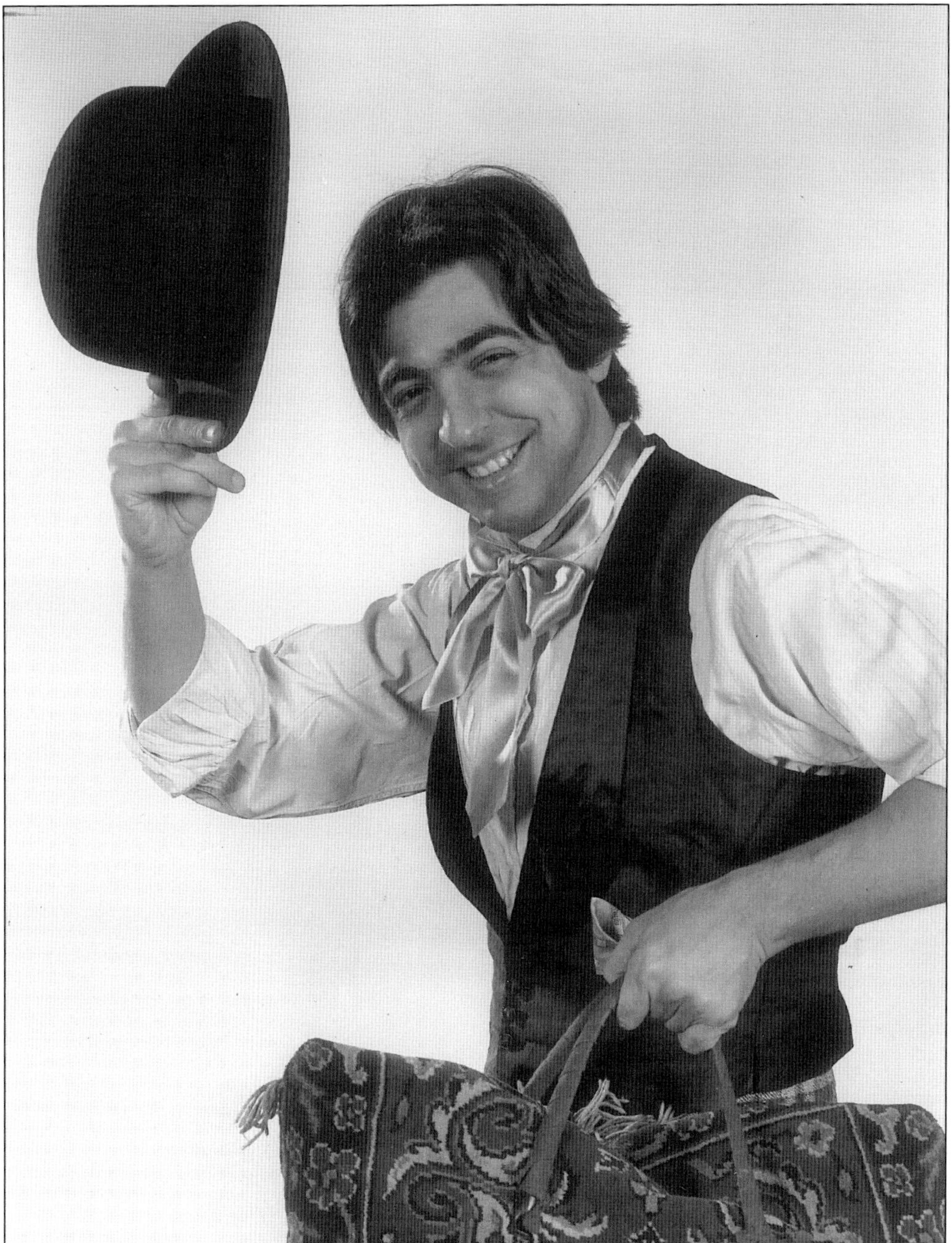

JOE MANTEGNA, AS "THE DUKE." One of Morton's most famous alumni is Joe Mantegna, who began his acting career in the '60s in school productions of *West Side Story* and *Carnival*. This photo, soon after his Morton days, shows Joe as "The Duke" in the Chicago Organic Theater production of *Huckleberry Finn*. In 1999, Joe credited Jack Leckel as the person most responsible for his career. "He was a little unorthodox...he made theater come alive...he produced shows with so much excitement, care, and interest that I have rarely seen them surpassed, not even on Broadway." (Courtesy *Life* Newspaper.)

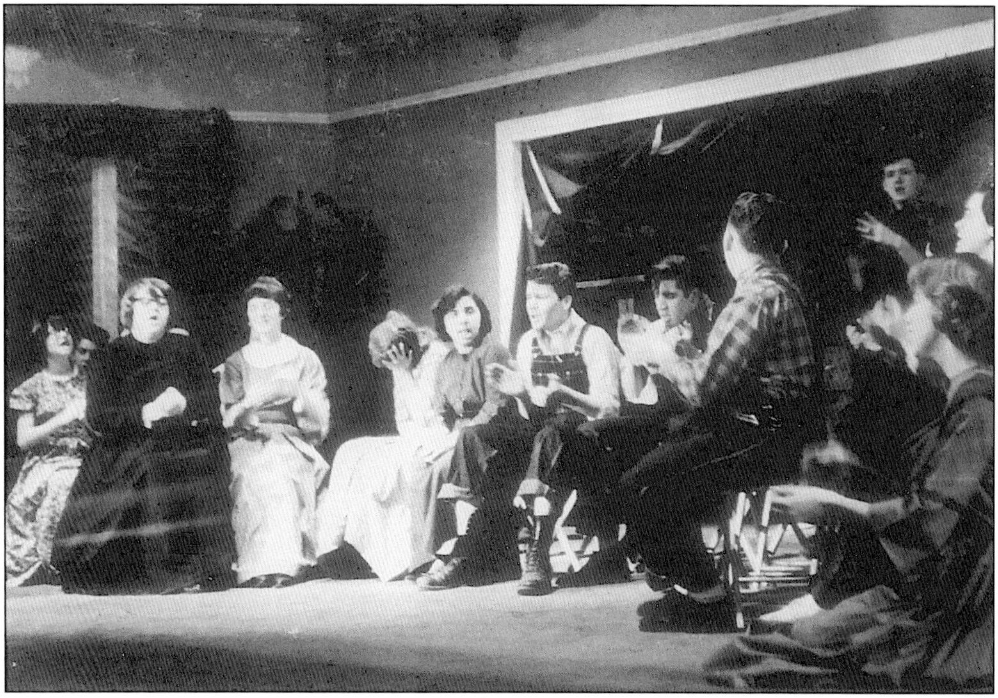

DARK OF THE MOON, CONTEST PLAY. In the 1963–64 school year, the play *Dark of the Moon* won fourth place at district competition. In this rehearsal picture, the cast consists of John Heitmanek, David Helsil, Navaab Fisher, Marilyn Hetzel, Lynn Conner, Mary Rocco, Lee Rybacek, Rudee Benda, and Dave Marek.

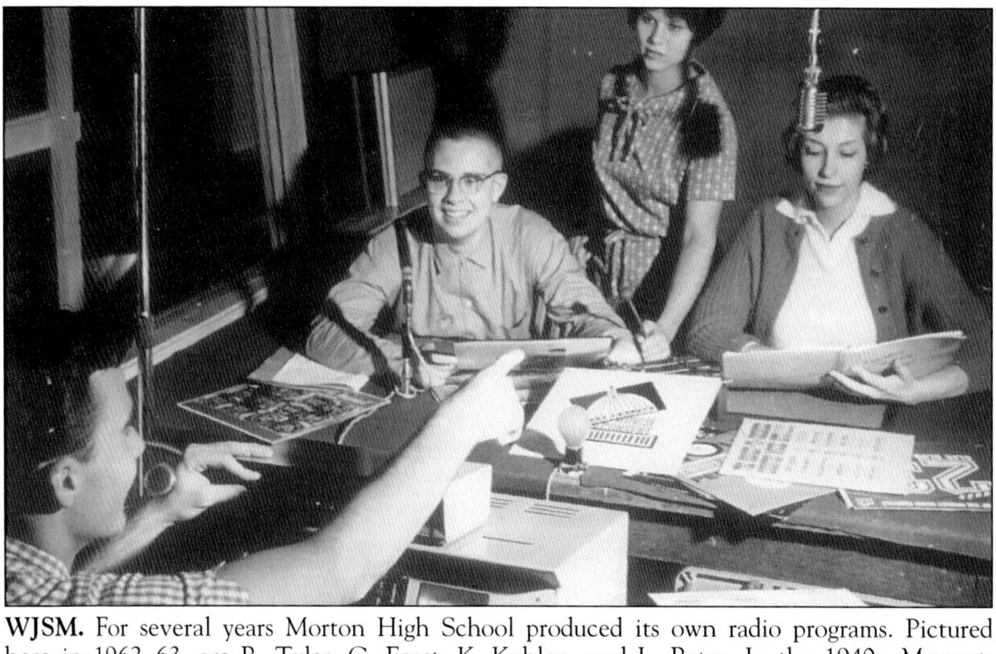

WJSM. For several years Morton High School produced its own radio programs. Pictured here in 1962–63, are R. Tyler, G. Ernst, K. Kuhlen, and L. Bates. In the 1940s, *Moments from Morton* was an active project in the Radio Guild, under the guidance of "Pop" Green. (Courtesy Morton Archives.)

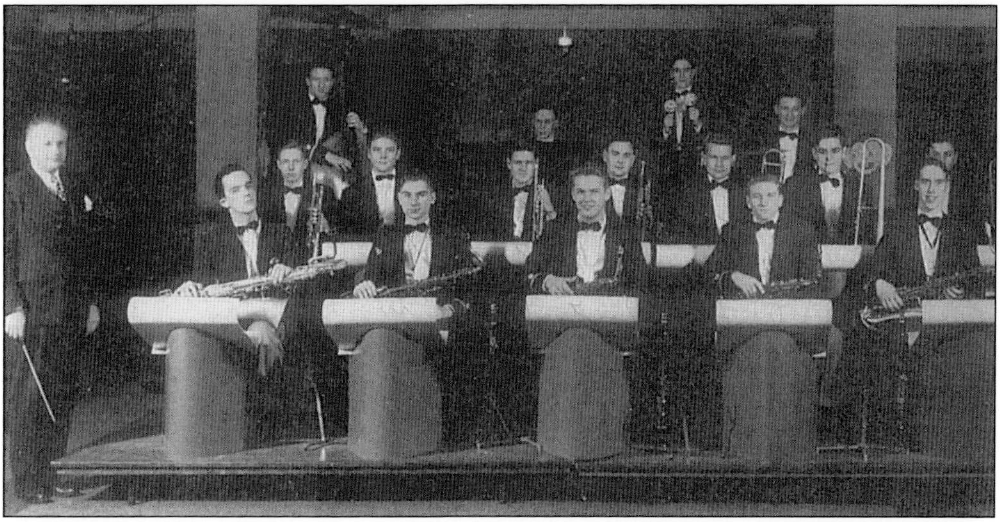

The Morton Dance Band. The 1940s were great times for dancing, especially after the war, and the Morton Dance Band provided music for many occasions, including afternoon dances. The band came complete with its own set up and bow ties. (Courtesy John Husa.)

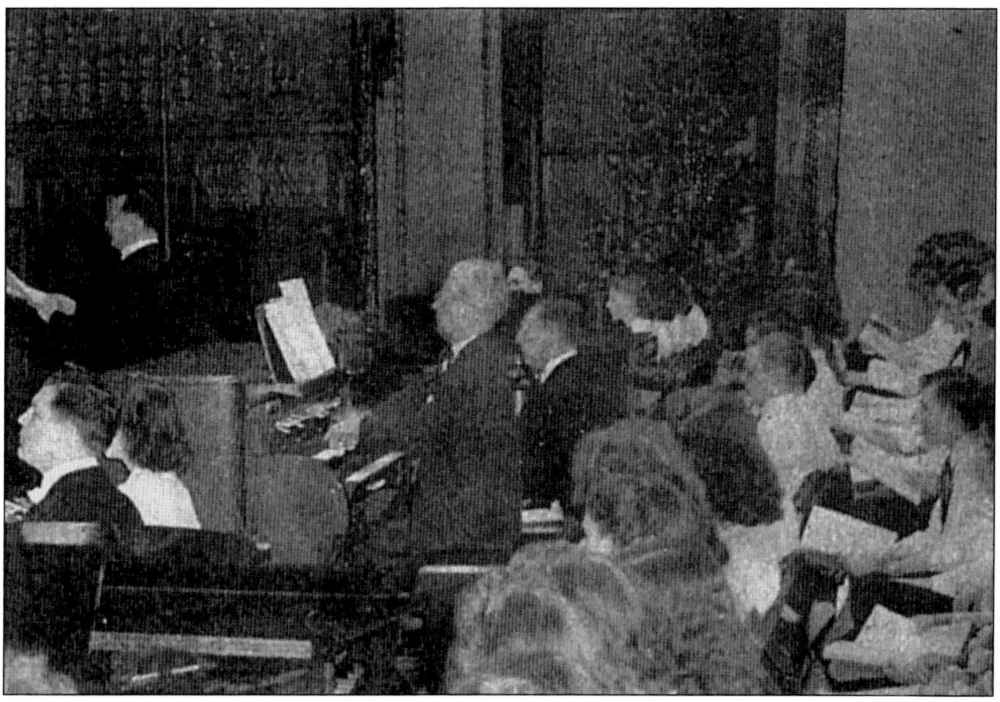

The Organ in Chodl Auditorium. A careful scrutiny of this photo indicates that it is the Christmas holiday season, and that there must be a sing-along going on. The organ was fully retractable so that it was out of the way and out of sight for basketball games and theater productions. (Courtesy John Husa.)

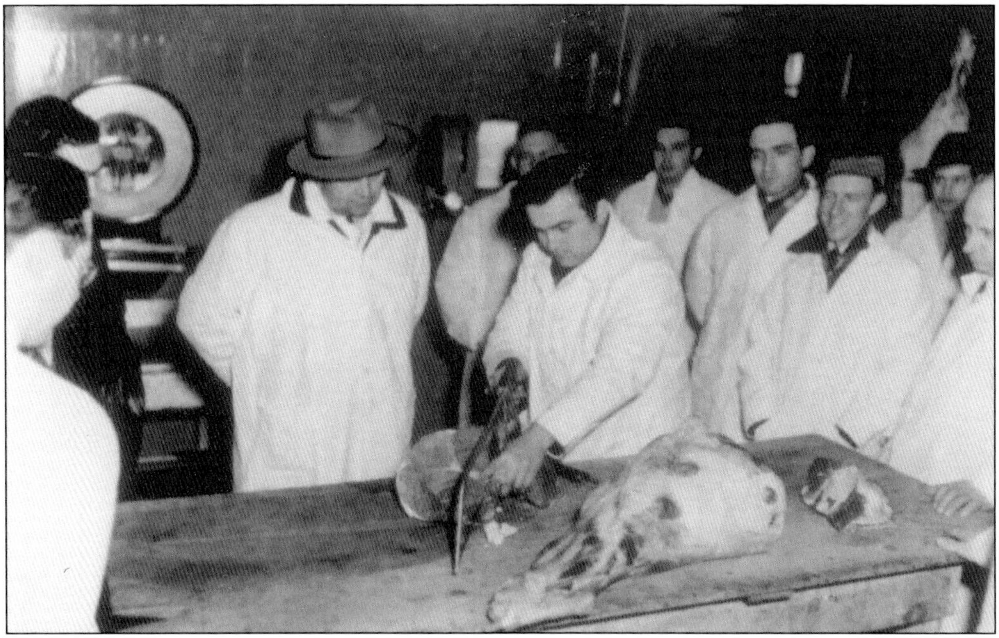

Meat Cutting Class. Adult evening classes were also offered through Morton High School. Here is a photo of the meat cutting class in the 1940s. Many adults took part in the adult classes offered on Monday and Thursday nights. Classes ran the gamut from TV repair and stenography to sewing and auto repair. (Courtesy Morton Archives.)

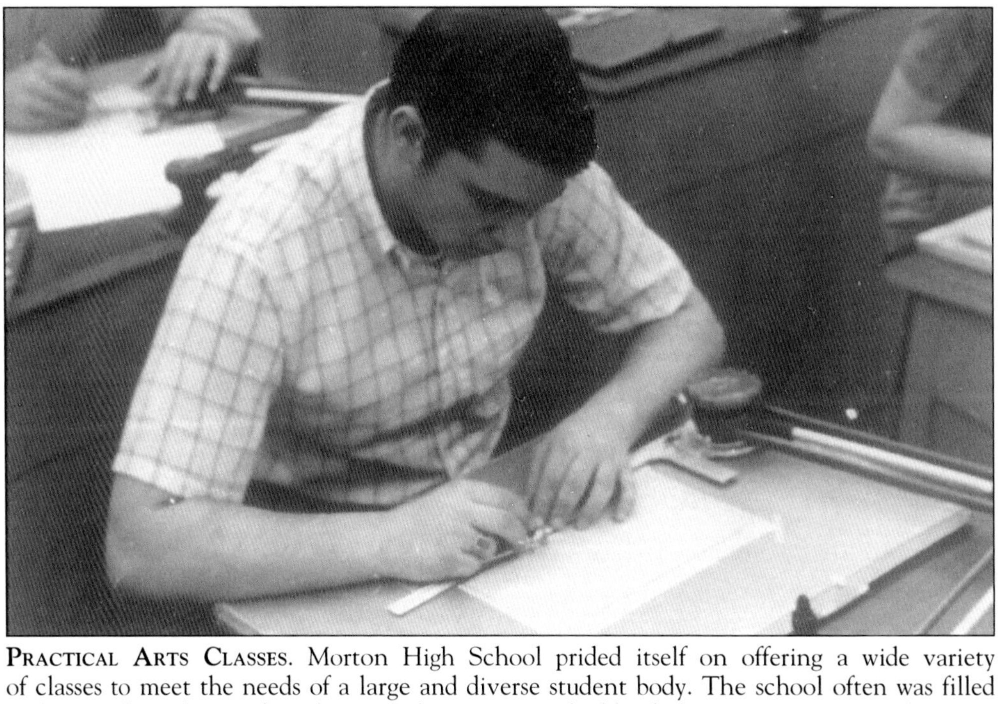

Practical Arts Classes. Morton High School prided itself on offering a wide variety of classes to meet the needs of a large and diverse student body. The school often was filled with over four thousand students, and some years double shifts were necessary. Classes in Industrial Arts were offered, as this photo of a student working at a drafting table shows. (Courtesy Morton Archives.)

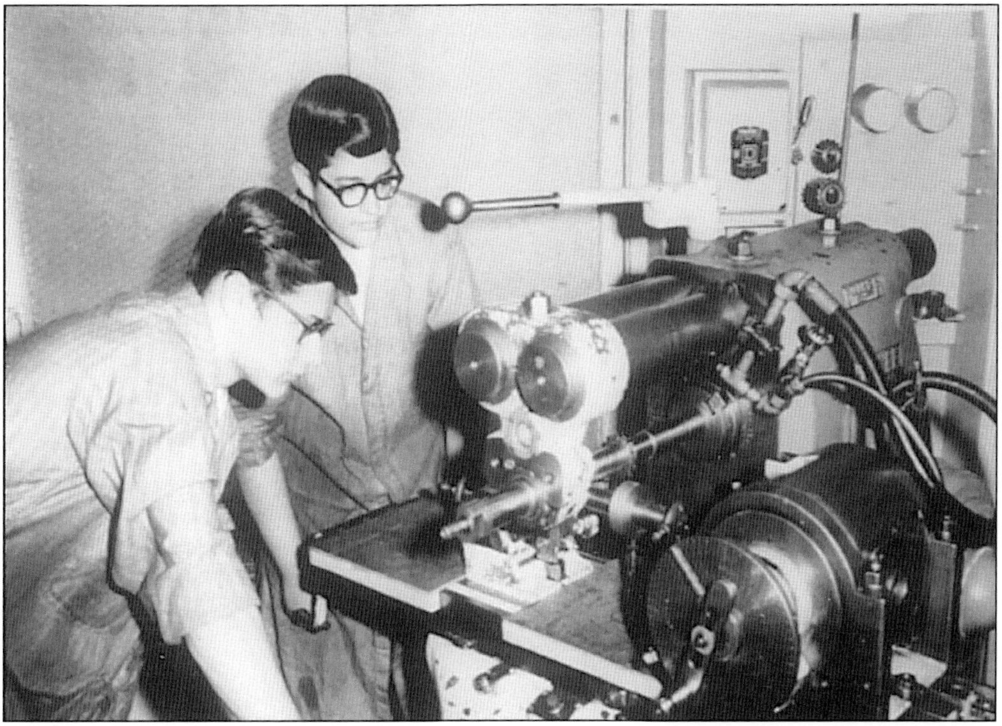

INDUSTRIAL ARTS. This photo from the '60s shows classes being taught in the machine shop. In the evenings, adult education took place in some of the same classrooms. (Courtesy Morton Archives.)

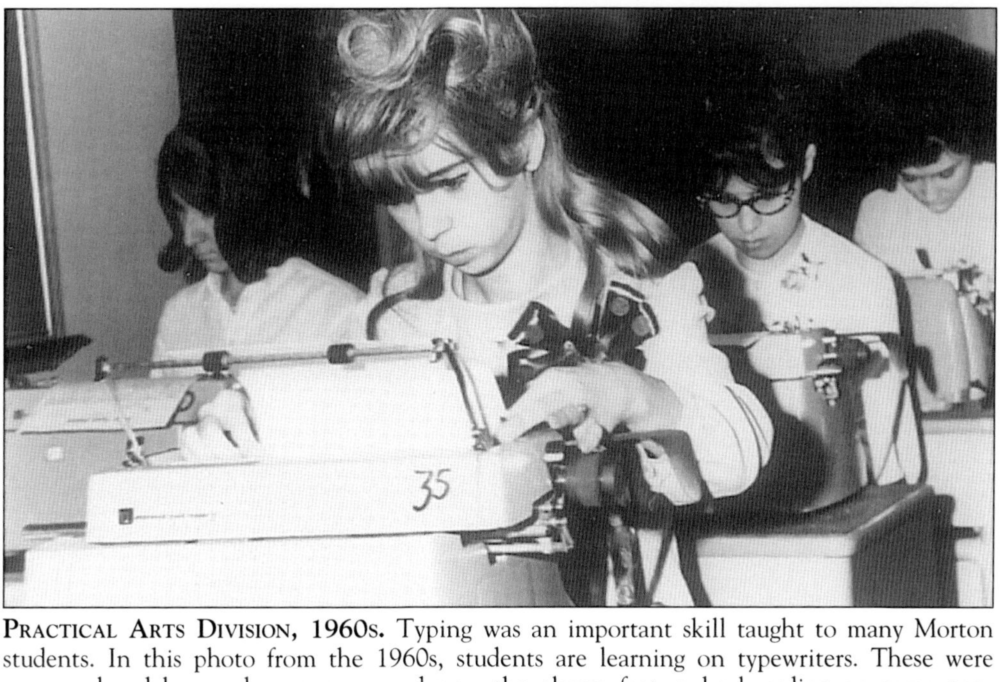

PRACTICAL ARTS DIVISION, 1960S. Typing was an important skill taught to many Morton students. In this photo from the 1960s, students are learning on typewriters. These were soon replaced by word processors, and now the classes feature keyboarding on computers. (Courtesy Morton Archives.)

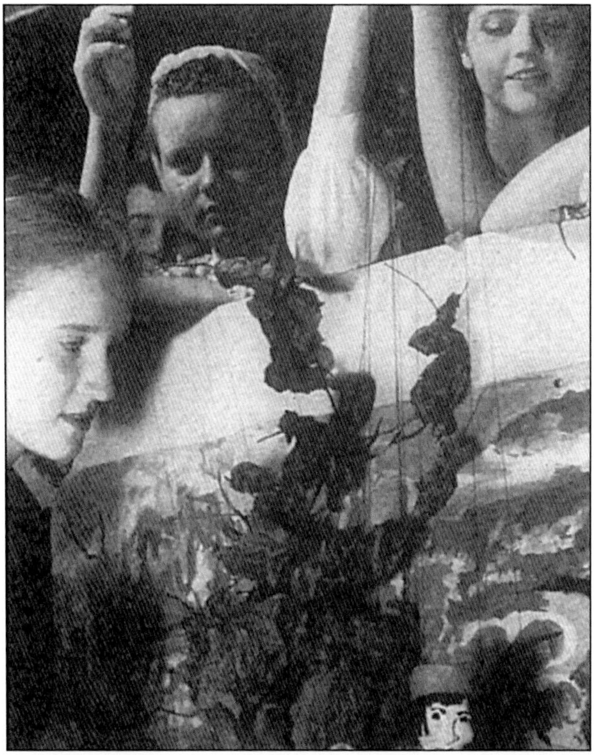

Marionette Club. More familiar clubs, such as Spanish Club, Booster Club, and Photography Club seem mainstream when compared with the Marionette Club of the '40s! In 1948, under the guidance of Miss N. Bredfeldt, members experimented with marionette construction and staging. (Courtesy John Husa.)

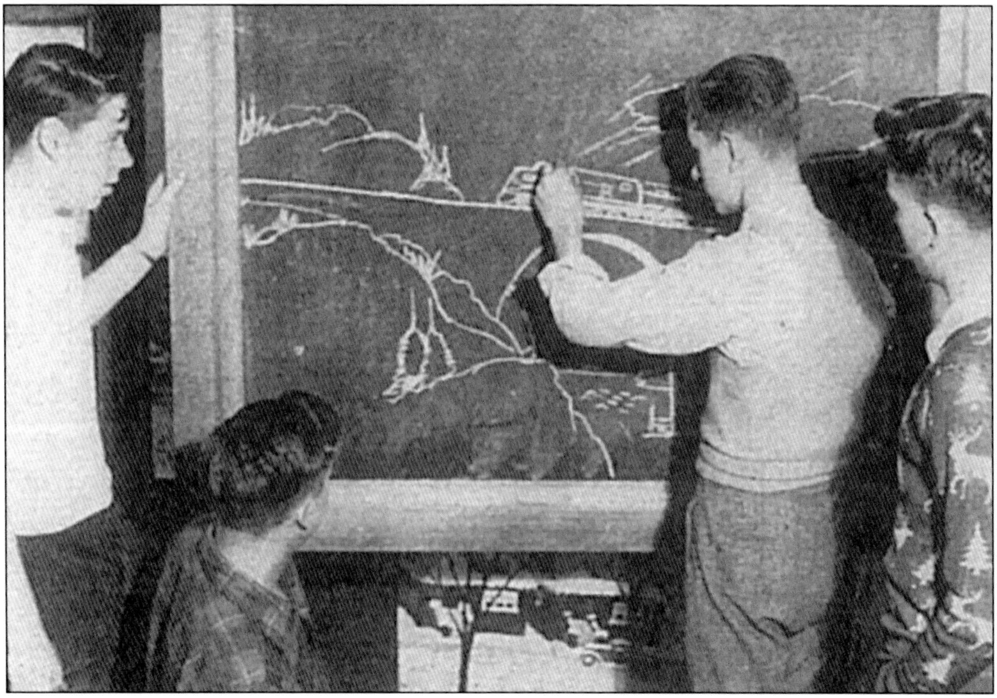

Cartoon Club, 1948. Another unique club, under the advisorship of Miss C. Stevenson, Cartoon Club was offered as an outlet for those interested in art who could not squeeze another course into their busy, full schedules. (Courtesy John Husa.)

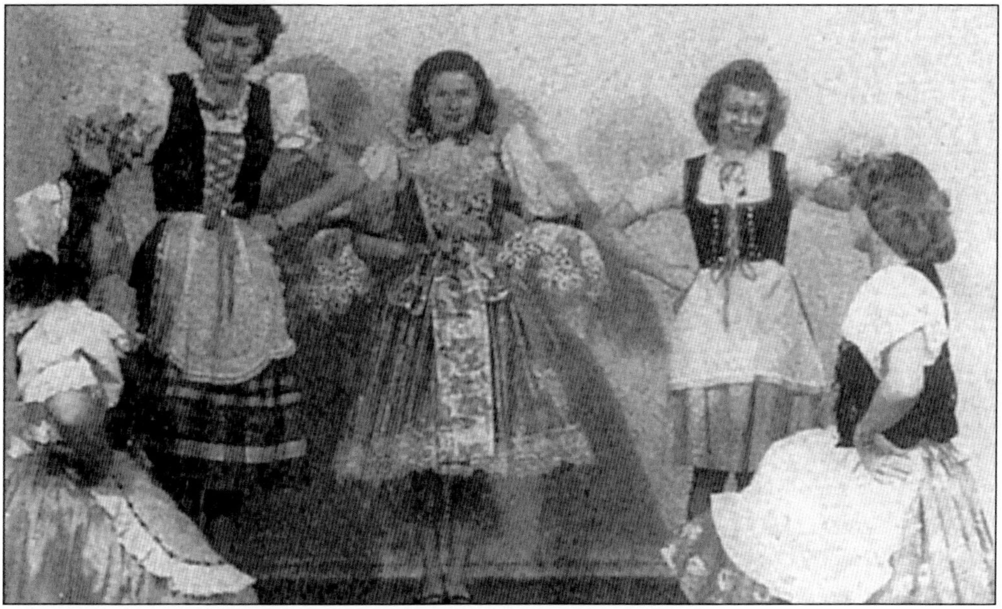

Folk Dancing Club. Folk Dancing Club in the 1940s was an outgrowth of the Czech Club. This club learned dances from many nations, while emphasizing the traditional Czech dances. The foyer of the auditorium was their meeting place. Lively music was furnished by Mrs. West. The advisor was Miss E. Jahelka. (Courtesy John Husa.)

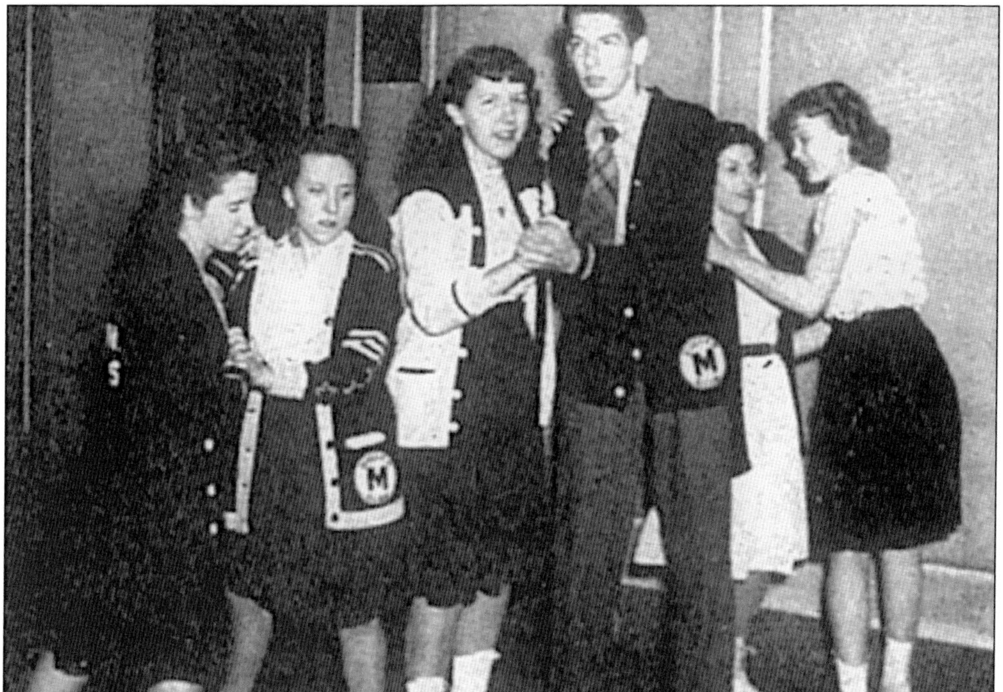

Skating Club. With a membership of over two hundred, the Skating Club was one of the largest clubs at Morton. The club sponsored many parties in the '40s, under the guidance of Mr. A.P. Kovanic. (Courtesy John Husa.)

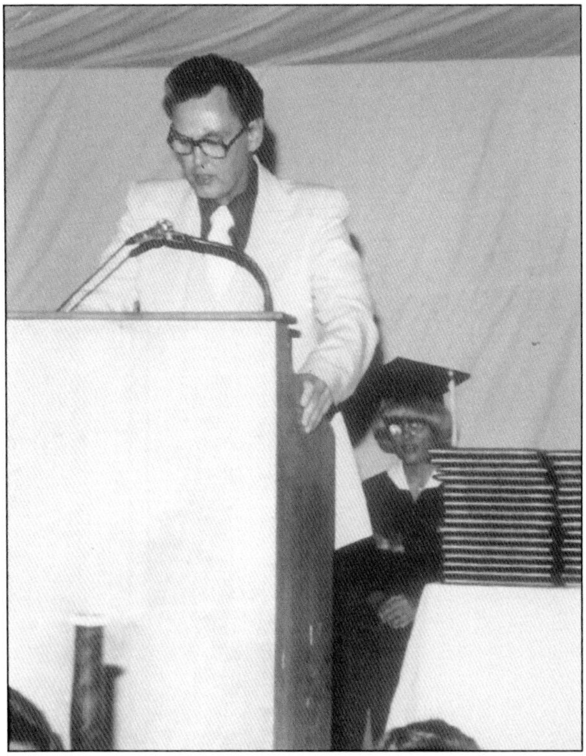

Dr. Kavanaugh at Graduation. Dr. Kavanaugh was principal for many years at Morton East, arriving for the 1964–65 school year. Here (about 1978) he is presenting graduation certificates, including one to Diana Para, a visually impaired student. (Courtesy Morton Archives.)

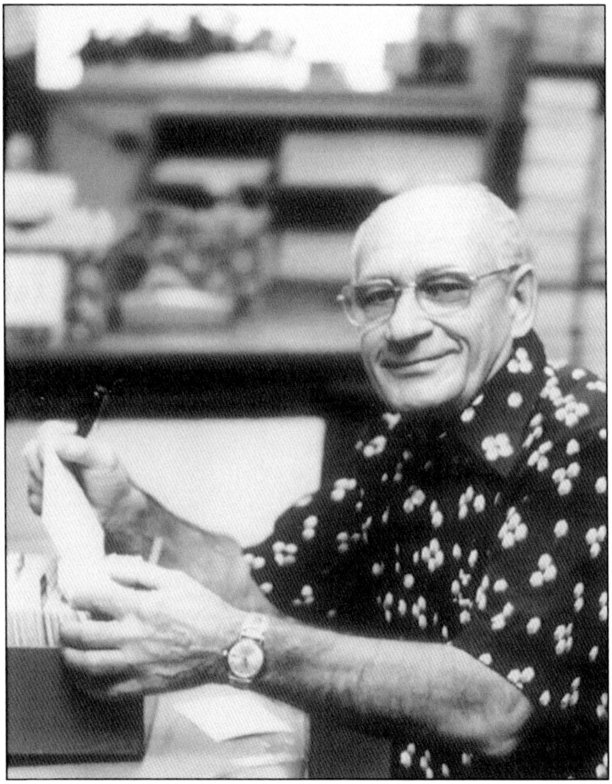

Mr. Henry West. Morton was the first school in the state to supply students with free textbooks. Before we end the pages on Morton, we must remember Hank West, who ran the textbook library. On his shelves were kept all the textbooks for every class offered in the school. Thank you, Mr. West, for all the years you cared for the books and the students of Morton East. (Courtesy Morton Archives.)

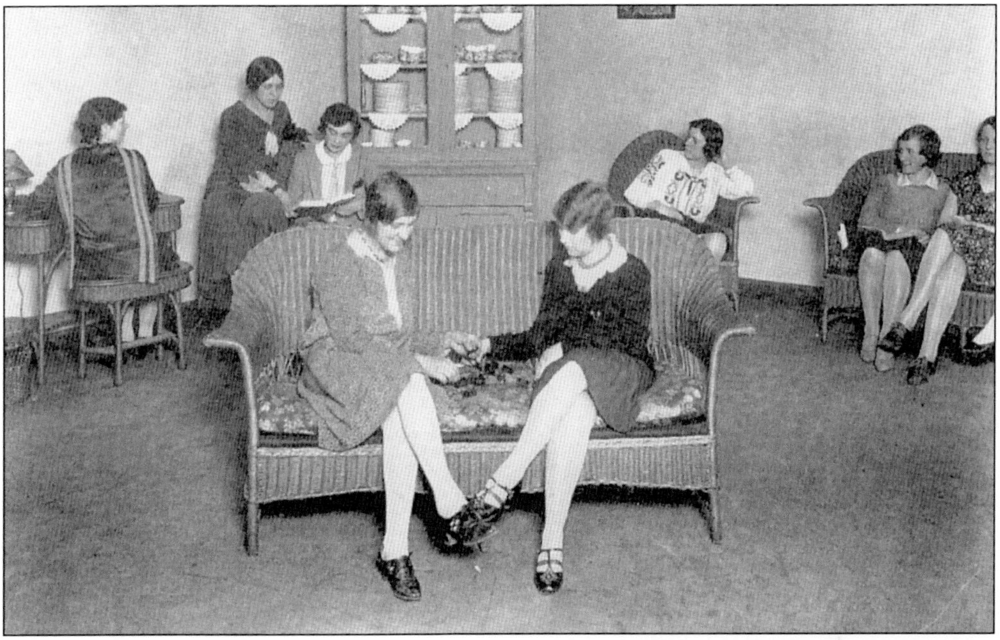

MORTON JUNIOR COLLEGE, WOMEN'S LOUNGE. The end of WWI saw the need for continuing the education process in Cicero. In 1924, Morton Junior College was founded on the fourth floor of the high school. It was the second Junior College in Illinois. Thus, Morton continued to be the town's center for learning, arts, and culture, post high school. This photo shows the women's college lounge in the 1930 yearbook, *The Pioneer*.

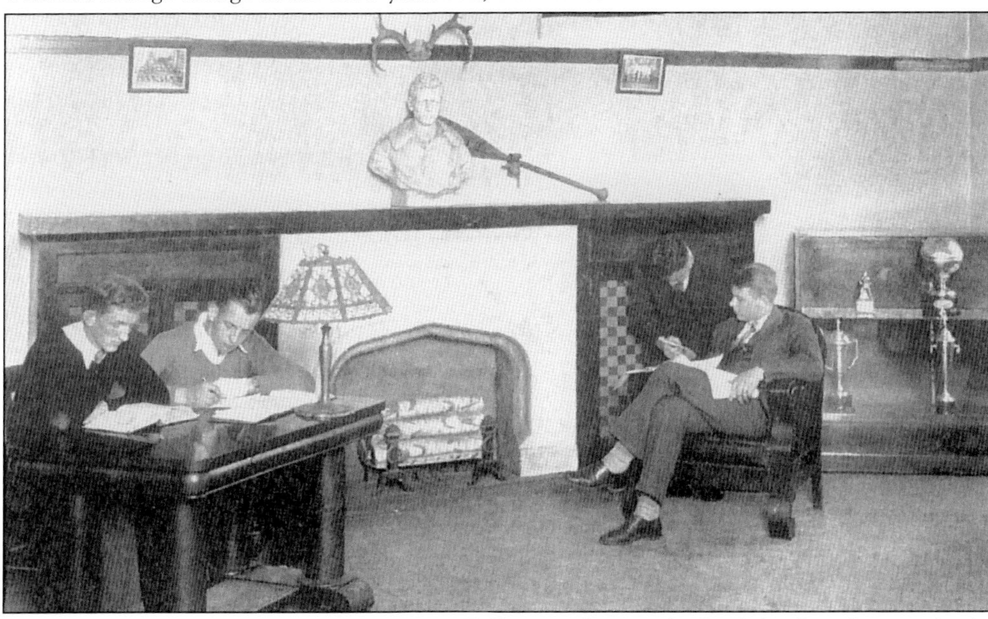

MORTON JUNIOR COLLEGE MEN'S LOUNGE. Following the standards of the day, the men had a separate lounge, sometimes referred to as "The Smoker." Morton Junior College met the needs of returning soldiers from the two world wars and Korea, and thanks to the farsightedness of the Morton administration and board of education, a modern, separate facility called Morton College was built on Pershing Road in the 1970s.

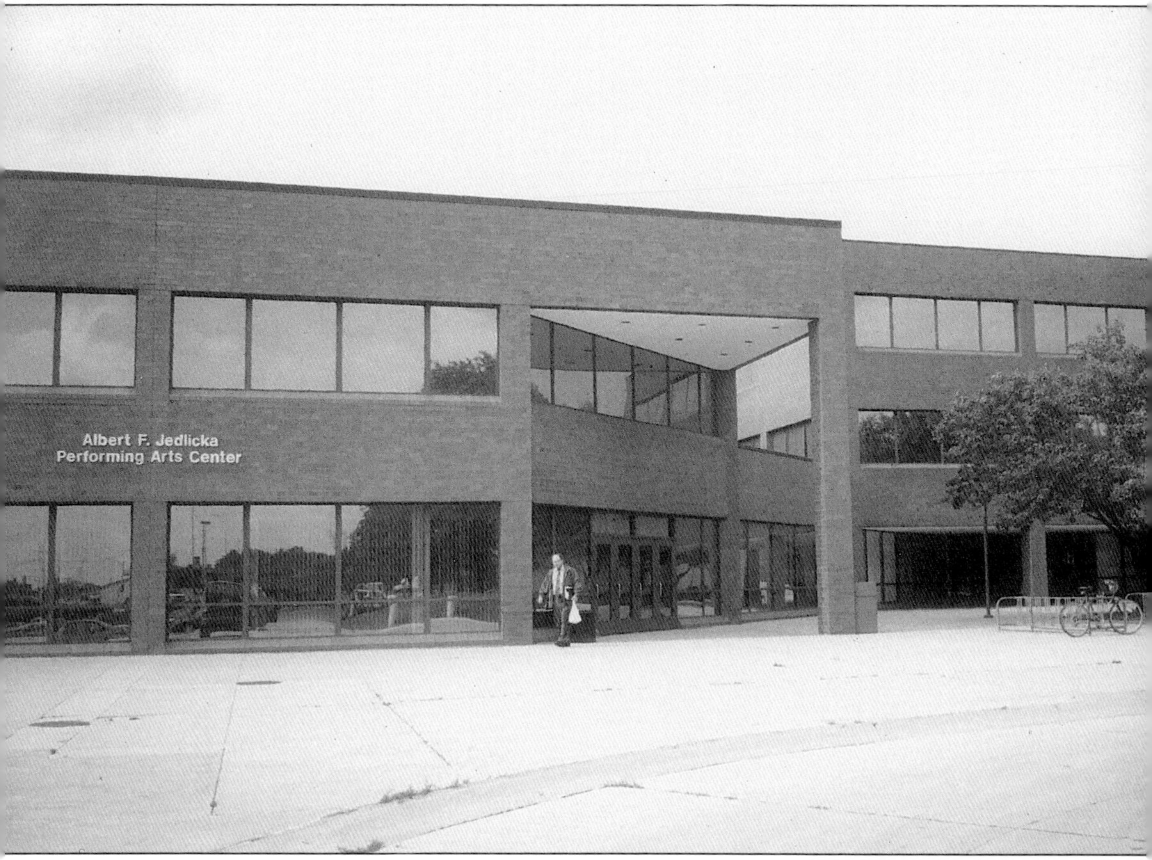

Morton College Today. In December, 1966, voters of the district gave Morton Junior College the go-ahead to separate from the high school and become an independent college. The new campus opened for business in the fall of 1975. It was formally dedicated in November, with Governor Dan Walker serving as the keynote speaker. Today the campus of Morton College graces the north side of Pershing Road at Central Avenue. Though it is no longer called a junior college, it still has connections to Morton High School and offers the students of Cicero an economical start on their college education. Seen here is the Albert J. Jedlicka Performing Arts Center of the college.

Six

Churches

It is the 1880s. Folks are moving west into the prairies of Cicero, struggling to shelter their families from the elements and feed their hungry bodies. But how to feed their hungry souls? How to find comfort and peace and hope in a very challenging situation? The answer for some was to return to old neighborhoods, usually on the west side of Chicago, and continue to attend their old churches in the areas they had left. But more often, the answer was to gather together with like-minded neighbors and build a new church of their choice right in their new neighborhood.

The largely Catholic population that came to Cicero built many churches to meet the desires of the different nationalities represented. Hence, there were Irish Catholic churches, Italian Catholic Churches, Polish Catholic Churches, and a Catholic Church whose members hailed from Luxembourg. Then, as now, the members wanted the Masses said in their native tongues. Hence, priests were hired who spoke Polish or German or Lithuanian, just as Masses are now said in Spanish to meet the needs of the present population. Protestant churches included the Methodist Church, the German Lutheran Church, the Swedish Lutheran Church, the Presbyterian Church, and the Baptist Church. Cicero was a melting pot of many nationalities and religious traditions.

The growth of the parishes can be directly related to the growth of Cicero, from east to west. The earliest churches were near Cicero Avenue, like St. Mary of Czestochowa (1885) and St. Dionysius (1889). With the opening of Western Electric in 1903, and its remarkable growth, the churches found themselves straining to meet the needs of their growing congregations. In 1911, Mary Queen of Heaven, St. Anthony's, and St. Valentine's were built. The ebb and flow of attendance in the Cicero churches reflect the ebb and flow of the factories that employed Cicero residents.

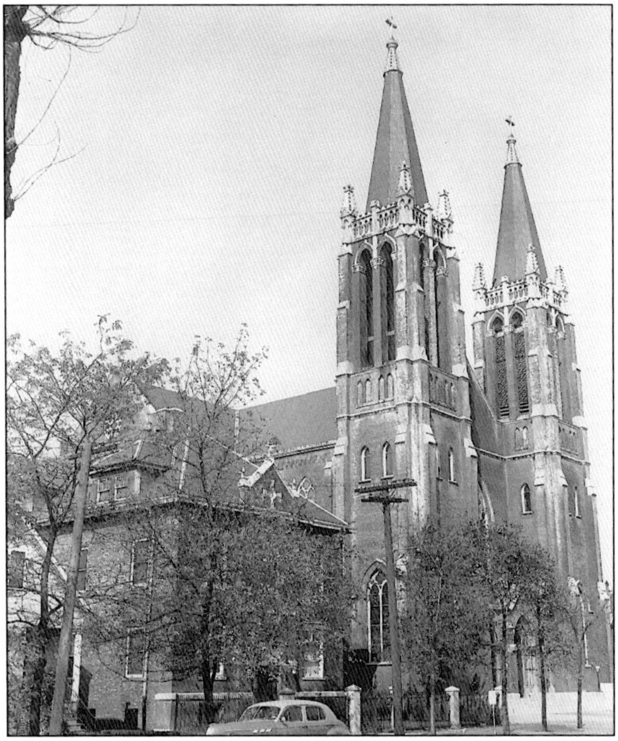

St. Mary's of Czestochowa, 1951. Eighty-six pioneer families, many of whom worked in the Dolese-Shepard Quarry on the east side of Cicero Avenue, met in 1892 to discuss having their own parish where they could build a church and a school and carry on their Polish traditions and language. They bought six lots on Linden Avenue (now Forty-Ninth Avenue) and erected a small church in 1895. Soon the need to expand was evident, and in 1918 a new church was constructed that seated one thousand people. (Courtesy *Life* Newspaper.)

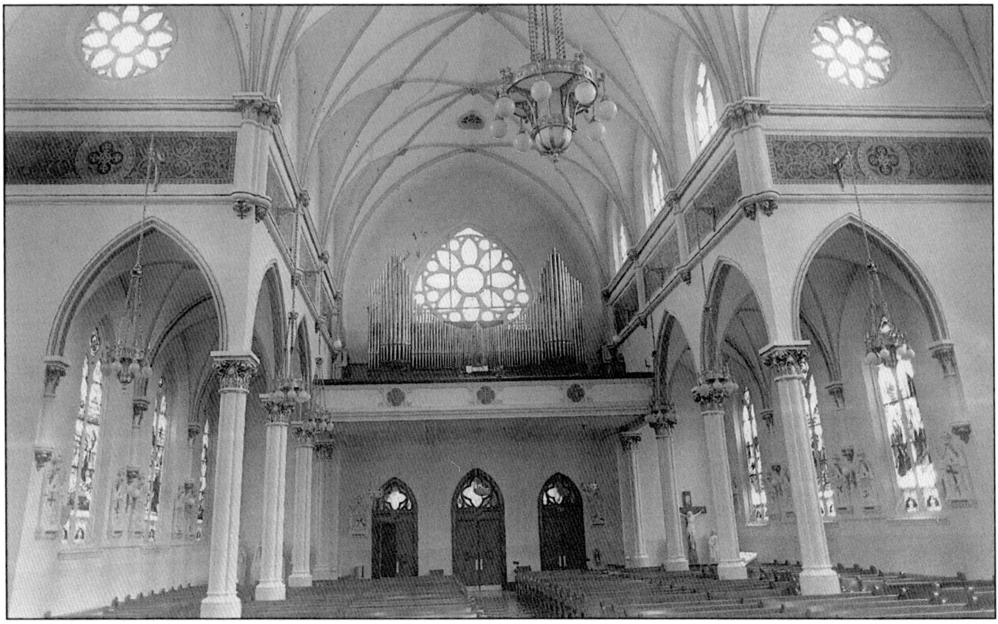

St. Mary's of Czestochowa, Renovated, 1980. The construction of this huge church continued from 1918 until 1927, when the altar of Italian marble was completed. On the left side was placed a life-sized statue of St. Hedwig, Queen of Poland, and on the right, a life-sized statue of St. Stanislaus Kostka, Patron of Youth. In 1934, a fire heavily damaged the altar, which took months to replace. Here, after another renovation in 1980, is the rear of the beautiful sanctuary. (Courtesy *Life* Newspaper.)

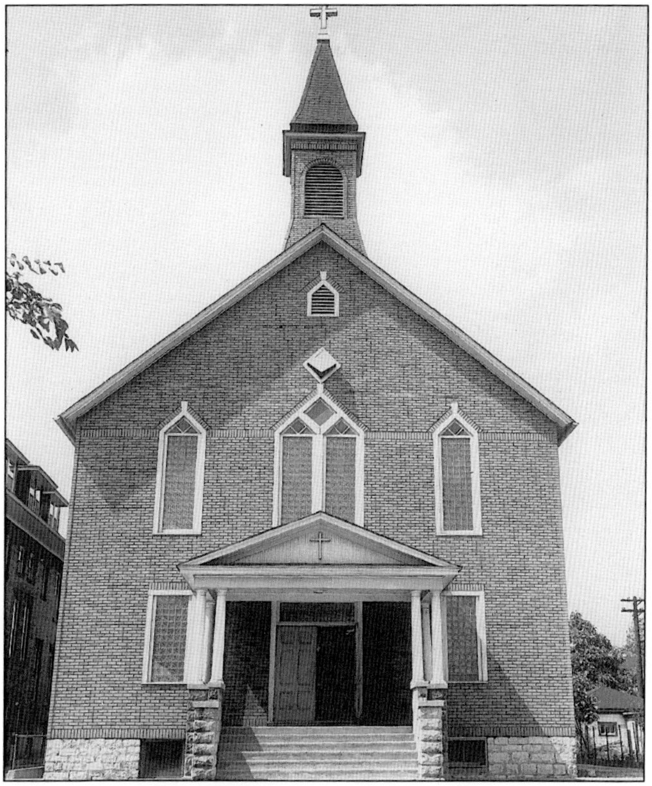

ST. DIONYSIUS CHURCH. The beginnings of St. Dionysius go back to 1889, when a group of immigrants, mostly Catholics from Luxembourg, petitioned the Archbishop of Chicago to organize a parish and build a church. They purchased nine lots on Forty-Ninth Avenue and Twenty-Ninth Street. The original building had wooden siding. This photo shows a later renovation, including the use of imitation brick siding. (Courtesy *Life* Newspaper.)

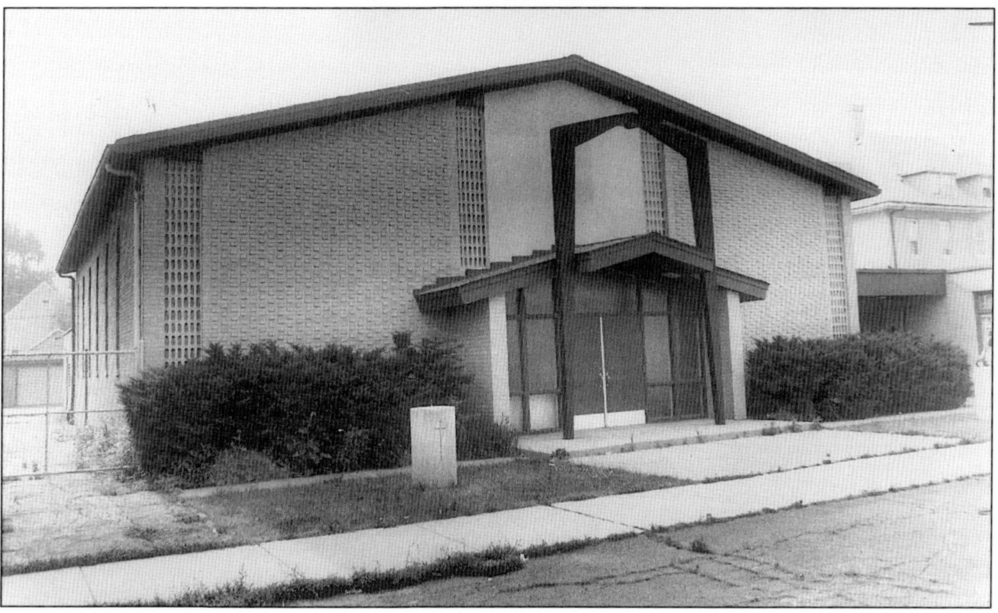

THE NEW ST. DIONYSIUS CHURCH, BUILT IN 1963. The much loved old church, with the sanctuary above the schoolrooms, met the needs of the parish well for over 70 years. But in the 1960s, it was decided to build a modern facility, one that could be reached without stairs. The new church and school were dedicated in the fall of 1963, with furnishings designed to incorporate the new liturgical changes of Vatican II. (Courtesy *Life* Newspaper.)

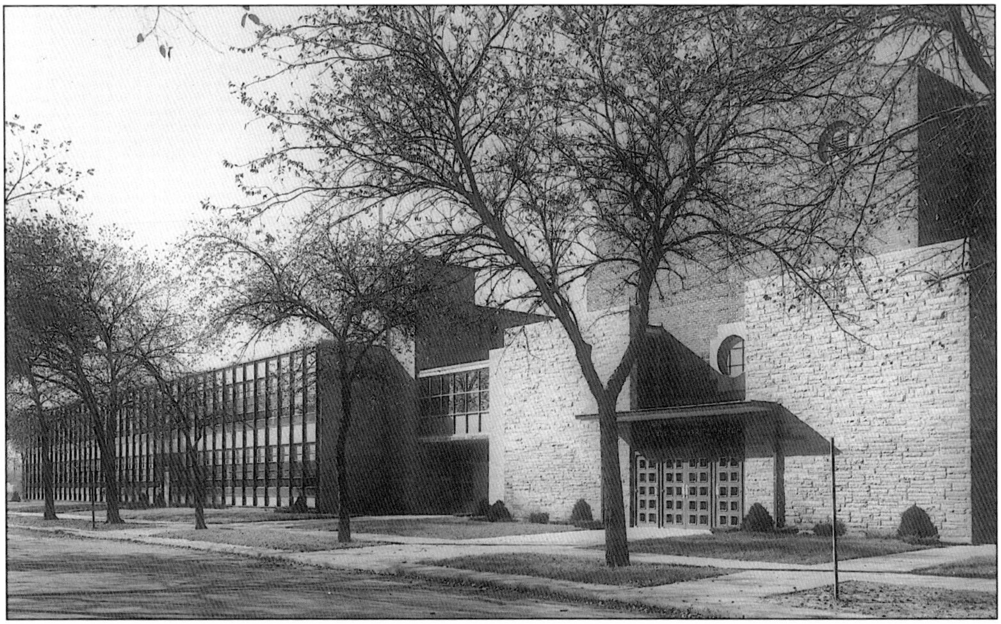

Our Lady of Charity. In the 1940s, with war production needs running the Cicero factories full tilt, many more people moved into the Drexel-Boulevard Manor area. The Rev. Edmund H. Long of St. Dionysius recognized the need for a Catholic Church in this area, and in 1943, established Our Lady of Charity Mission at 3620 S. Fifty-Seventh Court. It consists of a hall upstairs and eight classrooms downstairs. (Courtesy *Life* Newspaper.)

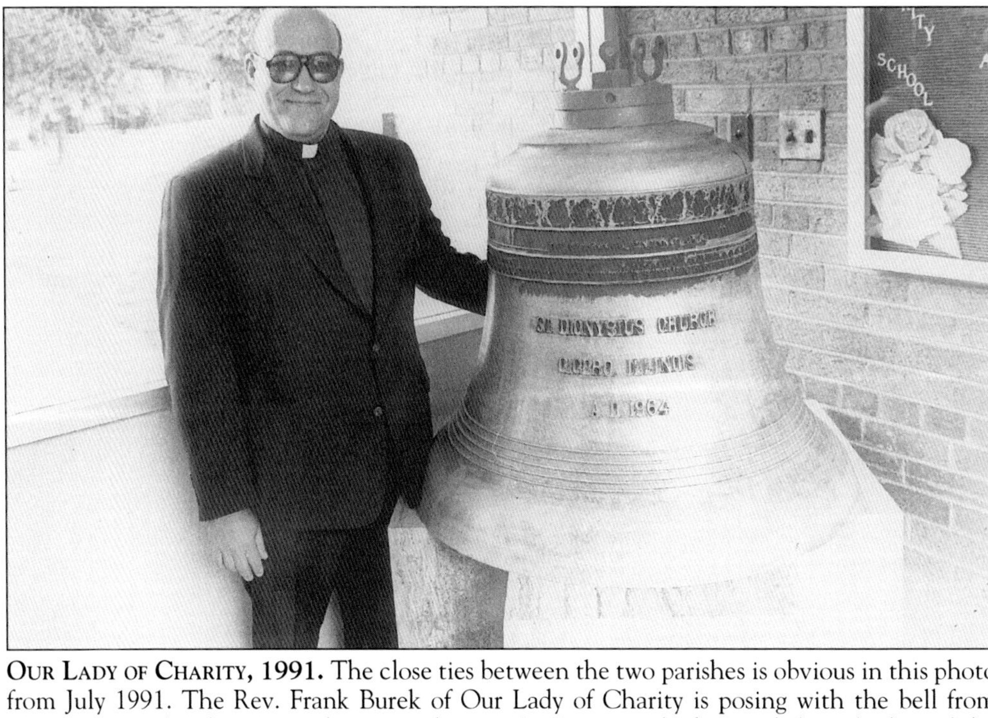

Our Lady of Charity, 1991. The close ties between the two parishes is obvious in this photo from July 1991. The Rev. Frank Burek of Our Lady of Charity is posing with the bell from St. Dionysius, dated 1964. At that time, the new St. Dionysius had recently been built, and the old bell was gifted to the sister parish. (Courtesy *Life* Newspaper.)

ST. ATTRACTA'S. Irish families who had built their homes in the prairie that was north Cicero were the first members of St. Attracta. Father Kiely became the pastor in 1920, and organized the parochial school. In its heyday, the church of St. Attracta held four Masses on Sunday mornings, at 7:30, 9:00, 10:30, and 12:00. In 1986, during the declining days of the parishes, St. Valentine consolidated with St. Attracta. (Courtesy *Life* Newspaper.)

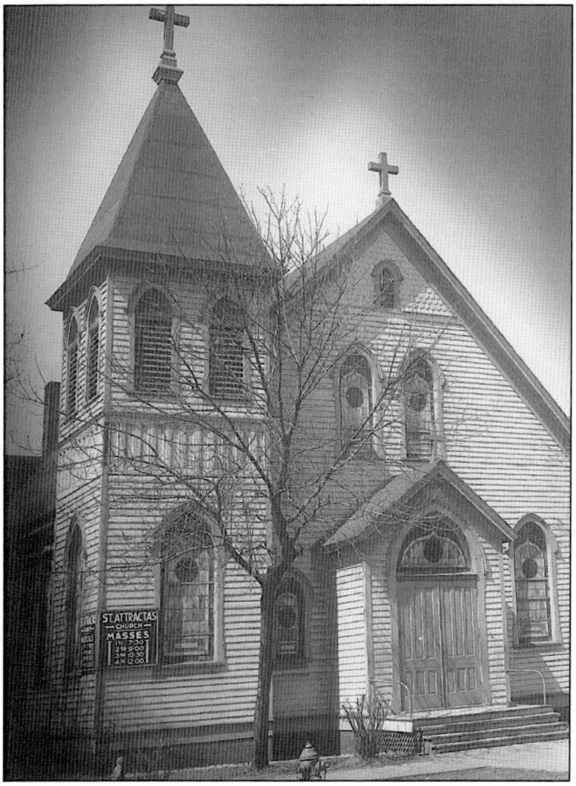

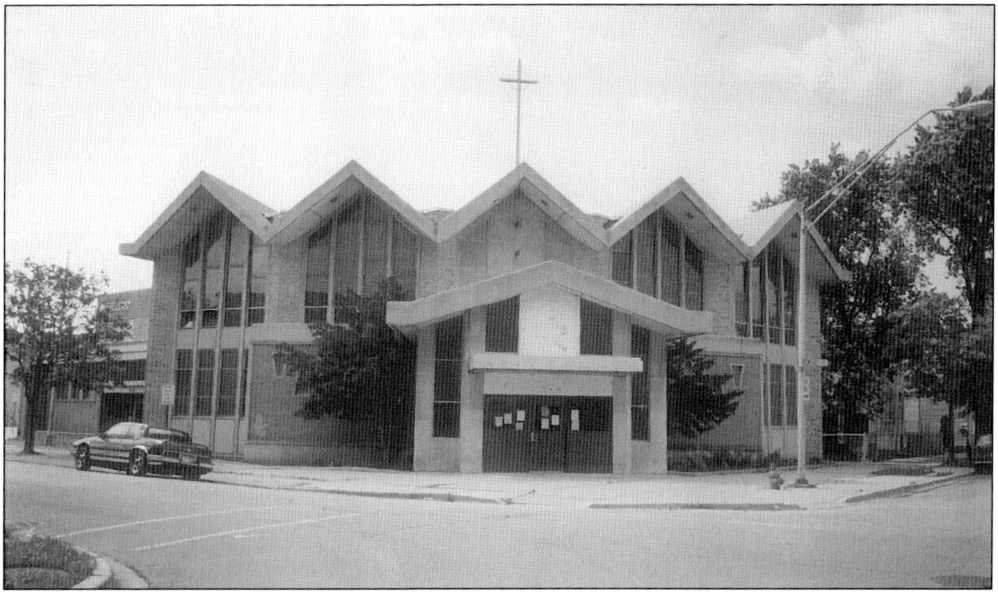

LIFE LINK, 2000. Today, the building that had housed St. Attracta's Church since the 1960s is used as headquarters of Life Link, a food bank.

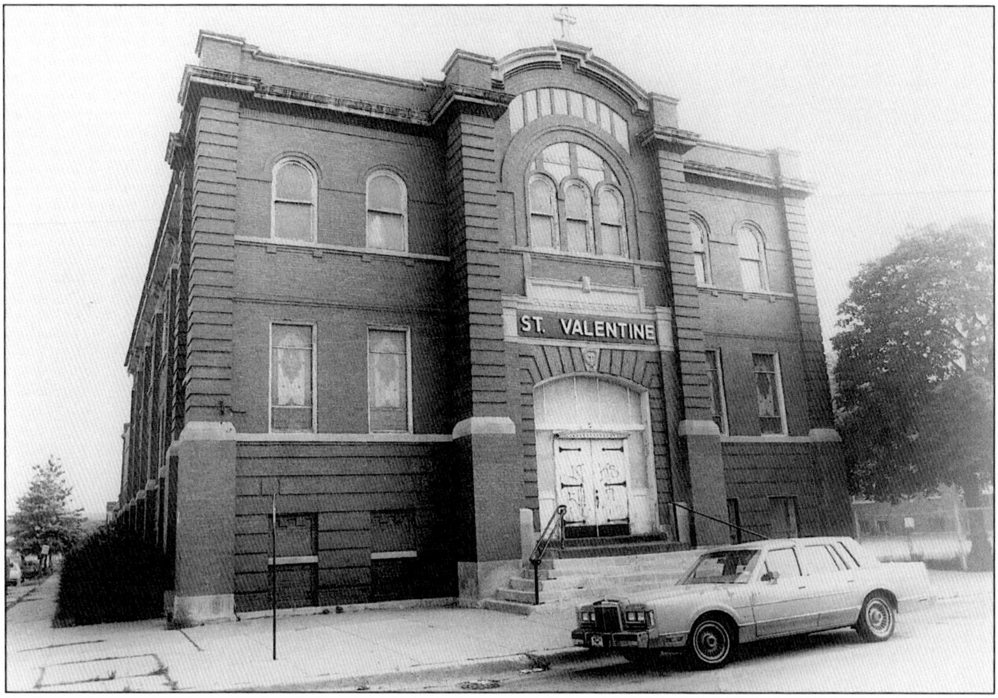

St. Valentine Church. In 1910, Polish-speaking people up in the Grant Works area had to go all they way to St. Mary of Czestochowa in Hawthorne to attend services in Polish. They built their own church and school in 1912, so that they could more conveniently attend church, and their children could easily attend a school which taught Polish language as well as English. They even offered Polish scouts. A new rectory was built in 1925 and a new convent was built in 1928. (Courtesy *Life* Newspaper.)

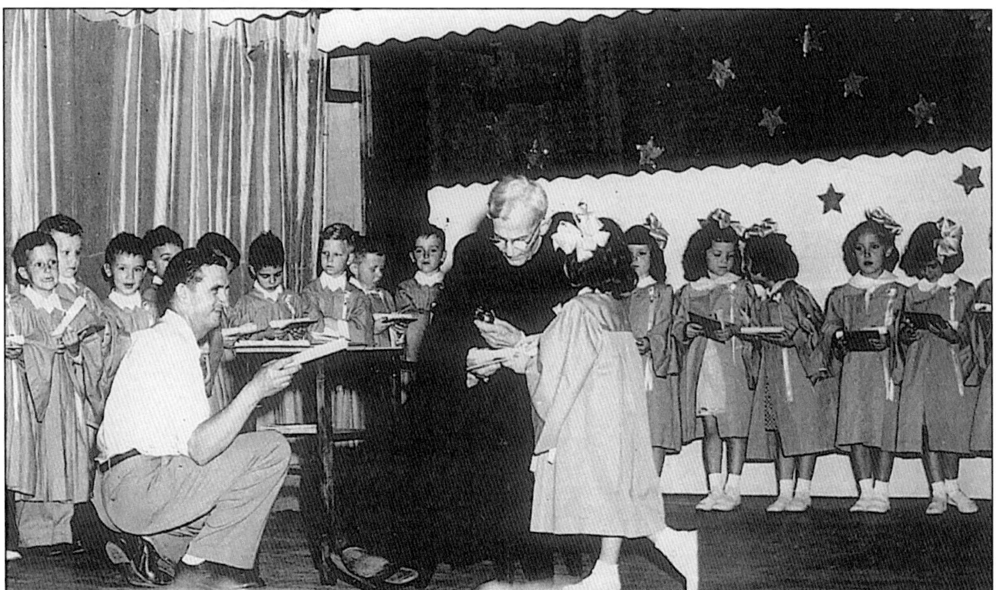

Kindergarten Graduation at St. Valentine, 1954. Receiving her kindergarten diploma on the stage at St. Valentine's is Michal Morganti. (Courtesy Michal Morganti Murphy.)

Eighth Grade Graduation at St. Valentine. Sitting in blue caps and gowns, the class of '62 is graduated from St. Valentine. (Courtesy Michal Morganti Murphy.)

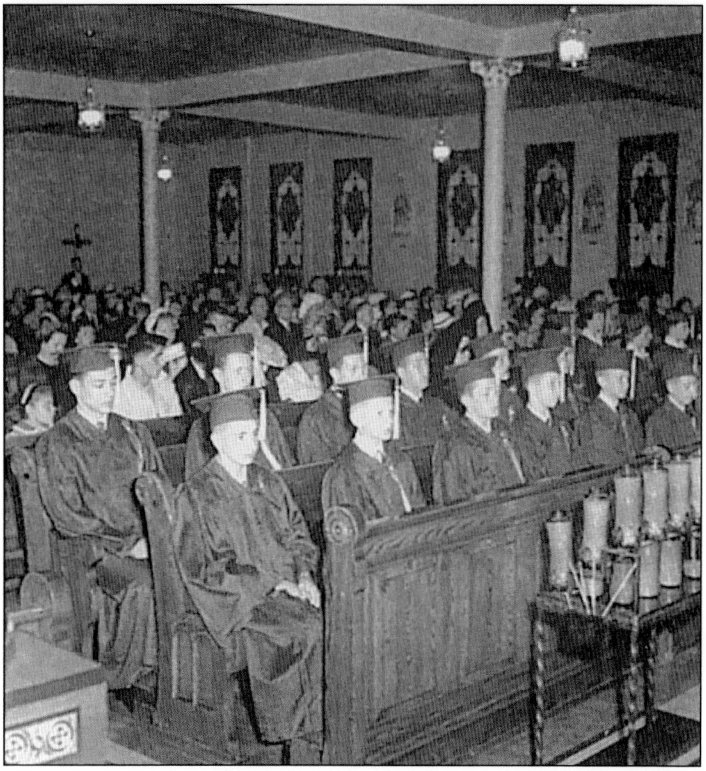

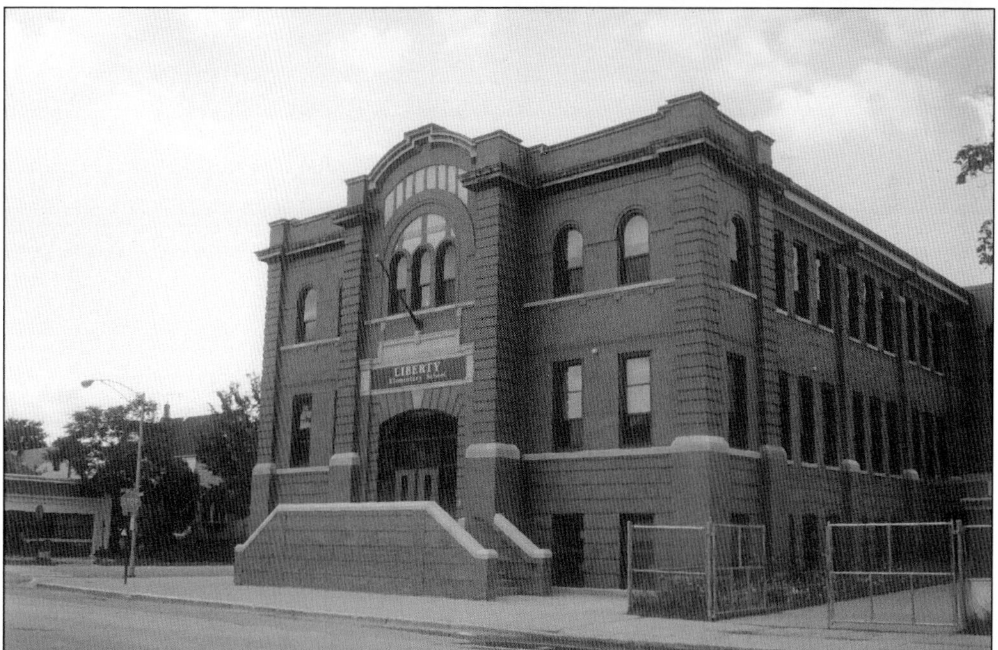

Liberty School, 2000. The St. Valentine Church no longer exists as a parish but the building still stands as a testament to quality building practices. It is currently the home of the Liberty School.

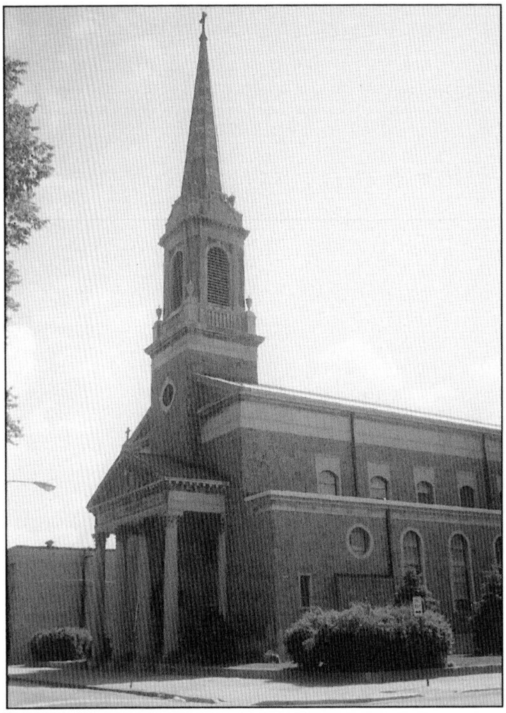

MARY QUEEN OF HEAVEN. The corner of Fifty-Third and Twenty-Fourth Streets has long been the home of Mary Queen of Heaven Catholic Church. It was built in 1911, as were St. Valentine and St. Anthony, in response to the great influx of people coming to work at the Cicero factories being built at the time. The first service was a Requiem Mass for 13 parishioners who died on the *Eastland*.

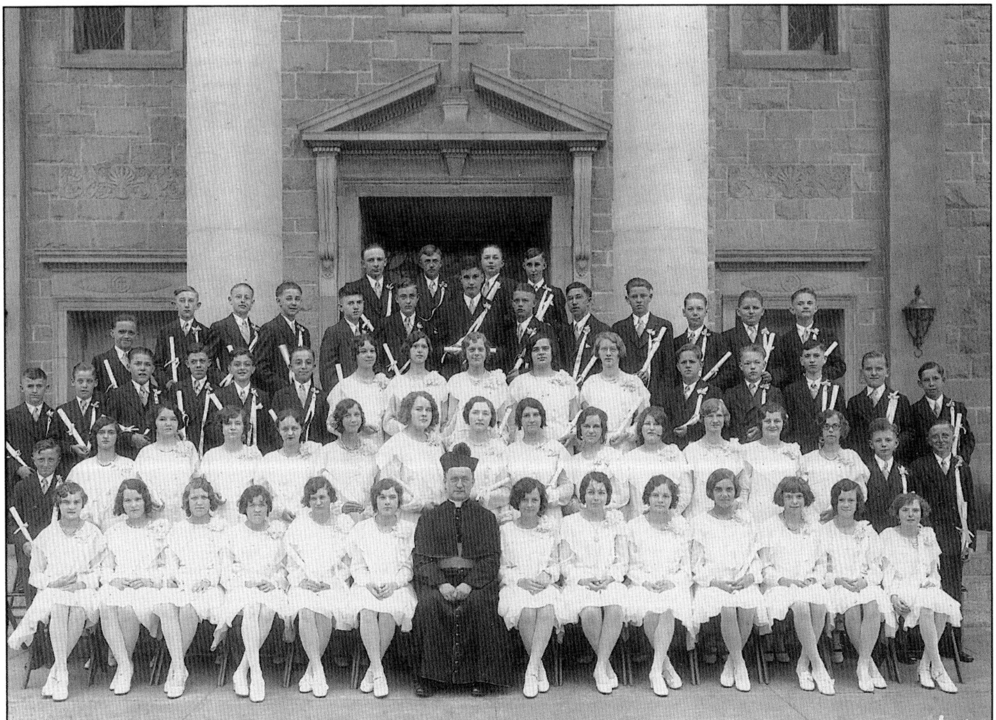

GRADUATION DAY, 1930. Photographed here outside the front door of Mary Queen of Heaven is the eighth grade graduating class of 1930. Note that the girls are dressed in identical dresses. One of the graduates is the mother of Bob Fuka, Morton East Class of '66. (Courtesy Bob Fuka.)

St. Anthony's Church and School. The first St. Anthony's Church (1911) was a combination church and school building founded by the Rev. Anthony Ezerskis, to meet the needs of the predominantly Lithuanian community members. In 1926, a brick edifice was built on the corner. A new convent was soon built for the Sisters of St. Casimir who taught at the parochial school.

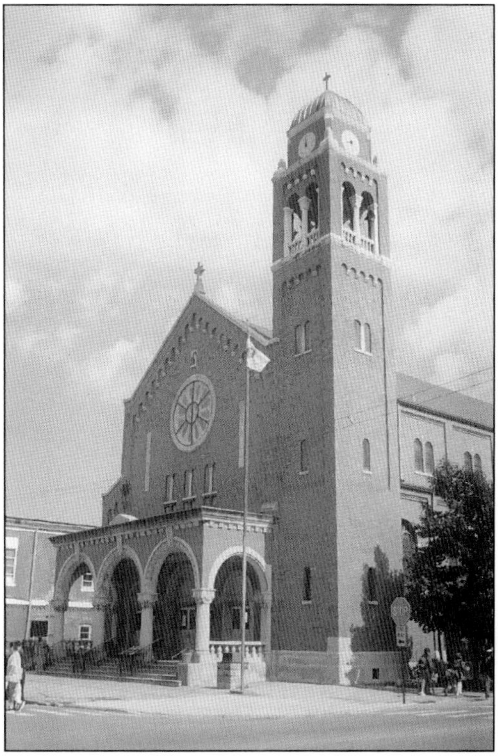

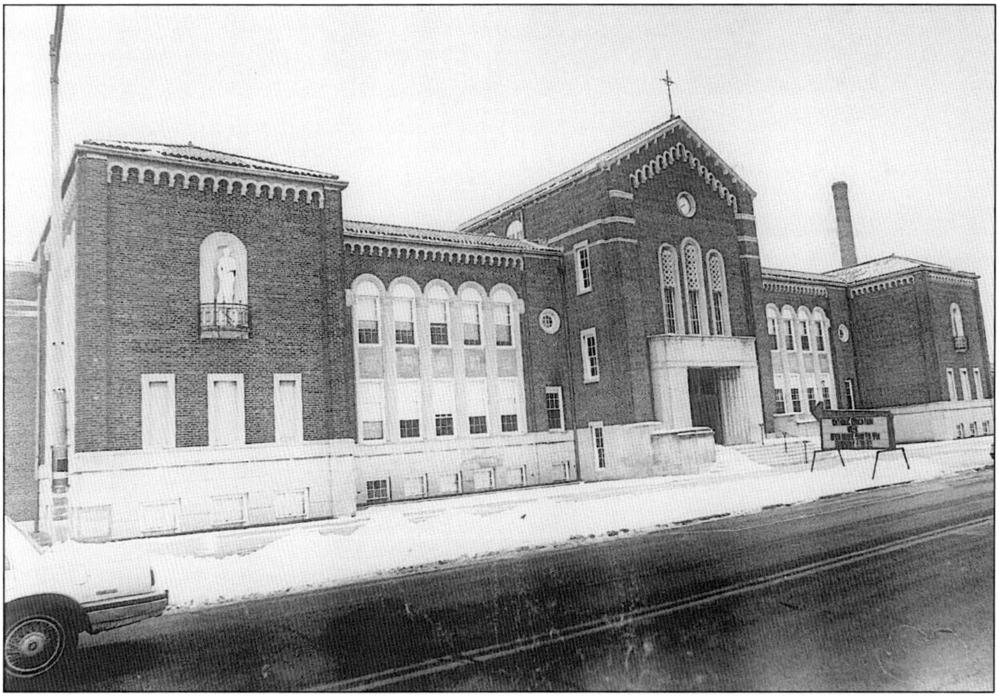

St. Francis of Rome School. The St. Francis of Rome School at 1401 Austin Boulevard is advertising Catholic Education Week here on a wintry day. The Rev. John L. Kelly was the founder of St. Francis and served as pastor until his death. (Courtesy *Life* Newspaper.)

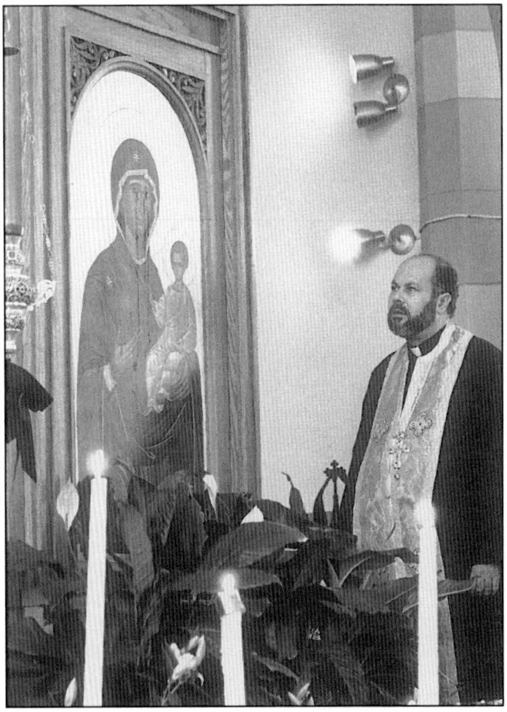

St. George Antiochan Orthodox Church, 1220 S. Sixtieth Court. The Rev. Nicholas Dahdal is pictured here looking up at the Icon of the Holy Theotokos, whose eyes were found to be weeping on April 22, 1994. His Eminence Metropolitan Philip formally declared it "The Miraculous Icon of Our Lady of Cicero." Even now, years later, the icon weeps occasionally, "over the violence, suffering, and death throughout the world." (Courtesy *Life* Newspaper.)

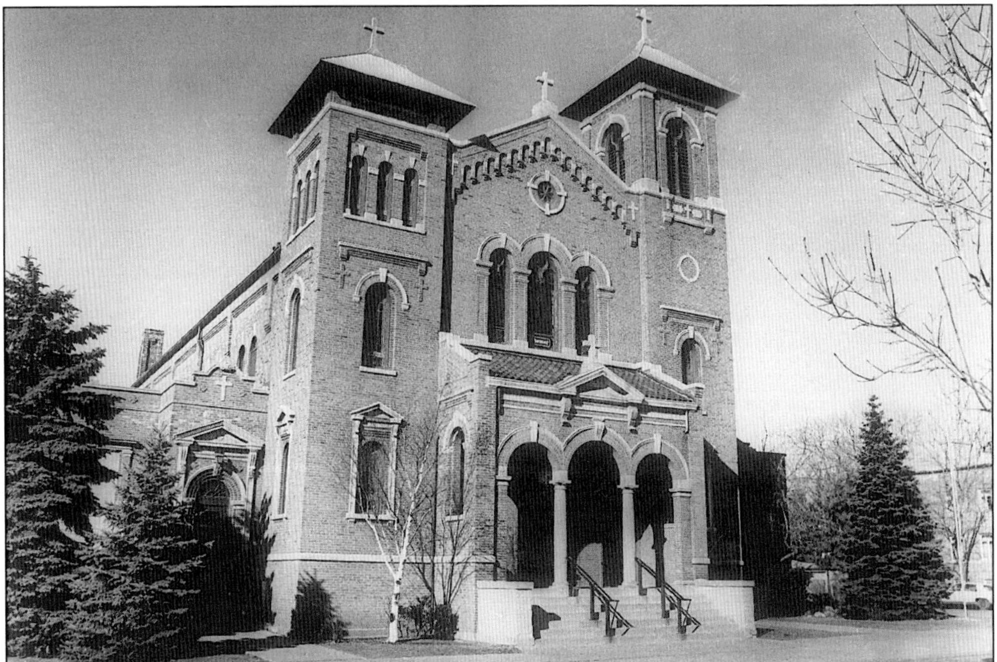

Our Lady of the Mount Church. In 1919, responding to the needs of a burgeoning population in Cicero, a wooden structure was first erected at the corner of 24th and 61st Court, and named for Czechoslovakia's famous Holy Mount site near Prague. The graceful Our Lady of the Mount Church was built in 1926. The Rev. Dedera, who had organized Mary Queen of Heaven, was appointed pastor of the church. (Courtesy *Life* Newspaper.)

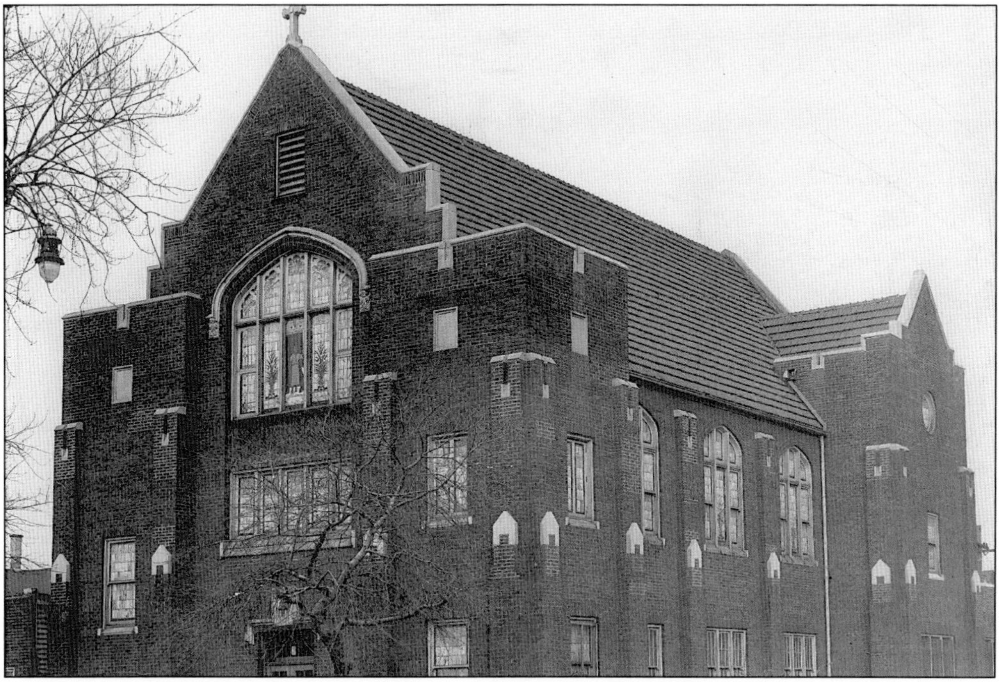

CLEMENT PRESBYTERIAN CHURCH. In 1893, the Christian Endeavor Society of the First Presbyterian Church of Austin, under the leadership of A.H. Clement, began meeting on a regular basis in an old schoolhouse. The church was formally organized on November 2, 1919, and about 1921, they built the church at 1447 Fiftieth Court as a mission project. (Courtesy *Life* Newspaper.)

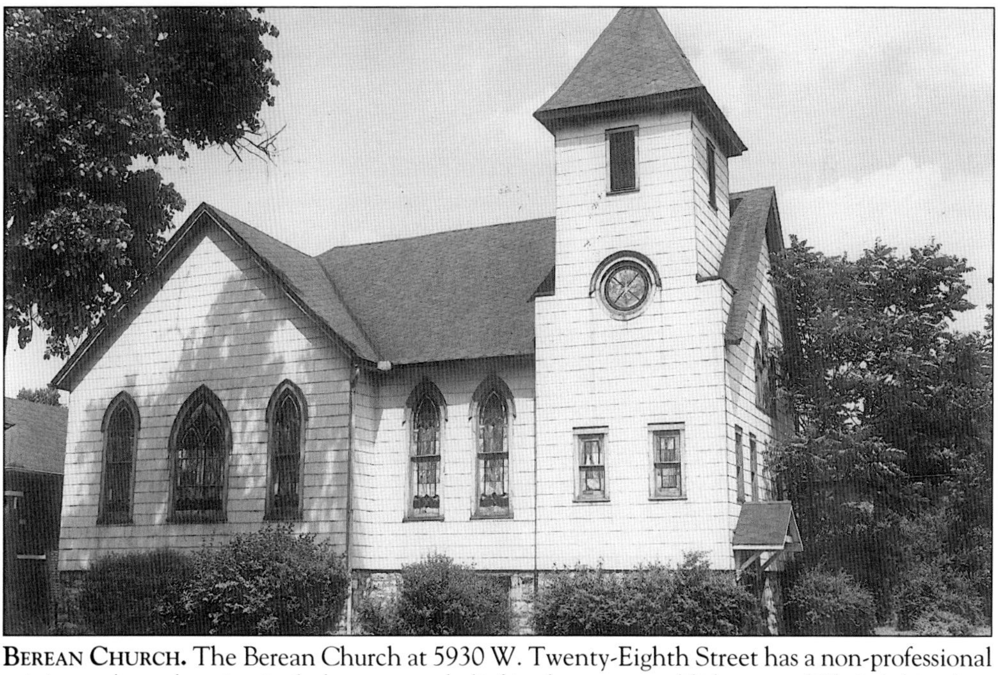

BEREAN CHURCH. The Berean Church at 5930 W. Twenty-Eighth Street has a non-professional ministry whose doctrine includes a strong belief in the near-establishment of Christ's kingdom for a "thousand-year duration on earth, for the blessing of all the people."

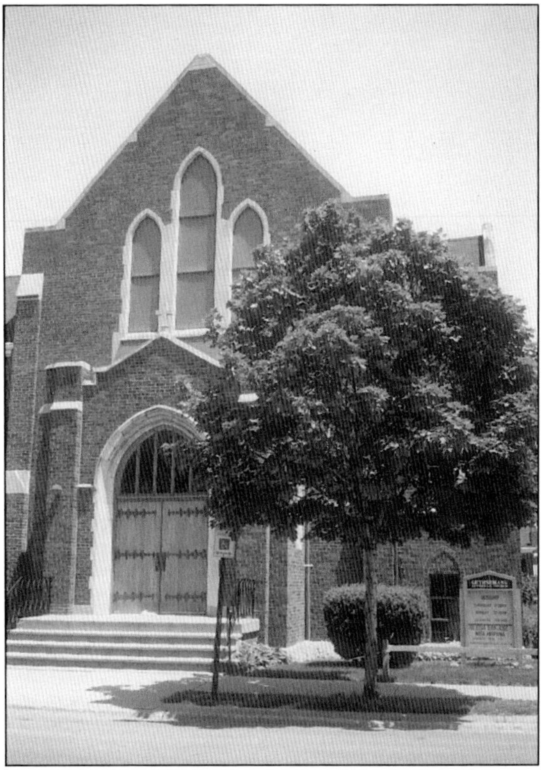

GETHSEMANE LUTHERAN CHURCH. The first service of the Gethsemane Lutheran Church was held in a store front at 5129 Cermak Road on March 23, 1912. In 1918, lots were purchased at 1937 S. Fiftieth Avenue, and a brick bungalow chapel was built at the rear of the lots. In 1956–57, a superstructure was built at a cost of $120,000 and has been a landmark at the corner of Fiftieth and Twenty-First Streets since then. Today, it is also known as the Iglesia San Jose. There are worship services in Spanish and in English.

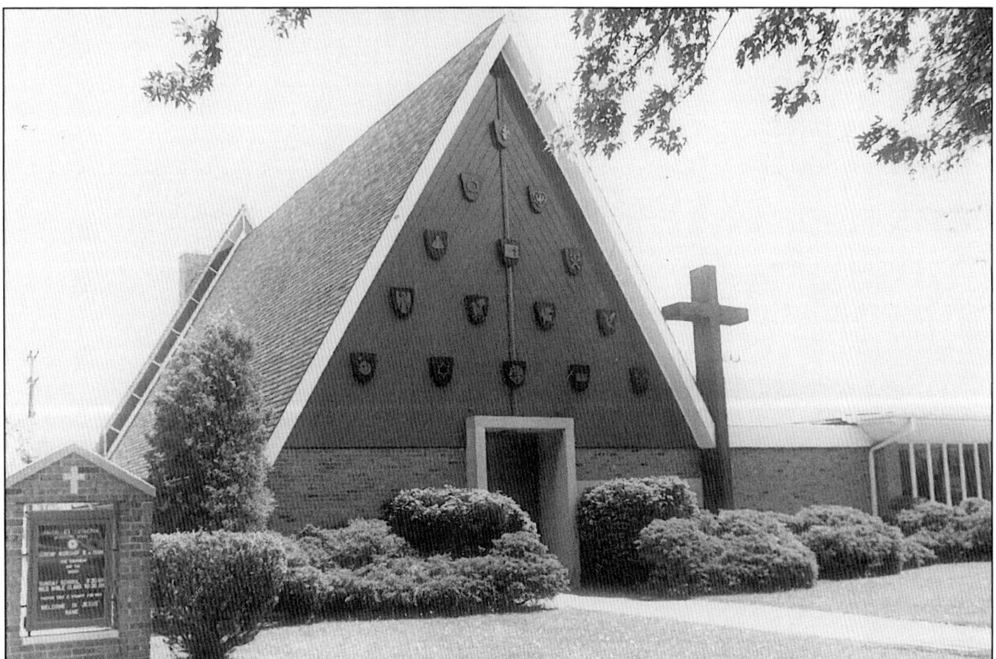

FAITH LUTHERAN CHURCH. The modern-looking Faith Lutheran Church was built in 1952 at 3601 S. Sixty-First Avenue. The Rev. Ernest Wenz was installed as the first pastor. (Courtesy *Life* Newspaper.)

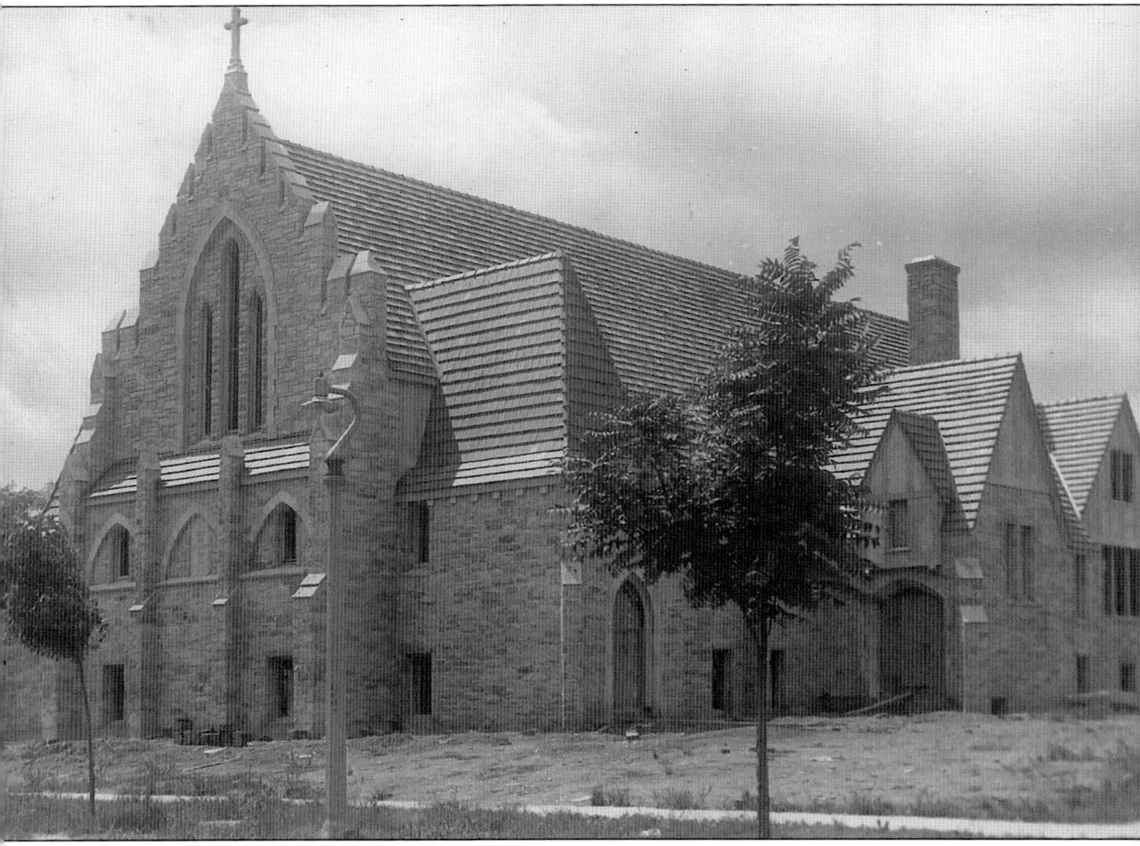

Warren Park Presbyterian Church, 1935. "The Most Beautiful Small Church in America," the Warren Park Presbyterian Church, was organized in 1926 by Rev. Stuart S. Pratt. A church in Tabor, Czechoslovakia was used as the model for the building, which was erected in 1935. For the past four years, however, it has also been known as the Emmanuel Presbyterian Church, as well as the Warren Park Church. Worship services and Sunday schools are held each Sunday in both English and Spanish. The growing Spanish congregation offers weekly Bible study, a youth service on Thursday nights, and Friday evening worship, as well as English and citizenship classes and a Saturday Children's Club. It is located at 6130 W. Twenty-First Street. (Courtesy *Life* Newspaper.)

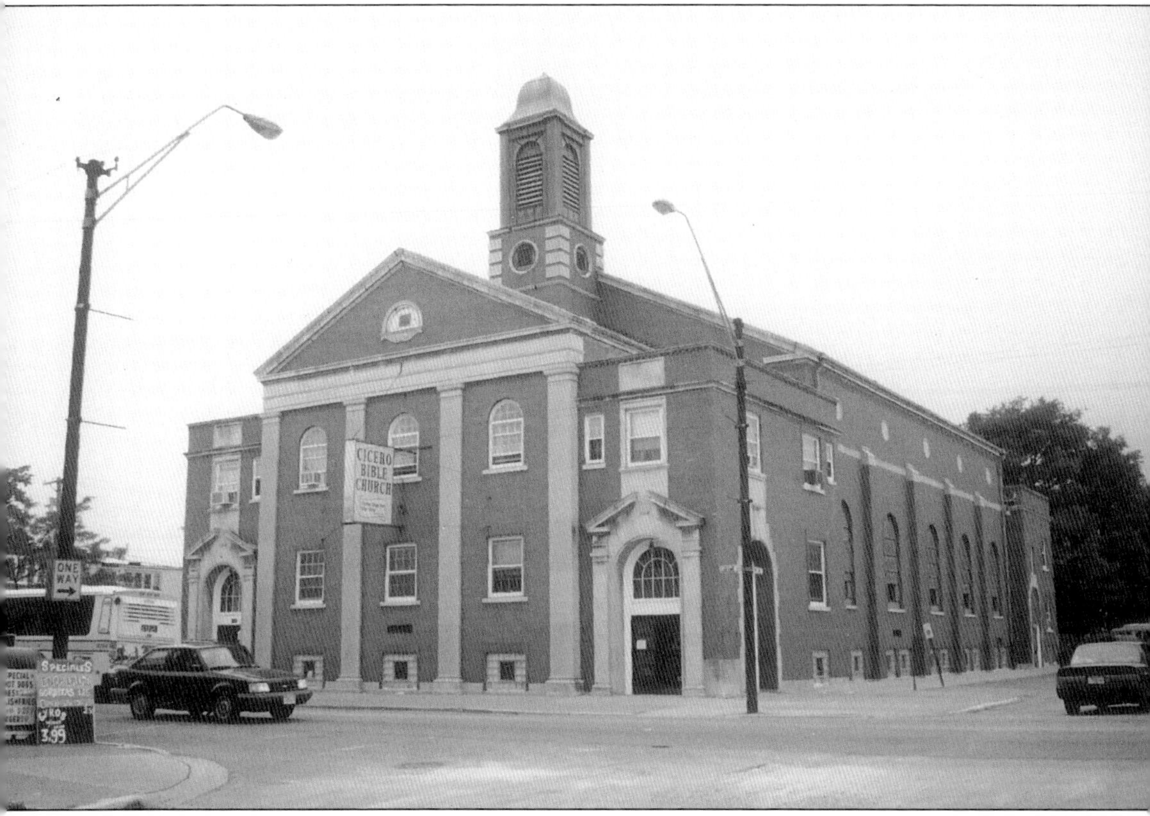

CICERO BIBLE CHURCH, 1929. "The church that did not close" grew from a small structure in 1913 that frequently had an evening attendance of eight people, to the 1929 red brick building which over the years has boasted over one thousand members. It began when a young graduate of Moody Bible Institute was invited to fill the pulpit on a Sunday in June of 1913, and stayed to become pastor of the church. His name, William McCarrell, has been held in great esteem. The church's phenomenal growth was due in part to the Cicero Fisherman's Club, an organization of evangelistic workers. Soon, the church expanded into the building at 2212 S. Fifty-Second (Laramie Avenue.)

Seven

Cicero Scenes

Cicero, a town of prairies, farms and a quarry, did not stay thinly inhabited very long. The great Chicago fire of 1871 encouraged rebuilding further west, as did the thousands of immigrants arriving in "the land of opportunity" at the turn of the 20th century. They came through Ellis Island or Boston and kept heading west, many to Chicago where there were job opportunities. The crowded conditions of Chicago flats and apartments lead folks to seek homes of their own, with a tiny plot of grass to lovingly tend. Cicero, the first suburb west, was right there to welcome them.

Families rejoiced in the space and kept chickens and geese and even cows in their yards. The fields not far away were a great place for kids to catch frogs in the summer and skate in the winter. Mud Lake was clean enough and deep enough for swimming on hot summer days.

Many homes were two-flats: one for living in and one for renting. Or, one floor for using when company came. Gradually, the streets filled with houses and people, and a few roads were raised with drainage ditches on either side. Streetcars ran down Cermak Road, Cicero Avenue, Laramie Avenue, and Twenty-Fifth Street. The "L" (elevated train) came out as far as Oak Park Avenue. Soon, roads were paved and stores and factories filled in the open land. Before long, Cicero had changed into a town with electricity and gas lines and pollution. People who lived through these changes are amazed at how fast they occurred.

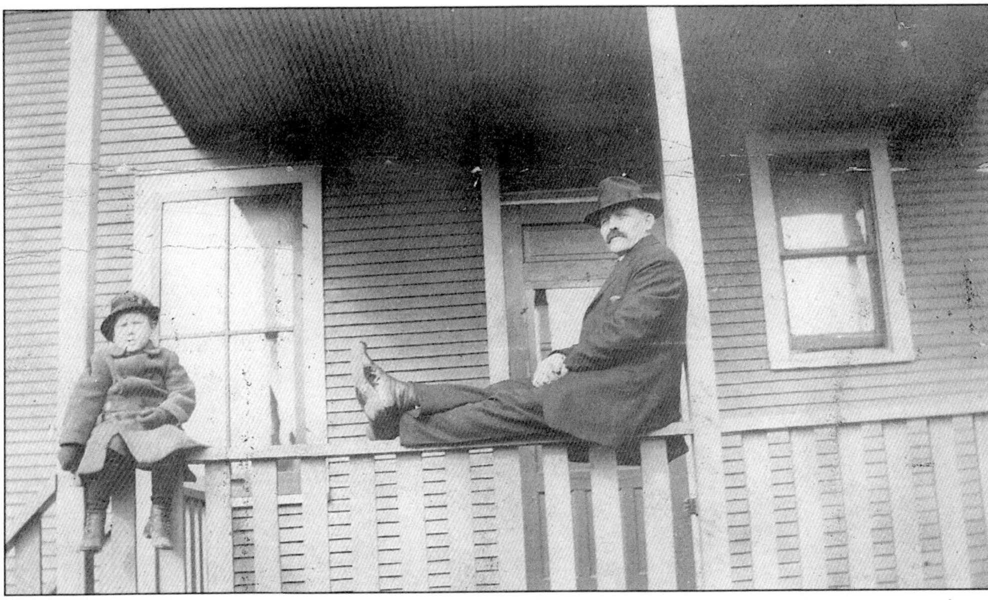

The House on Twenty-Second Place. Pride of home ownership is evident even without a smile. Emil Carlson emigrated from Sweden in the 1890s, worked at McCormick Works, married Emma Petersen, and by 1915 he was out of a small apartment on Chicago's west side and into his own home in Cicero. He lived in the Morton Park house until his death in 1950, and his son continued to live in the same house until his death in 1974.

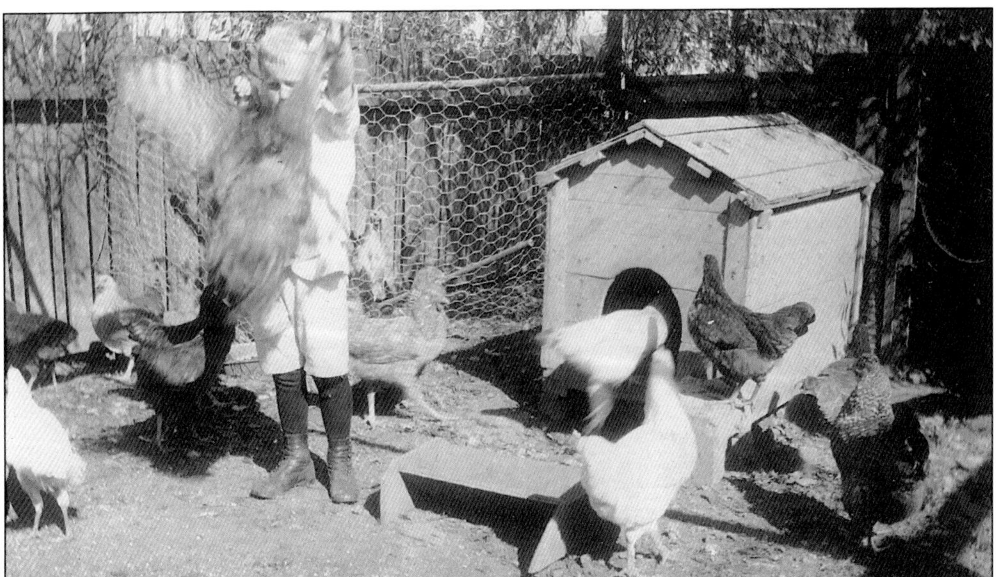

Raising Chickens. In 1915, it was not unusual for families to keep chickens, geese, and even cows in the backyards of Cicero. Playing with the chickens in his high top shoes and knickers is a new resident of the town in its early years.

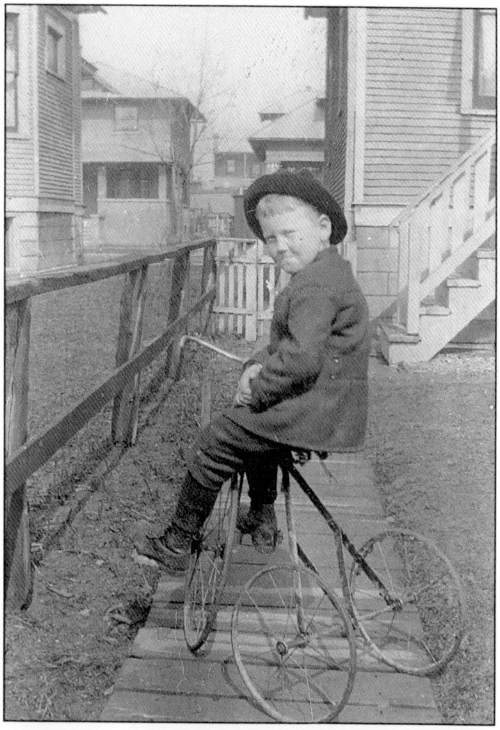

WOODEN SIDEWALKS. The wooden boards of the city's first sidewalks made walking and pedaling drier and easier. Here, Red Carlson rides his tricycle from the alley to the house on a wooden sidewalk. Note the original wooden siding on the house.

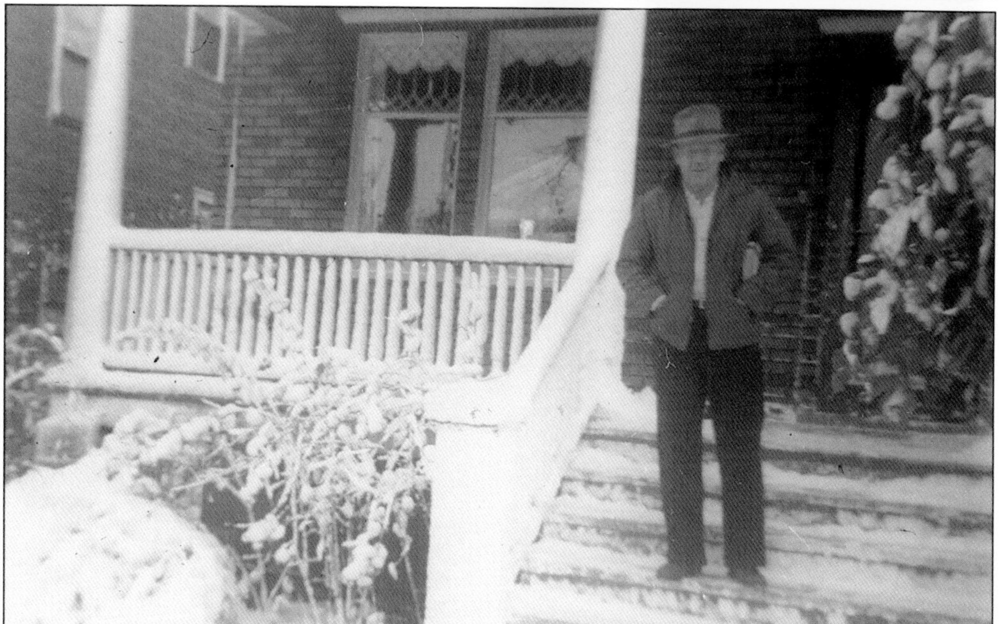

NEW "BRICK" SIDING, ADDED IN THE '40S. The little boy who moved into Cicero and played with chickens in his yard lived in the same house his whole life. Here he stands on a snowy day in 1955, heading for work at Commonwealth Edison. The wooden siding on the house is now covered with the very latest thing—imitation bricks! The streets were shaded by huge elm trees then, soon to be decimated by the Dutch Elm disease.

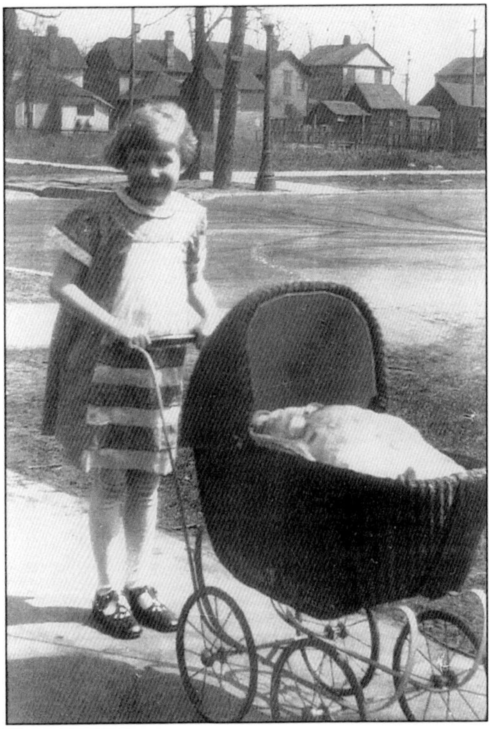

Lois Palmer, 1924. Pictured here wheeling her doll carriage near her family's home at Twenty-Eighth and Fifty-Ninth Court in Cicero is Lois Palmer, later to add Huth to her last name. Lois has many early Cicero memories of her father, a fireman who was also an artist, who painted the decorative curtain for the Clyde Park Pavilion in 1908. She herself is an artist, sculptor by choice. She is quite famous for her sculptures that she has exhibited and sold widely. (Courtesy Lois Palmer Huth Family.)

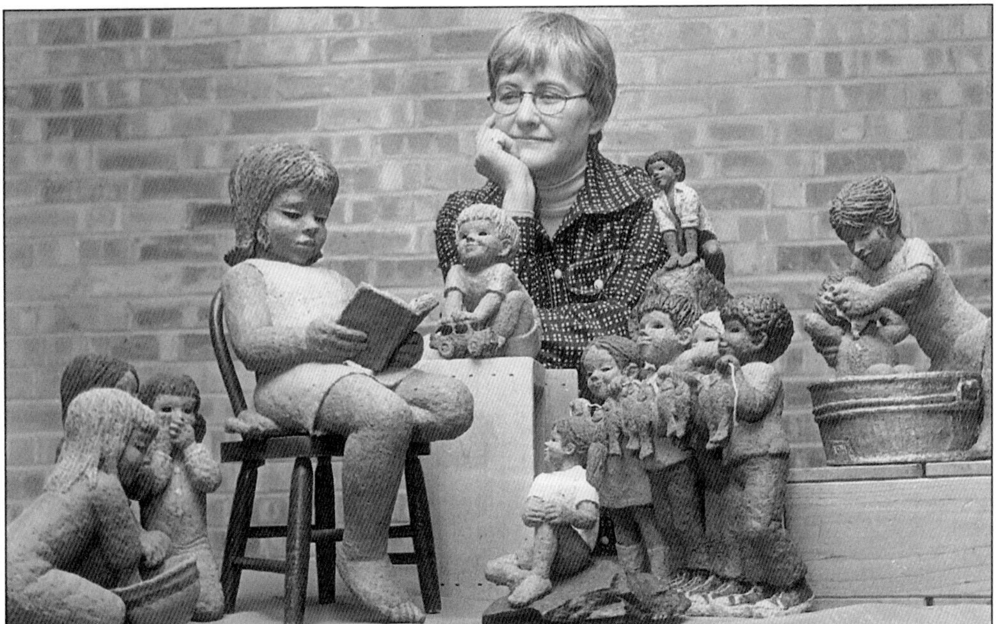

Lois Palmer Huth and Her Sculptures. Pictured here in the 1960s is Lois Palmer Huth and some of her "children." Lois remembers never being without a drawing pencil in her hand in her childhood. Both her parents were artists. Her son Jonathan is now a carver of wood, and a granddaughter is a graphic artist. Something special is in those genes! (Courtesy *Life* Newspaper.)

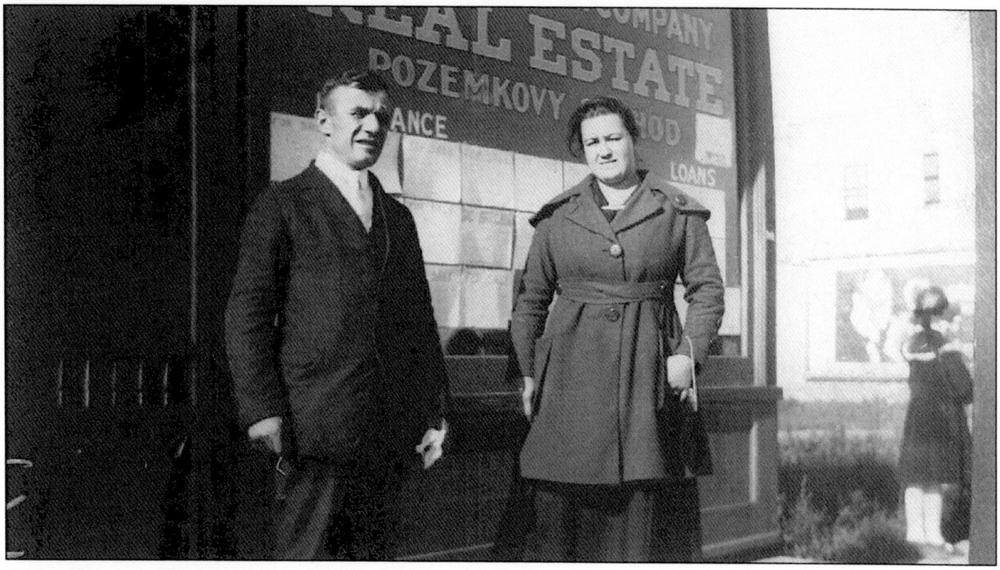

Real Estate Venture, c. 1919. Bohumil Machian was a very successful real estate broker in the Cicero area who had emigrated from Bohemia in 1890. He is pictured here with his wife Emma (Riha) Machian, and daughter Mildred. The advertisements were written in both English and Bohemian at this time. Bohumil was killed in a car accident in 1921, and Emma married Joseph Sup Jr., who delivered her milk (see cover.) (Courtesy Karl J. Sup.)

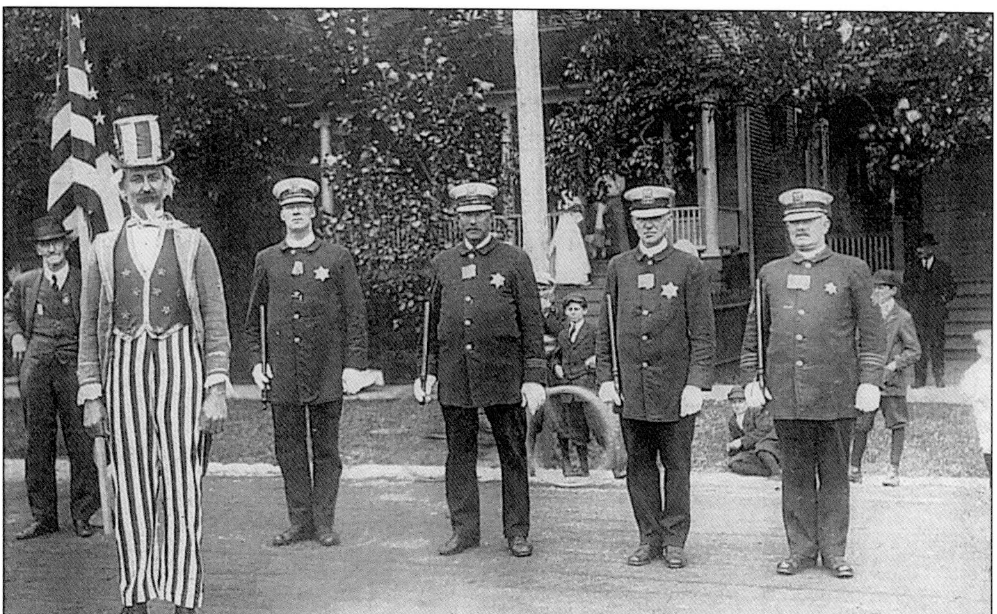

Fourth of July Parade, 1913. The Fourth of July Parade in Clyde was lead by Uncle Sam, a.k.a Otto Taeschner, the tallest man in Cicero at six feet, six inches. Mr. Taeschner, a machinist by occupation, lived at 2745 S. Fifty-Eighth Court. Once the president of the Clyde Park District Board, he is seen here flanked by Cicero's finest, ready to lead the Fourth of July Parade. (Courtesy Lois Palmer Huth Family.)

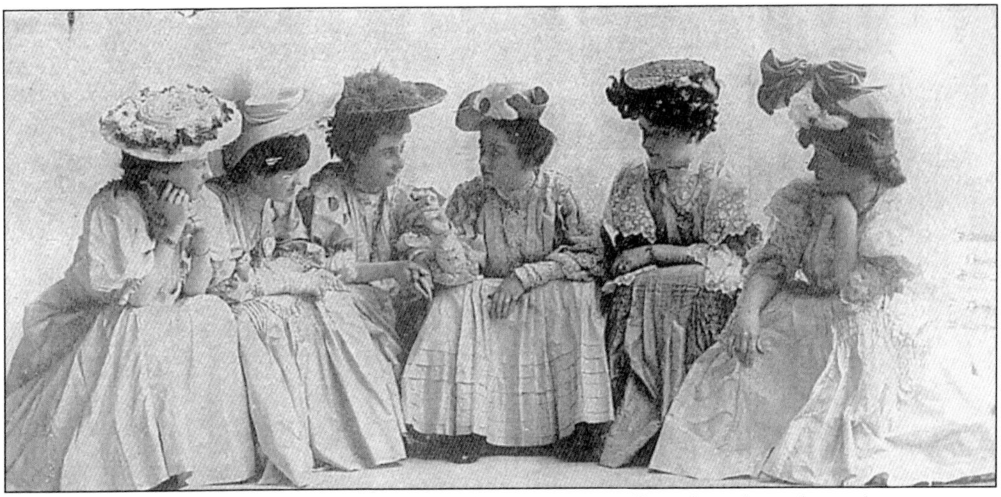

Cicero Belles, 1902. Lest one thinks that life in 1902 was all work and no play, take a moment to enjoy this charming picture from the 1929 *City Directory*. The interesting pose makes one wonder what the women are sitting on, and why they are sitting like this! But it sure makes for a cute pose! The title of the photo says, "Cicero Belles Talking Over the Paris Styles in 1902."

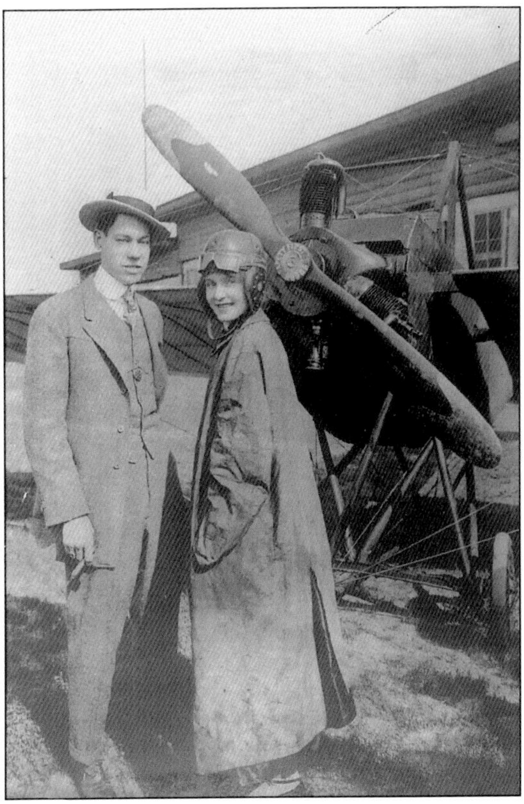

Cicero Airfield, 1914. Mr. and Mrs. J. Lee Fitzgerald are seen here in 1914 at the Cicero Airfield, which stretched from Sixteenth to Twenty-Second, and from Forty-Eighth to Fifty-Second. It opened with a flying exhibition on the Fourth of July in 1911. But even the opening of a flight school in 1912 was not enough to compete with the much larger Midway airport being cleared on the south side. (Courtesy *Life* Newspaper.)

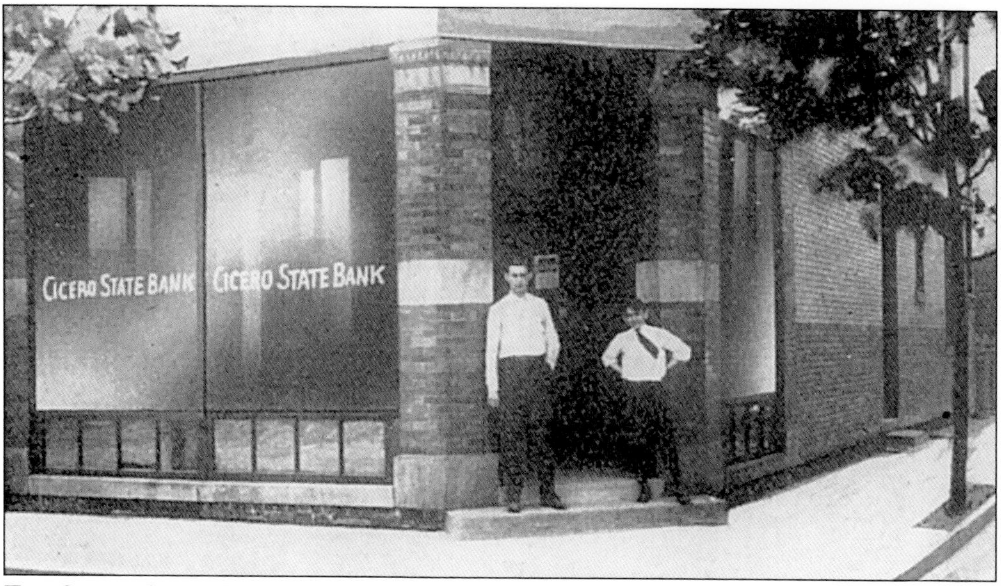

THE CICERO STATE BANK, 1907. The Cicero State Bank was founded in 1907, in a store in Hawthorne at 4929 W. Twenty-Ninth Street. Standing in front of this building, which bravely began during the panic of 1907, are Stanley Witkowski and Charles C. Stoffel. G.H. Hughes, the founder of the bank, worked long hours, often driving around the neighborhood in an old Ford picking up deposits. The bank "made it possible to do business in practically everyone's native tongue." (*City Directory*, 1929.)

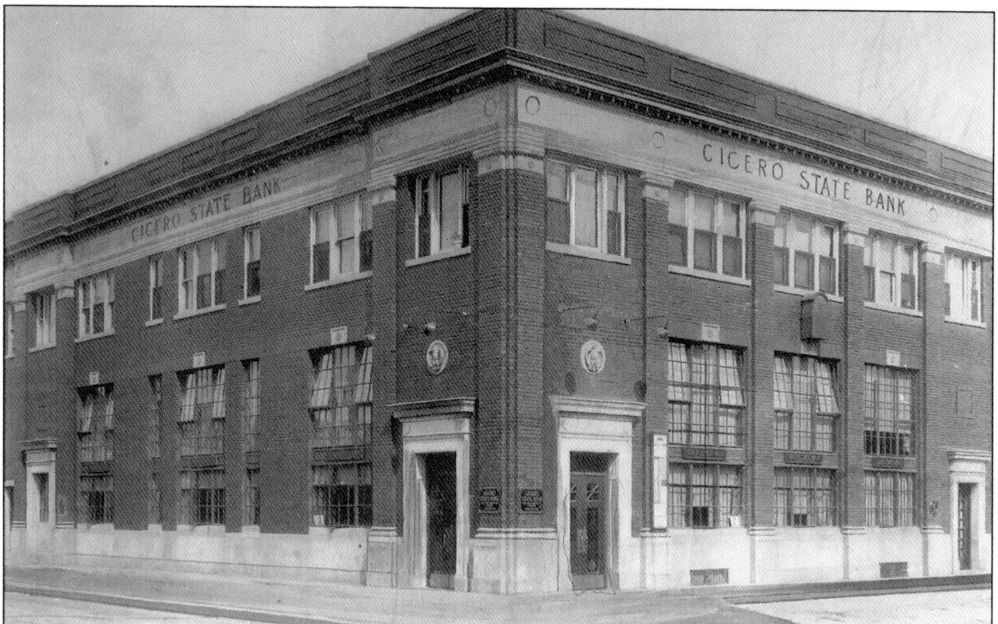

THE CICERO STATE BANK, 1930. Growth in business encouraged the bank to move to the corner of Cicero Avenue and Twenty-Fifth Street in January of 1924. At first built of red brick, the bank later was given a white facade. Though the Cicero State Bank is no longer standing, the Harris Bank, built in 1997 at Twenty-Ninth and Cicero, meets the needs of the present-day Hawthorne residents. (Courtesy Stan Loula.)

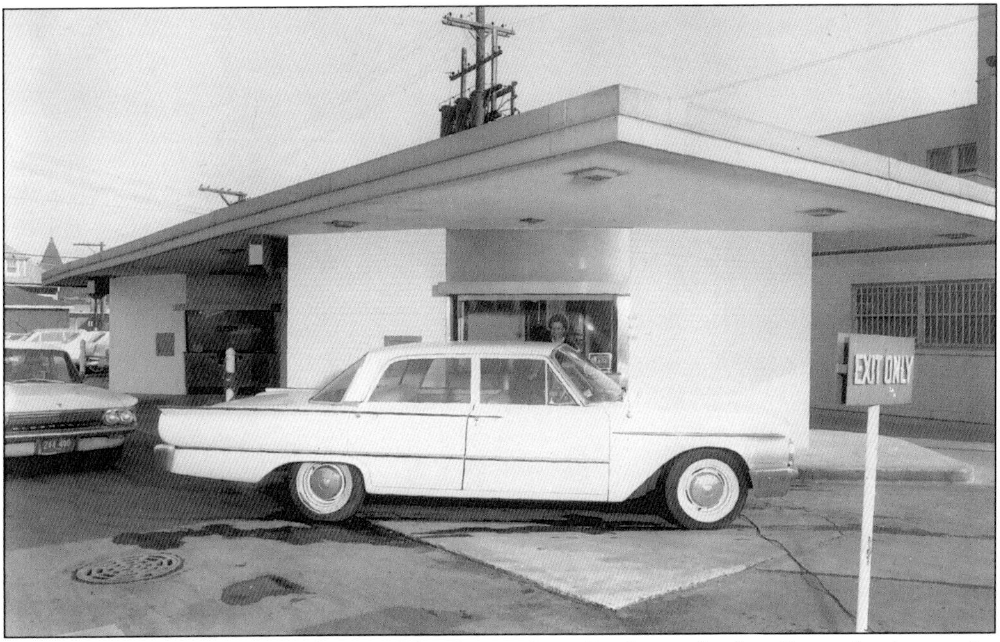

First Drive-Up Window in Cicero. The Cicero State Bank was the first Cicero bank to make automobile loans, beginning in the early days of the Model T. It was also the first bank to offer full trust services, the first with a parking lot, and the first with automobile drive-in facilities. (Courtesy Stan Loula.)

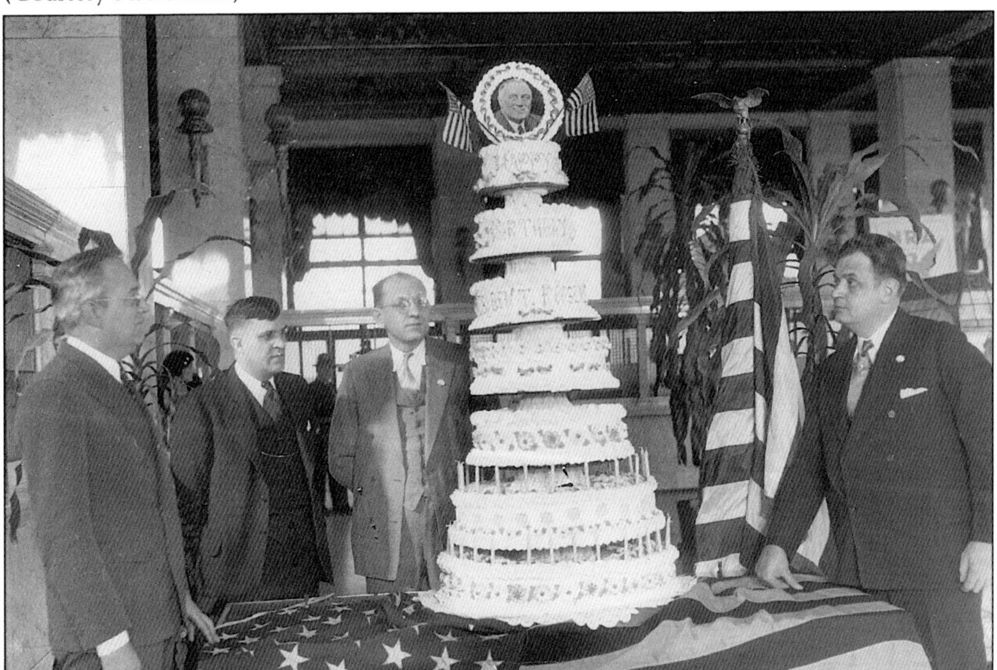

Celebrating President Roosevelt's Birthday. Cicero helped celebrate President Roosevelt's 52nd birthday on January 30, 1934 at the First National Bank of Cicero. Second from left is Dr. L.M. Houdka, from Morton High School. (Courtesy Stan Loula.)

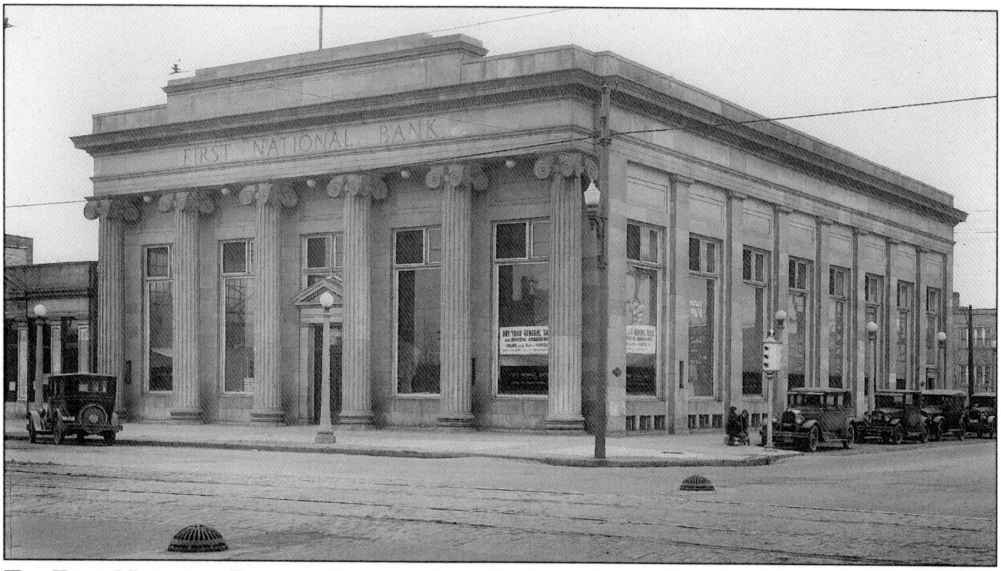

THE FIRST NATIONAL BANK OF CICERO, 1921. The First National Bank of Cicero was constructed in 1920, at a cost of $375,000. Mr. William Kaspar, founder of the bank and the first president, was born in Holice, Czechoslovakia in 1834. After fighting in the Civil War he moved to Chicago, where he started a real estate and mortgage loan business. Soon, he purchased the land on the corner of Cermak and Austin and organized the First National Bank of Cicero. (Courtesy Stan Loula.)

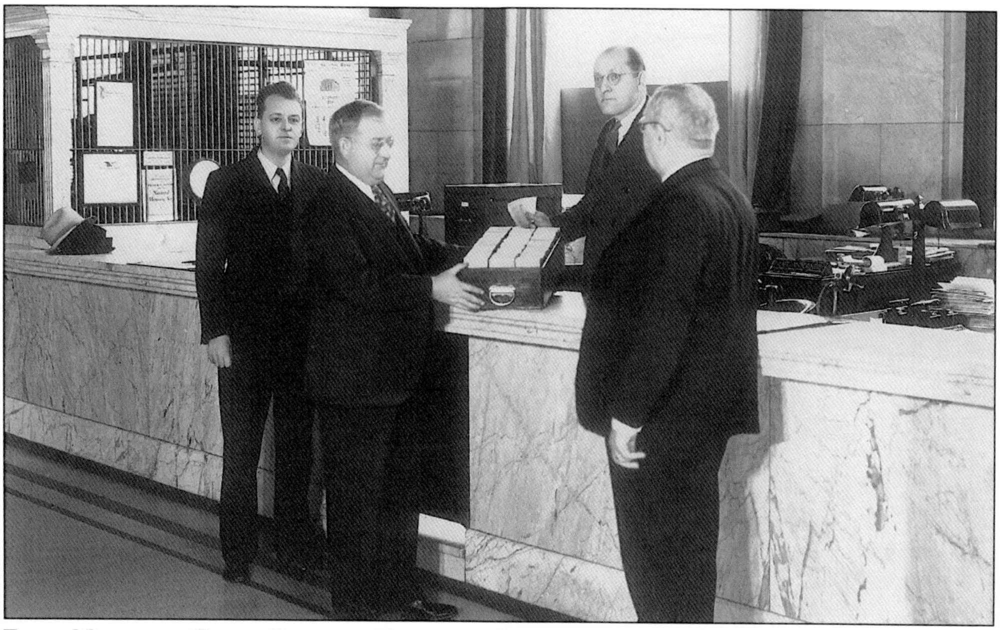

FIRST NATIONAL BANK ORIGINAL BUILDING, JANUARY 1935. The constant fear of another monetary catastrophe led people to put so much money into their savings each week that banks and savings and loans on Cermak Road in Cicero and Berwyn earned themselves the nickname, "The Bohemian Wall Street." Stanley Chleboun (behind the counter), a 40-year bank employee, was instrumental in maintaining the bank as a viable institution through the Depression. He was president from 1953 to 1961. (Courtesy Stan Loula.)

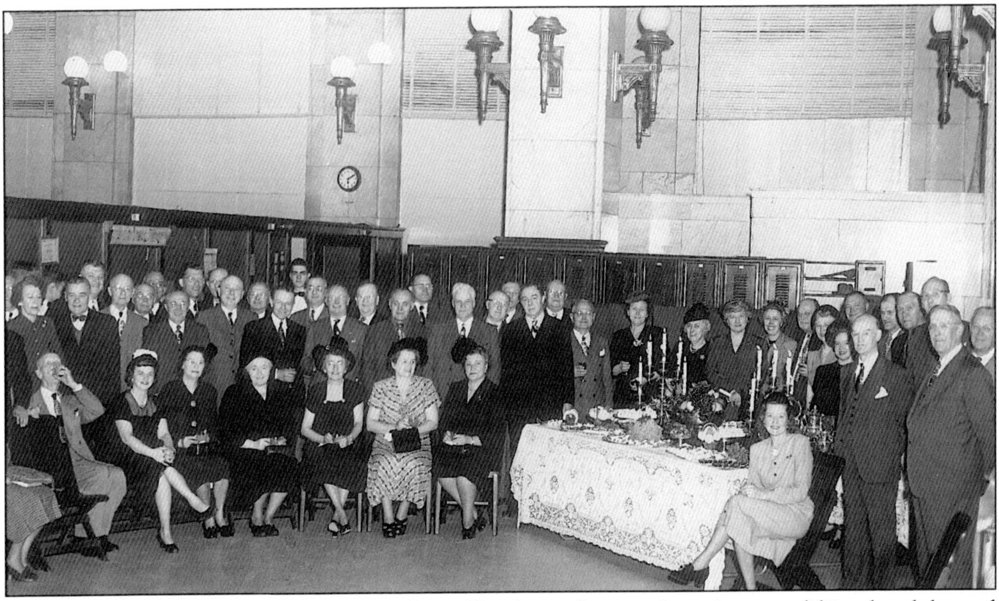

Celebrating the 25th Anniversary. Proud bank employees, depositors, and friends celebrated the 25th anniversary of the First National Bank of Cicero in 1946 on the main floor of the bank. (Courtesy Stan Loula.)

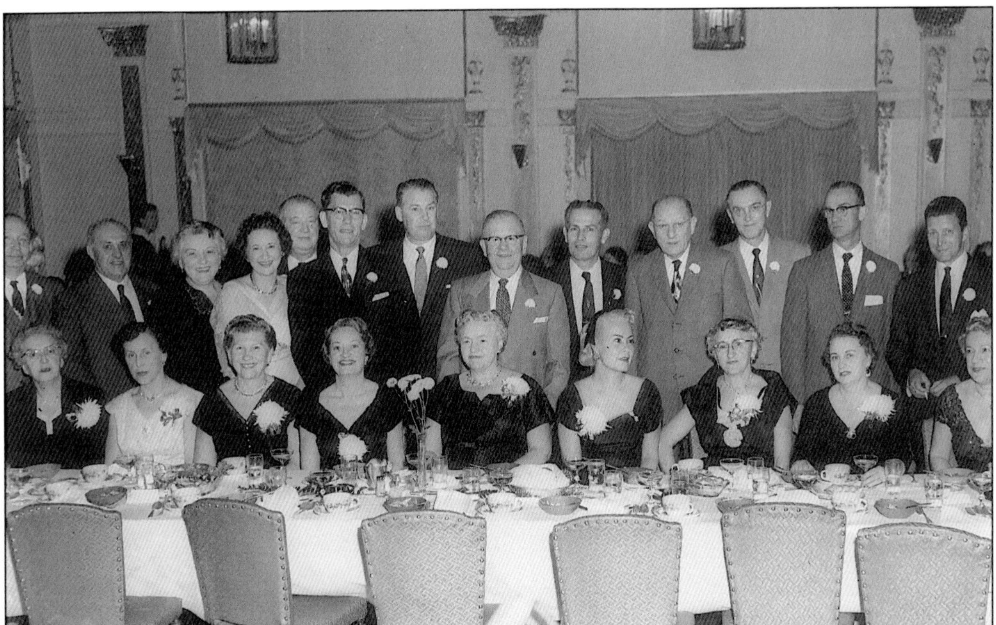

First National Bank Directors, 1956. Pictured at a dinner for the bank directors are, from left to right: (seated) Mrs. Vesecky, Mrs. Rose Krzmarik, two unidentified, Mrs. Anna Jecmen, Mrs. Edna Kaspar, Mrs. Betty Chleboun, Mrs. Betty Stava, and Mrs. Helena Kerner; (standing) Rudolph Vesecky, Jack G. Zajicek, Mrs. Bertha Zajicek, Helen Kralovec, Hugo Kralovec, Joseph E. Novak, Ted Bartnick, Anton Jecmen, James P. Krzmarik, Stanley L. Chleboun, John F. Stava, James Triner, and the Honorable Otto Kerner. (Courtesy Stan Loula.)

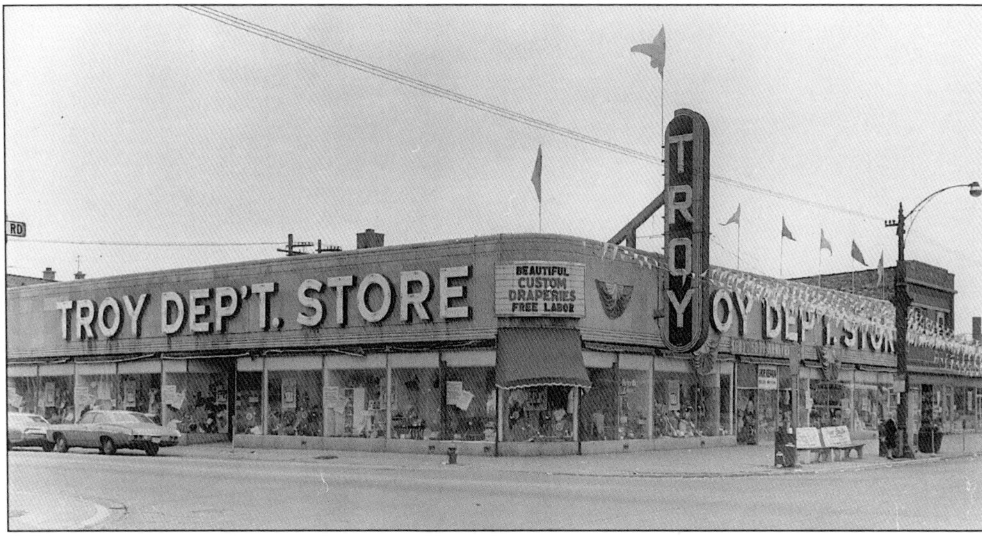

The Troy Department Store. The Troy Store was an important landmark for years on Cermak Road, first at 6217, and then at the new store at Cermak and Ridgeland. It was founded in 1919 in Chicago by Rudolph Vesecky, and offered quality merchandise at good prices. The department store included a shoe repair shop, a beauty shop, and a large candy department. Its presence made Cermak Road a good shopping area. (Courtesy *Life* Newspaper.)

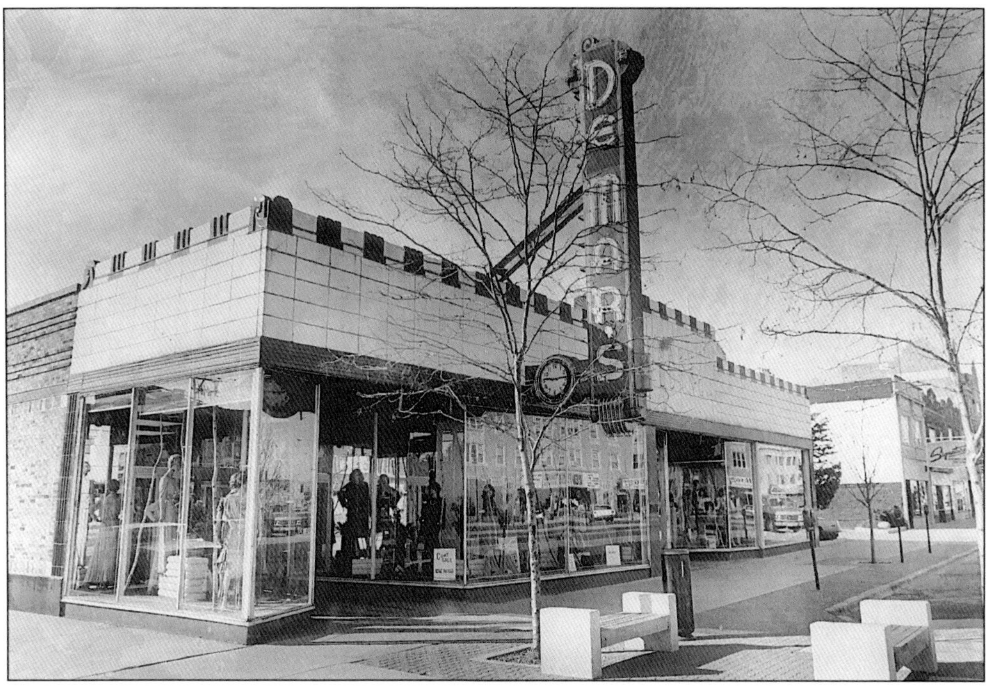

DeMar's Fashion Center. Further west on Cermak Road was DeMar's dress shop. Generations of women recall purchasing high quality, fashionable dresses from this store. (Courtesy *Life* Newspaper.)

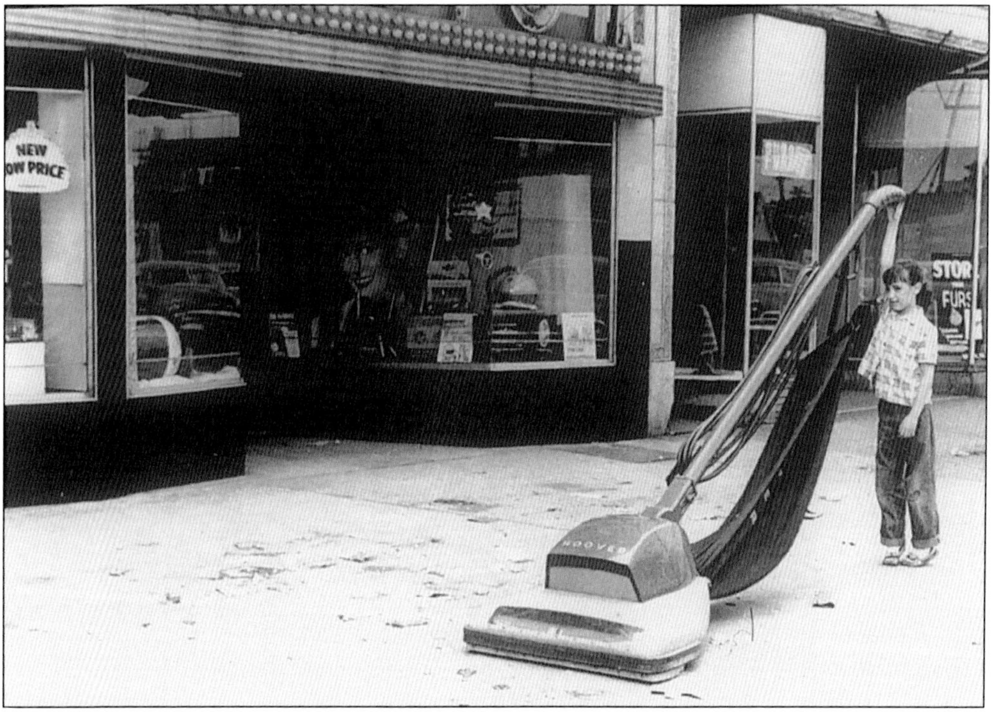

A Sales Promotion on Cermak Road. On the sidewalk in front of an appliance shop on Cermak Road, a young girl tested her strength against a giant, promotional Hoover vacuum. Shopping that day in the 1950s was a memorable event for Janice Morganti, who was raised on Twelfth Place. (Courtesy Michal Morganti Murphy.)

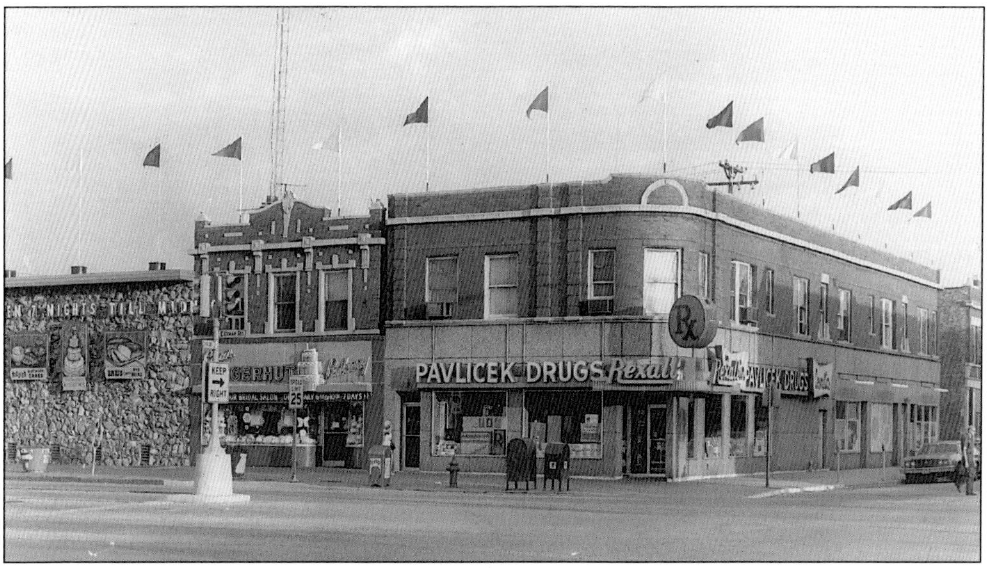

Pavlicek Drugs and Fingerhut Bakery. The history of the Fingerhut Bakeries begins in the 1700s in Bohemia, in a small bakery owned by Frantisek Fingerhut. In the 1890s, the bakery opened at 5403 W. Twenty-Fourth Place, then moved to the 5537 Cermak Road address. They provided the delicious hot dogs wrapped in a bun, topped with chunks of Kosher salt, which Morton alums recall fondly. (Courtesy *Life* Newspaper.)

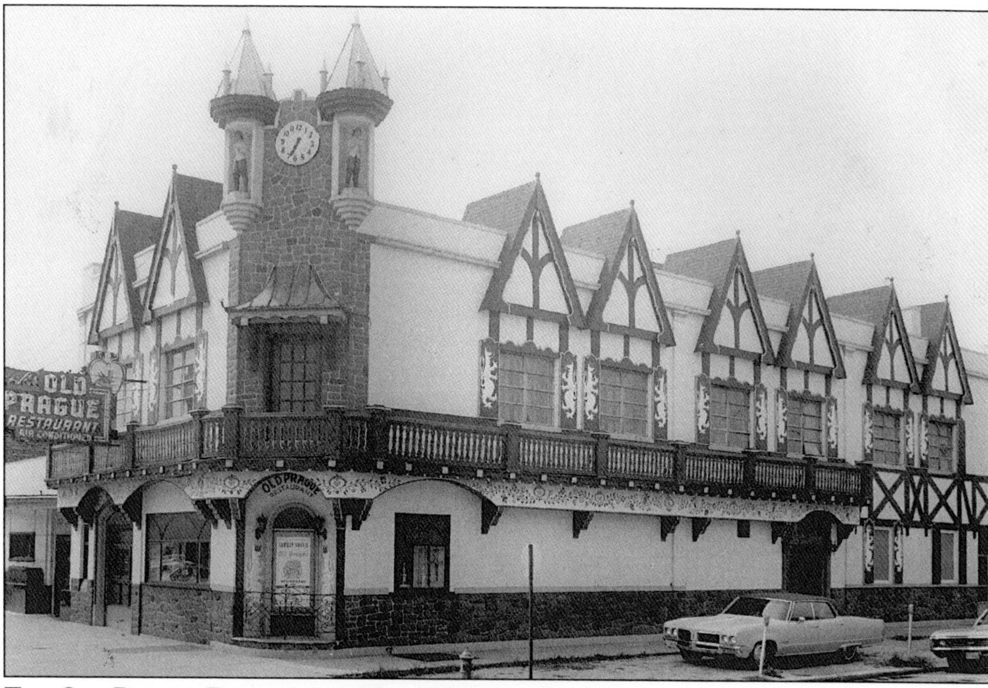

The Old Prague Restaurant. The Old Prague Restaurant on Cermak Road brought a bit of old world charm to Cicero for years, providing delicious meals in the Czechoslovakian tradition, from dumplings to duck. The architecture, complete with statues in the clock tower, was charming and memorable. Sadly, a fire destroyed the structure. (Courtesy *Life* Newspaper.)

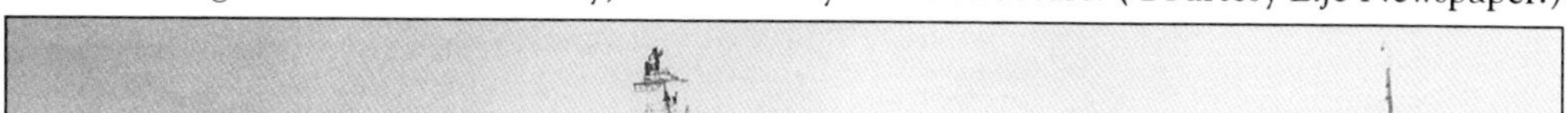

The Klas Restaurant, 1922. Reminiscent of a street in old Czechoslovakia, the restaurant features a bar, a banquet hall, and an outdoor garden, as well as a main dining hall. Two cuckoo clocks from Austria grace the premises as well as dishes and dolls that fill lighted shelves in the entrance hall. Sharp eyes will spot a deck of cards, reputed to have been used in a card game with Al Capone. (Courtesy *Life* Newspaper.)

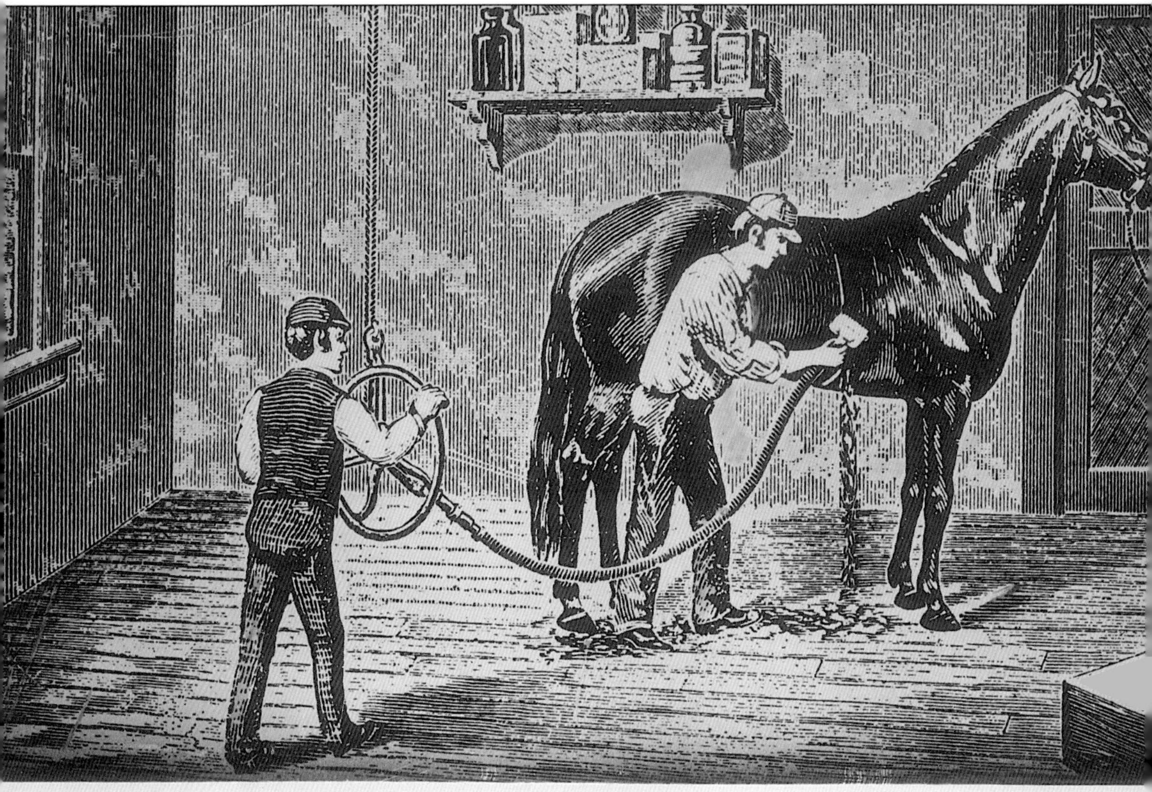

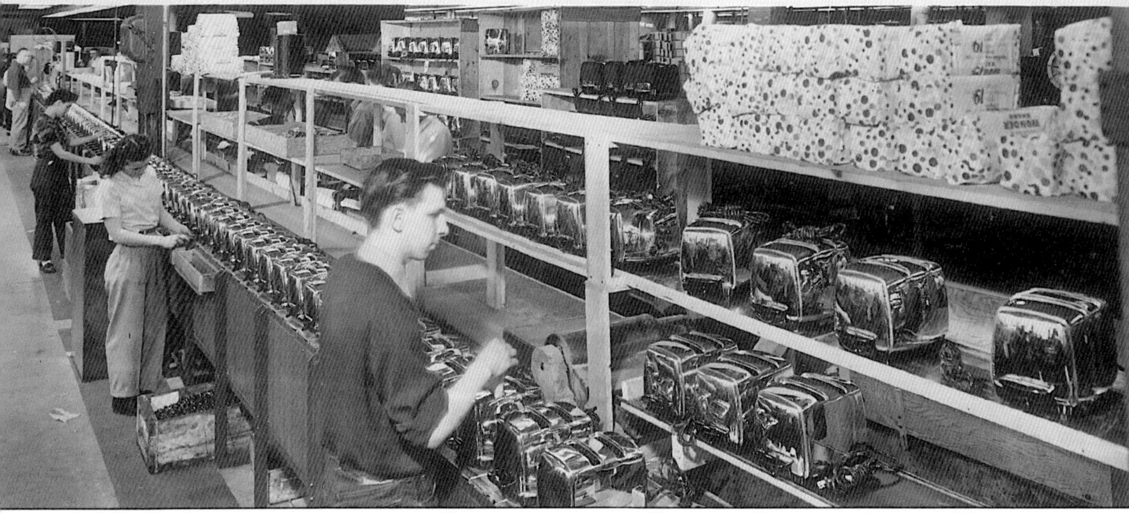

The Sunbeam Corporation. The Sunbeam Company was a large employer on the northeast end of Cicero during the days of heavy manufacturing. In this before and after photo, the Sunbeam Company depicts the remarkable progress made in their plant. The top picture shows the latest in helpful mechanics for clipping your horse, c. 1893. The bottom photo shows the product testing line of the Sunbeam toaster department. Note the loaves of Wonder Bread available for testing as each toaster comes off the assembly line. Founded by John K. Steward and Thomas J. Clark, the name Sunbeam did not appear on national advertising until 1921. (Courtesy *Life* Newspaper.)

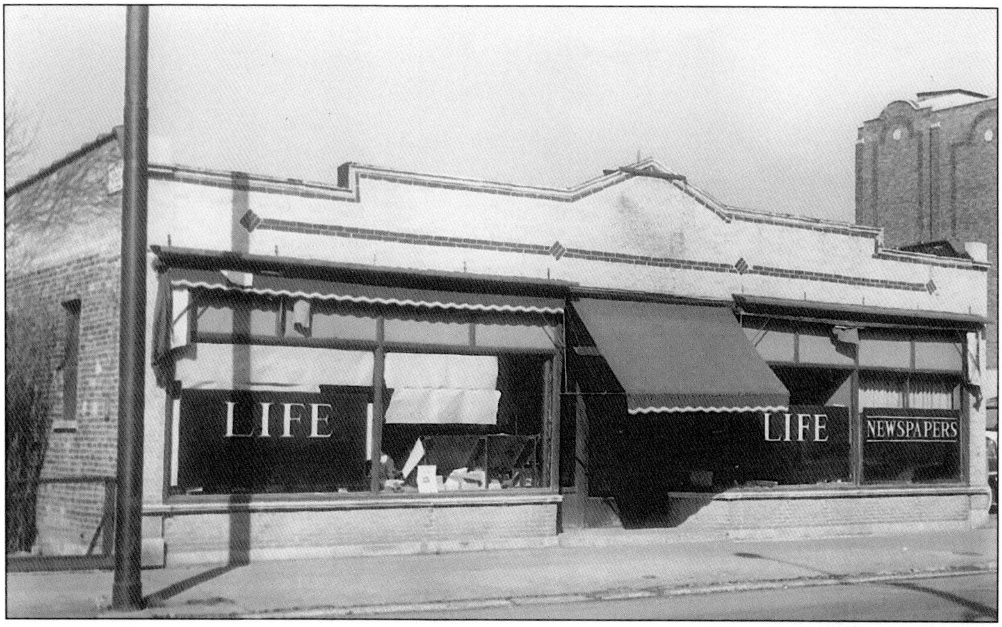

The *Life* Newspaper Offices, 1940s. Billy Cepak started the *Life* Newspaper in a basement on Cermak Road in 1926. In the '40s, the offices were at 5304 W. Twenty-Fifth Street until a fire in 1949 destroyed the presses. It was rebuilt, and in 1961 moved to Harlem Avenue. (Courtesy *Life* Newspaper.)

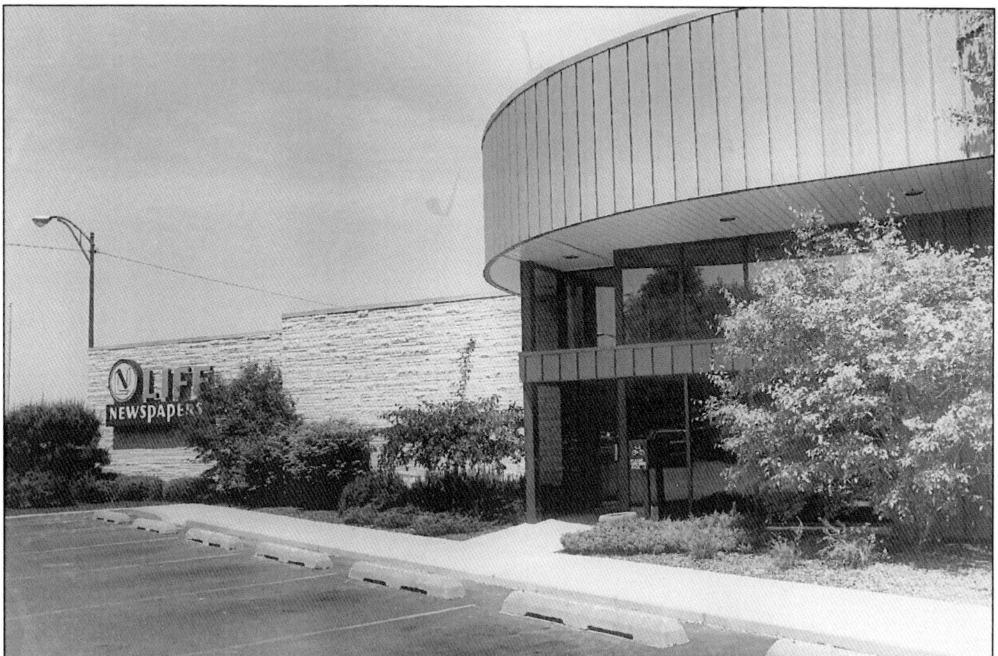

Main Offices on Harlem Avenue. The *Life* Newspaper covered the Cicero, Berwyn, and Stickney areas from its office at 2601 Harlem Avenue in Berwyn from 1961–2000. The offices then consolidated in Hodgkins, leaving a small staff at a location on Grove to handle the local news items. (Courtesy *Life* Newspaper.)

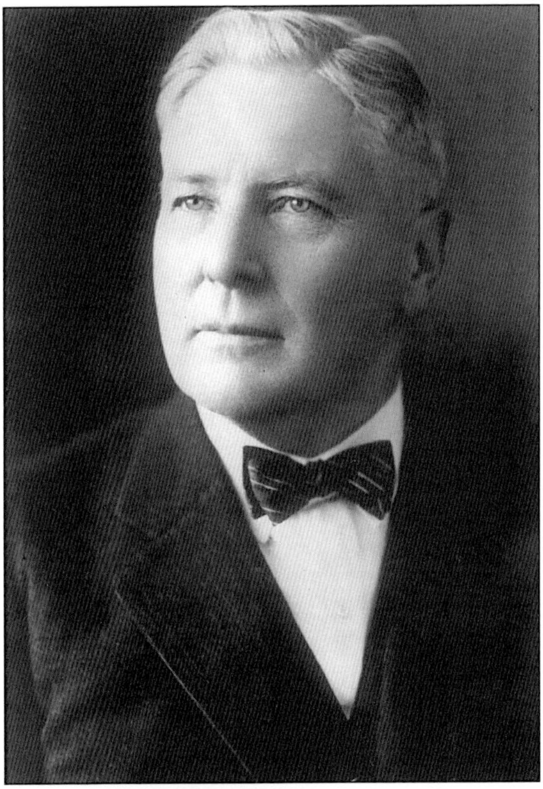

DR. ARTHUR W. MACNEAL, 1868–1932. Dr. Arthur W. MacNeal, M.D., was the first doctor in the Cicero area in the days when doctors made house calls in buggies pulled by horses. In fact, Dr. MacNeal made so many house calls, and rode so many miles, that he needed two horses, one for mornings and one for afternoons! He delivered many babies, at home of course, including Lois Palmer Huth. (Courtesy *Life* Newspaper.)

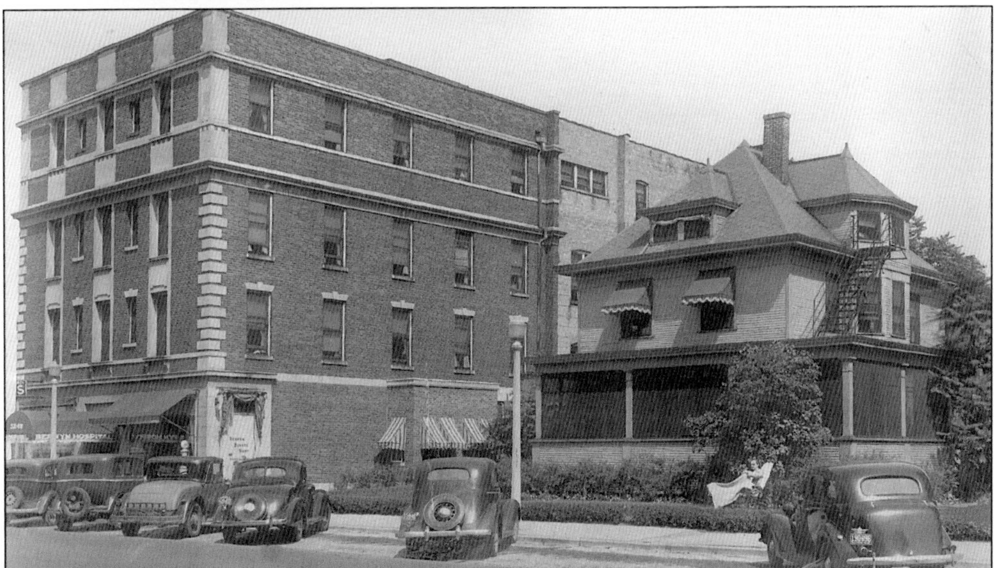

MACNEAL MEMORIAL HOSPITAL'S BEGINNINGS. A graduate of Rush Medical College in Chicago, Dr. MacNeal used his ten-room house on Oak Park Avenue and Thirty-Third as his offices as well as his home. As early as 1902, he had purchased an x-ray machine, and keeping up with the times, he was one of the first to use diphtheria vaccine. In 1925, the brick building next door was opened to patients, and Dr. MacNeal's house became a nurse's residence. (Courtesy *Life* Newspaper.)

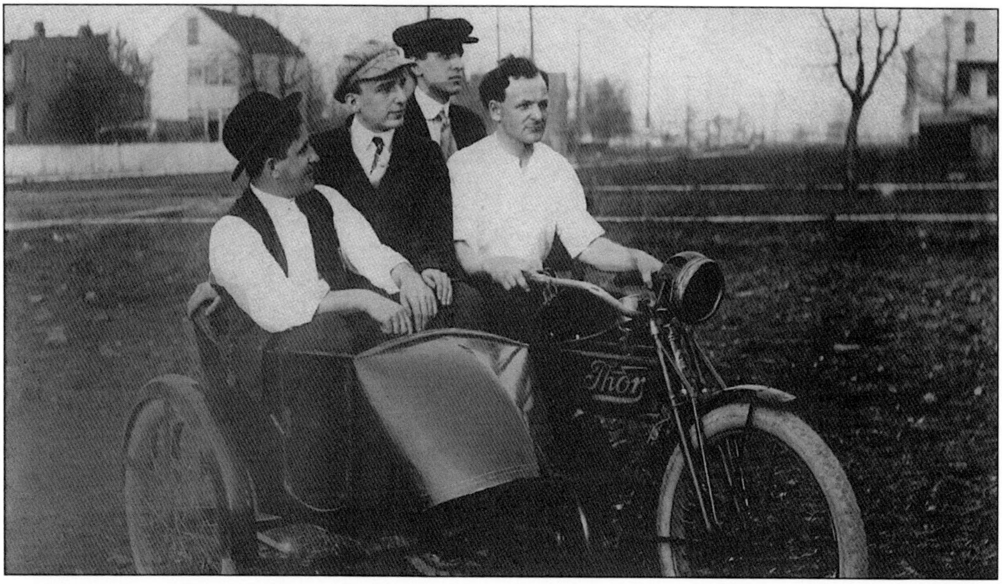

A Motorcycle Ride in 1917. The three Krause brothers, pictured here on this very modern motorcycle, were second-generation Americans whose parents hailed from Pomerania. From left to right are: Walter, Paul, Herman, and their cousin Otto Stroemer. Herman had survived the *Eastland* disaster in 1915, wearing an Uncle Sam costume in preparation for the parade and festivities that were never held in Michigan City on that fateful day. (Courtesy Karl J. Sup.)

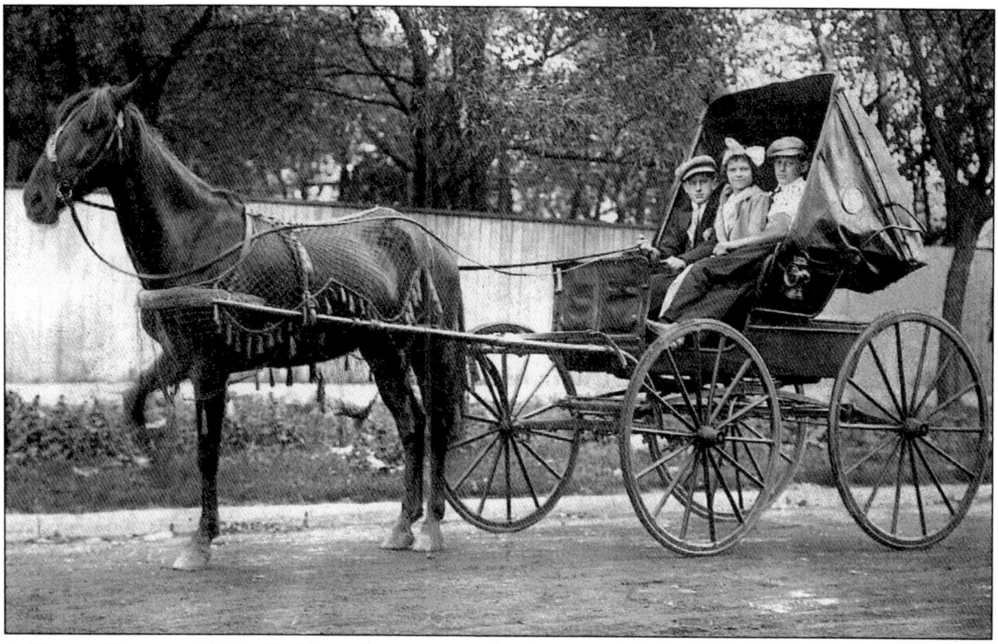

A Buggy Ride in 1912. Holding the reins on this buggy ride is 14-year-old Joseph James Sup Jr. Joseph's father, also Joseph James, emigrated from Bohemia in 1879. Joseph Jr. and his three brothers (Frank, Charlie, and James) ran the Sup Dairy in Cicero. The brothers lived in the Cicero/Berwyn area their whole lives, enjoying fishing in their leisure time. (Courtesy Karl J. Sup.)

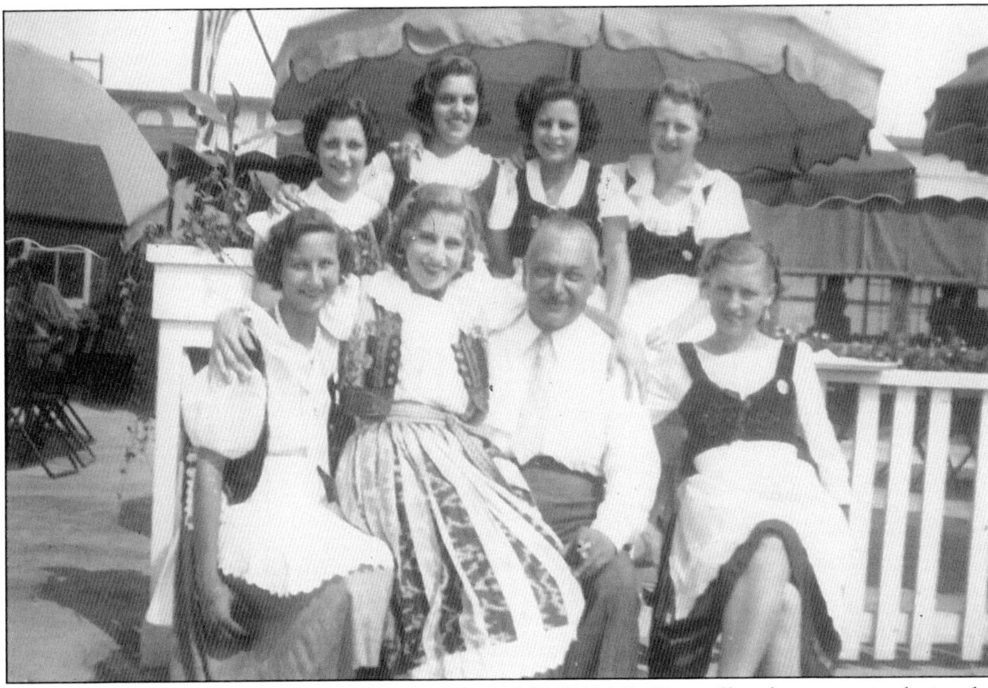

TAKING OUR ETHNICITY ON THE ROAD. The 1933 World's Fair offered many people in the Chicago area the opportunity to proudly display their old-world heritage to visitors. Posing here are several members of Bob Fuka's family, who are taking their Bohemian customs to the fair. They are dressed in native costume and enjoying the days of ethnic singing and eating. In the front row are, from left to right, Lill, Marion, Smeler, and Bessie. (Courtesy Bob Fuka.)

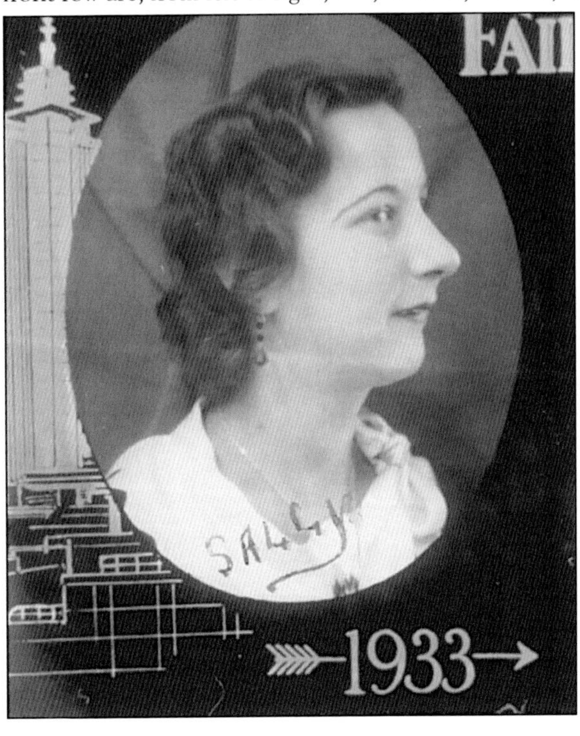

SALLY AT THE WORLD'S FAIR. These special souvenir photos were perhaps intended for giving away to a beaux. Here is Lillian Sally Sisul, who later married Jerry Fuka. (Courtesy Bob Fuka.)

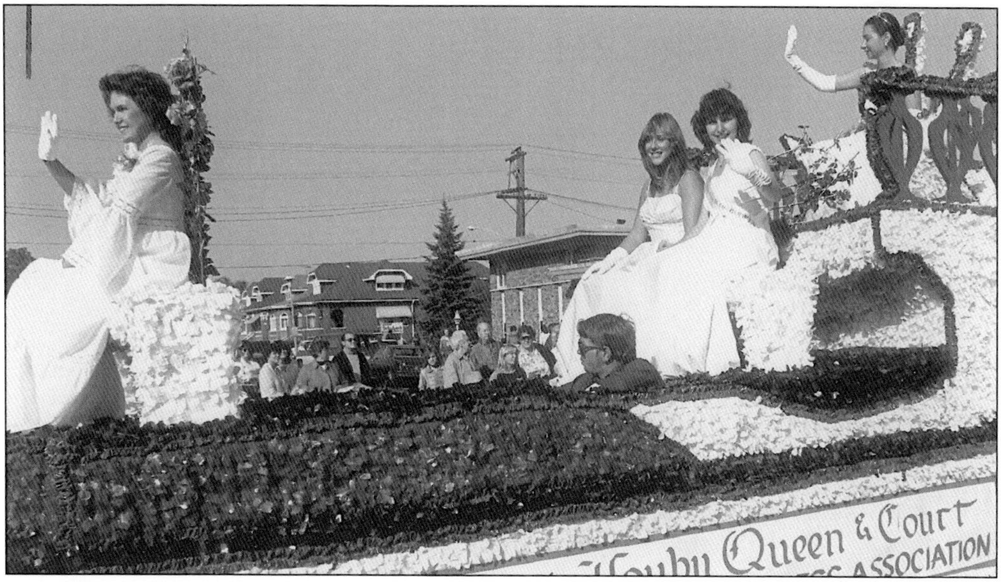

THE HOUBY QUEEN AND COURT, 1981. Unless you are from Cicero, you may not understand the desire to celebrate the houby. You may not even know that the houby is a mushroom, hard to find, and certainly prized. The parade has been a Cicero tradition for years. Recently, there has been interest in also having a Cinco de Mayo parade, in honor of the town's now heavily Hispanic population. (Courtesy *Life* Newspaper.)

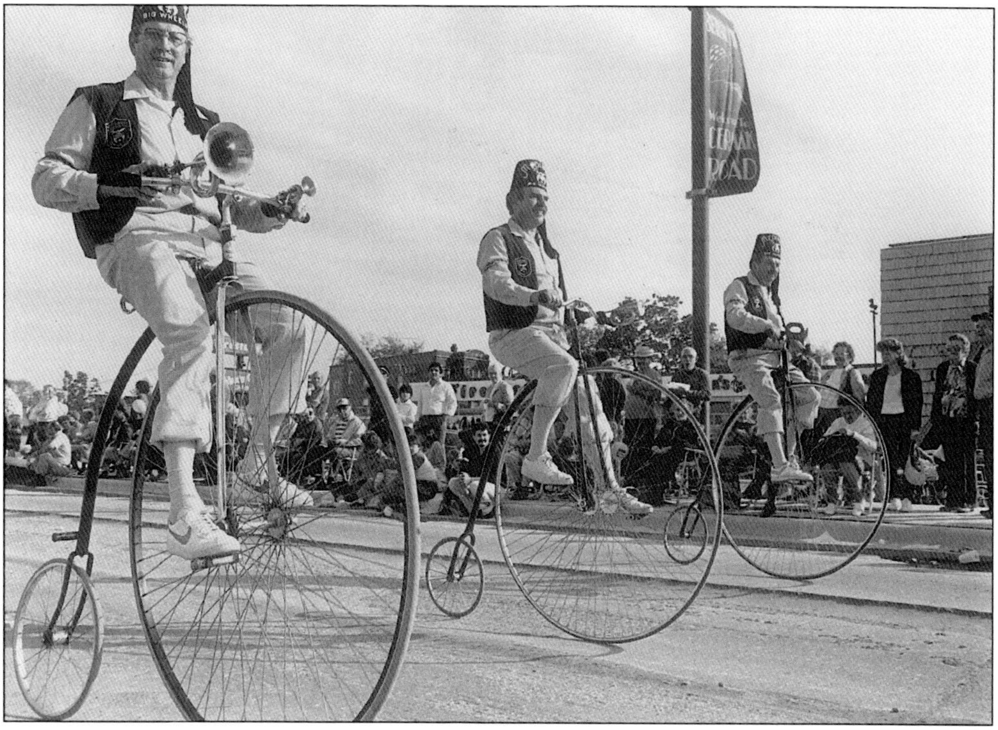

OLD-FASHIONED BICYCLE RIDERS. These old-fashioned bicycles are being ridden by volunteers from the Medinah Temple. Not only are these tricky to ride, they are tricky to mount! (Courtesy *Life* Newspaper.)

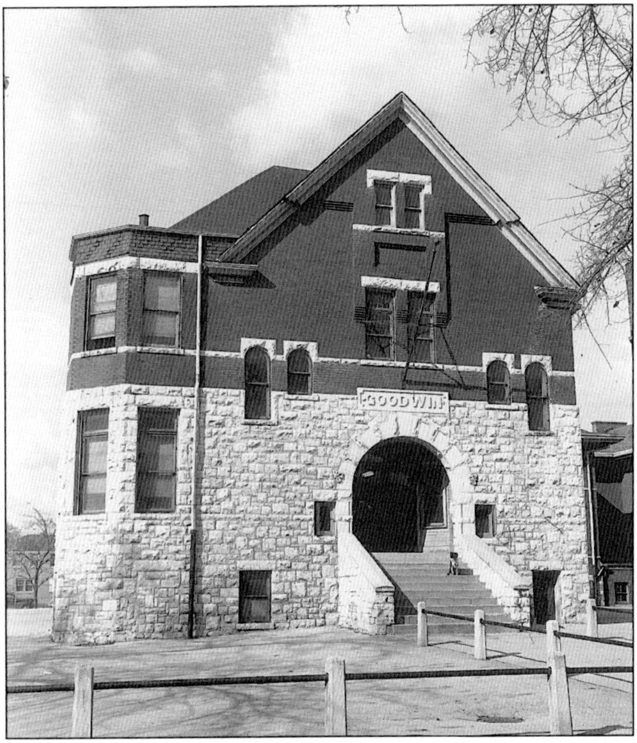

The Old Goodwin School. The little stone school known as Goodwin was built in 1888 at Twenty-Sixth and Austin Boulevard. (Courtesy *Life* Newspaper.)

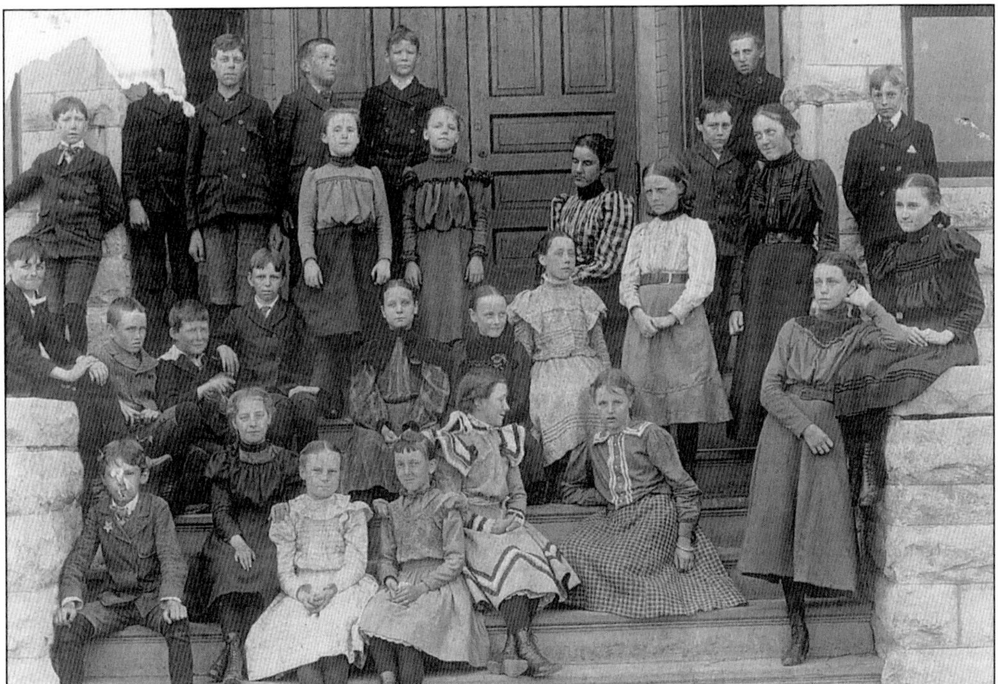

Students at Goodwin, 1896. Students and teachers pose on the steps of the first Goodwin in this vintage photo from 1896. The building had been built in 1888. (Lois Palmer Huth Collection.)

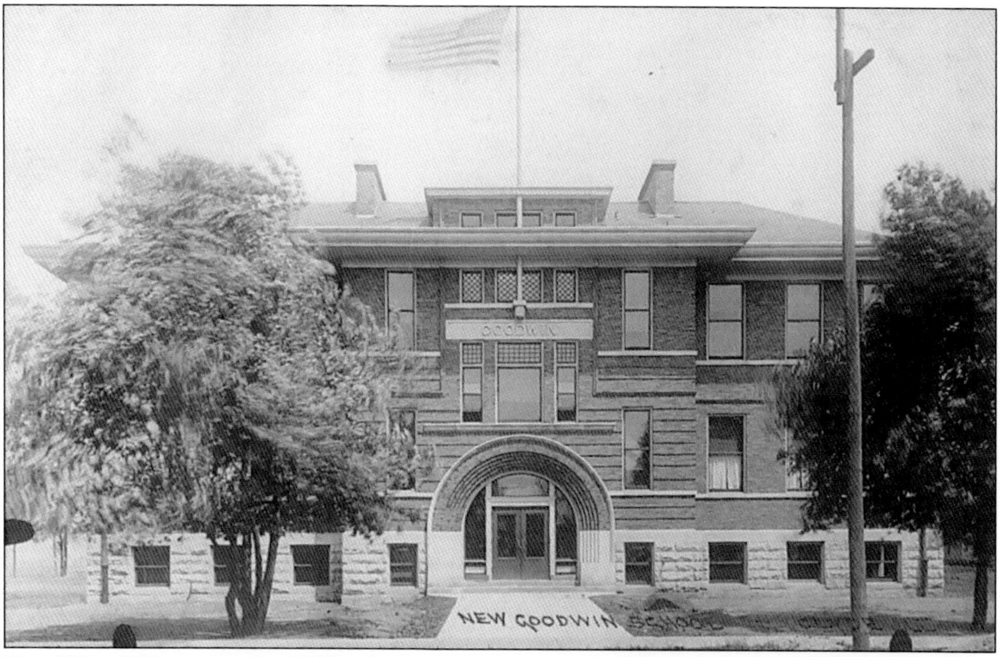

THE "NEW" GOODWIN. In 1898, a larger school was needed and so a new Goodwin was built. (Courtesy *Life* Newspaper.)

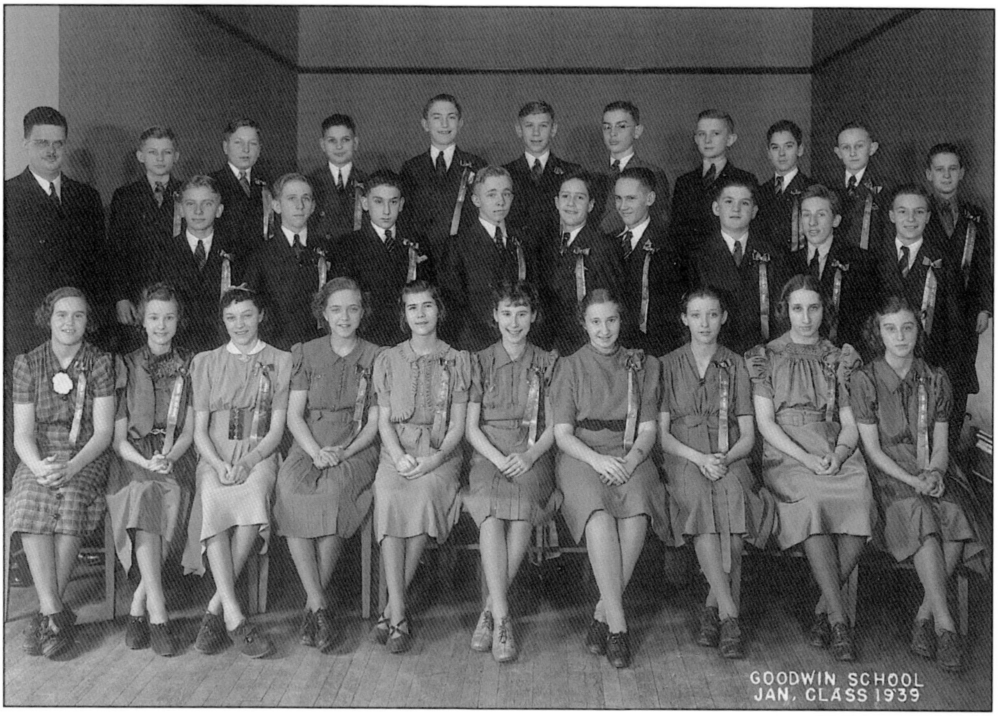

THE GOODWIN SCHOOL CLASS OF '39. The January class of '39 indicates that at this time, students were graduated mid-year. It probably means that students were also accepted as kindergartners mid-year, a practice ended long ago. The students are wearing ribbons with "Goodwin School" in gold letters. (Courtesy *Life* Newspaper.)

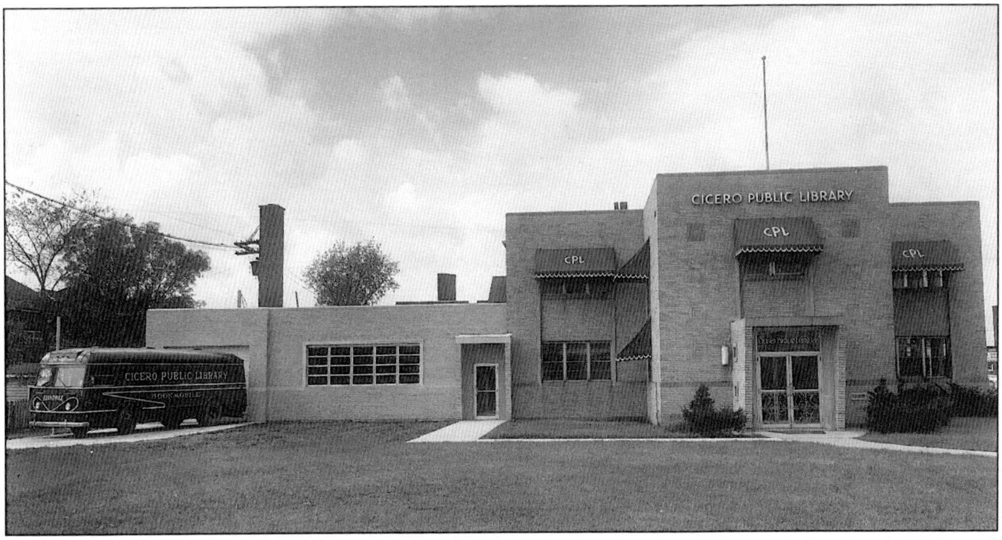

Cicero Public Library. Ideas for a public library were under discussion in March of 1920, and by 1929 the library was well established at 5225 W. Twenty-Second Street, with a circulation room on the first floor and a reference library on the second floor. By then, there were nearly 25,000 volumes and 10,000 borrowers. Here the library shows several additions and the bookmobile. In 2001, the library looks forward to further additions and renovations. (Courtesy Cicero Public Library.)

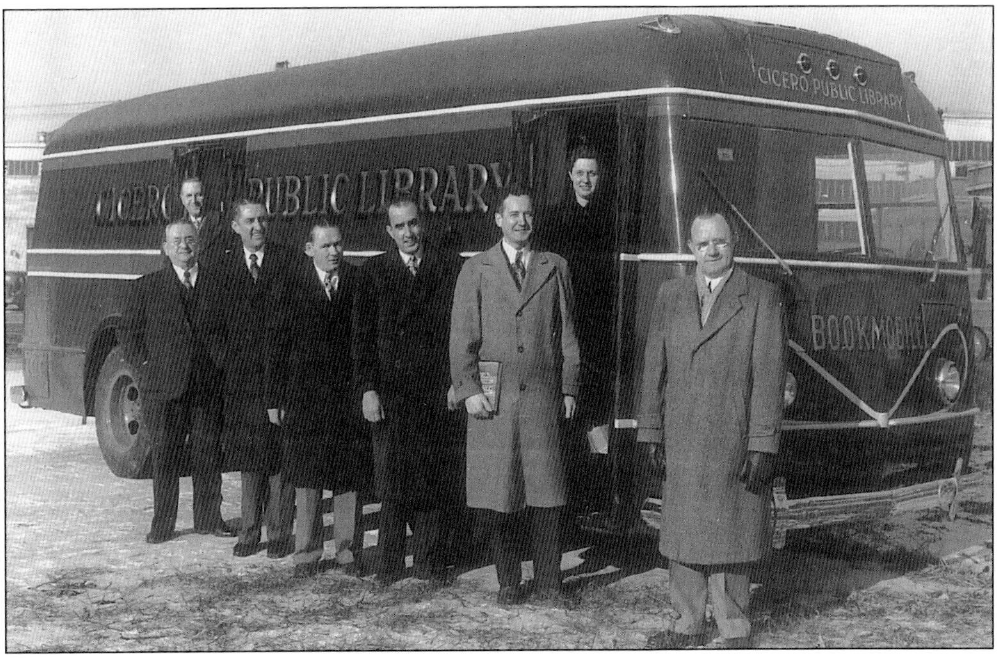

The New Bookmobile, 1960. In 1950, the Cicero Public Library was one of only a few libraries to set up a bookmobile service. An old bus was converted into a mobile library which made stops all around Cicero. During 1960, a new bookmobile was purchased at a cost of $19,650 and held 3,500 books. The new bookmobile was photographed on this cold, winter day, flanked by proud library directors. Note the librarian in the doorway. (Courtesy Cicero Public Library.)

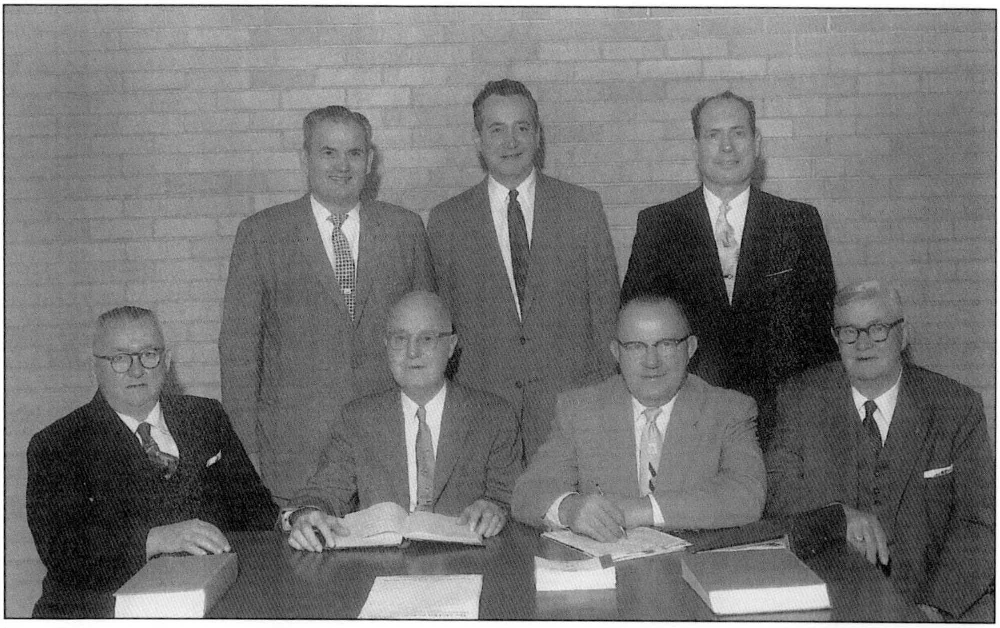

The Library Board of Directors, 1955. Pictured are the directors of the library in 1955. They are, from left to right: (seated) John Svoboda, William Bruner, Anton Dvorak, and Charles Cada; (back row) Matthew Witczak, George Mate, and Frank Mungai. (Courtesy Cicero Public Library.)

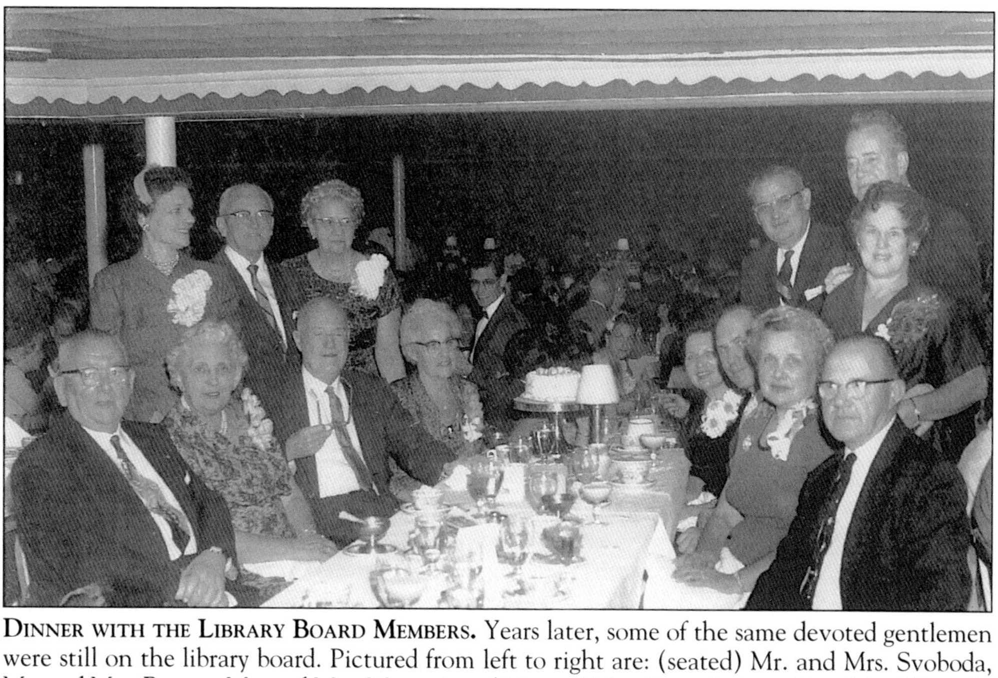

Dinner with the Library Board Members. Years later, some of the same devoted gentlemen were still on the library board. Pictured from left to right are: (seated) Mr. and Mrs. Svoboda, Mr. and Mrs. Bruner, Mr. and Mrs. Mungai, and Mr. and Mrs. Dvorak; (standing) Mrs. Witczak, Mr. And Mrs. Pertl, Mr. Witczak, and Mr. and Mrs. Mate.

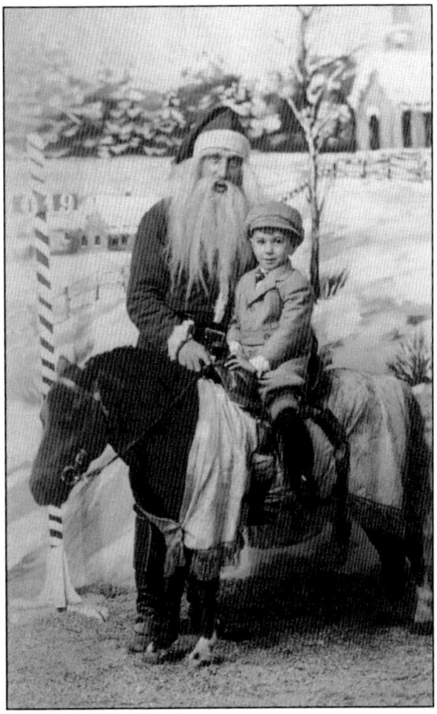

MEETING SANTA, CIRCA 1928. Pictured with Santa, about 1928, is Joseph James Sup III. His father, Joseph James Sup Jr., ran the Sup Dairy (as seen on the cover) with his brothers Frank, Charlie, and James. However, when this little boy grew up, he worked at Motorola, transferring to Phoenix in 1972. (Courtesy Karl J. Sup.)

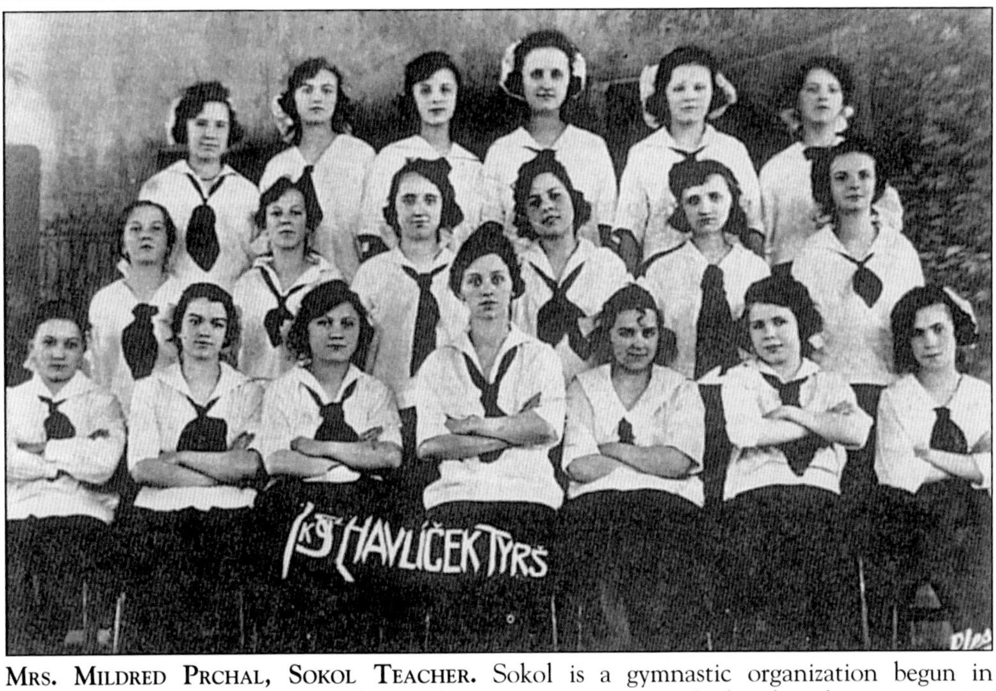

MRS. MILDRED PRCHAL, SOKOL TEACHER. Sokol is a gymnastic organization begun in Czechoslovakia in 1862, dedicated not only to maintaining strong bodies, but also to preserving the Czech language and culture. The word Sokol means "falcon," and Mildred Prochaska Prchal was one of those majestic soaring birds in the Cicero area for many years. Mildred became one of the first women teachers in the organization, and she wrote the book *Artistic Gymnastics, Floor Exercises for Women* in 1964.

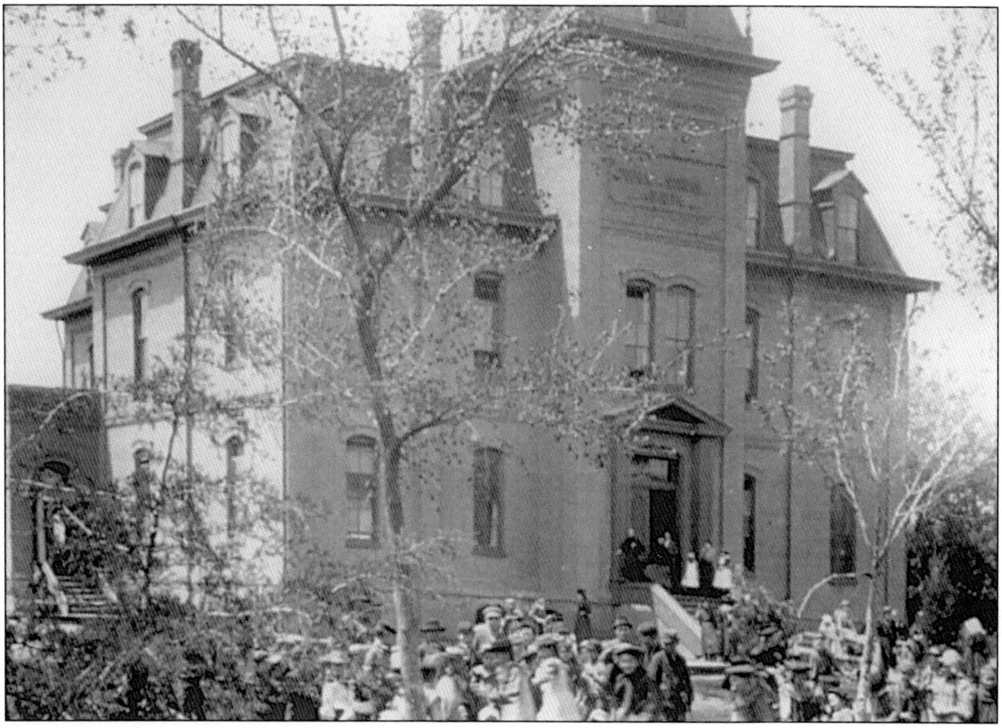

An Early School in Cicero. One of the earliest elementary schools in the area was the Hawthorne School, built on Thirty-First Street in 1894 for the children of the employees of the Dolese-Shephard Quarry, at Cicero Avenue. Drexel School (1893) was another early school, named after Mrs. Anthony Drexel, for whom the Drexel area was also named. The above photo is probably one of those two early buildings. (Courtesy Morton Archives.)

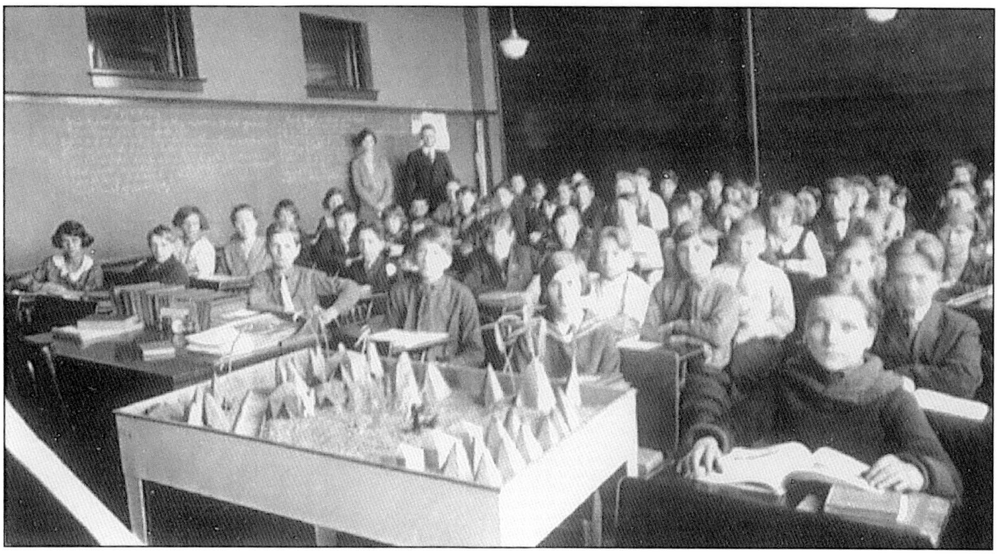

An Early Classroom. Even in the earliest days of education in Cicero, wise teachers knew how to make the textbooks come alive. Here, the children have built a diorama based on their knowledge of the Plains Indians, not so unlike the dioramas and visuals still enlivening classrooms today. (Courtesy Morton Archives.)

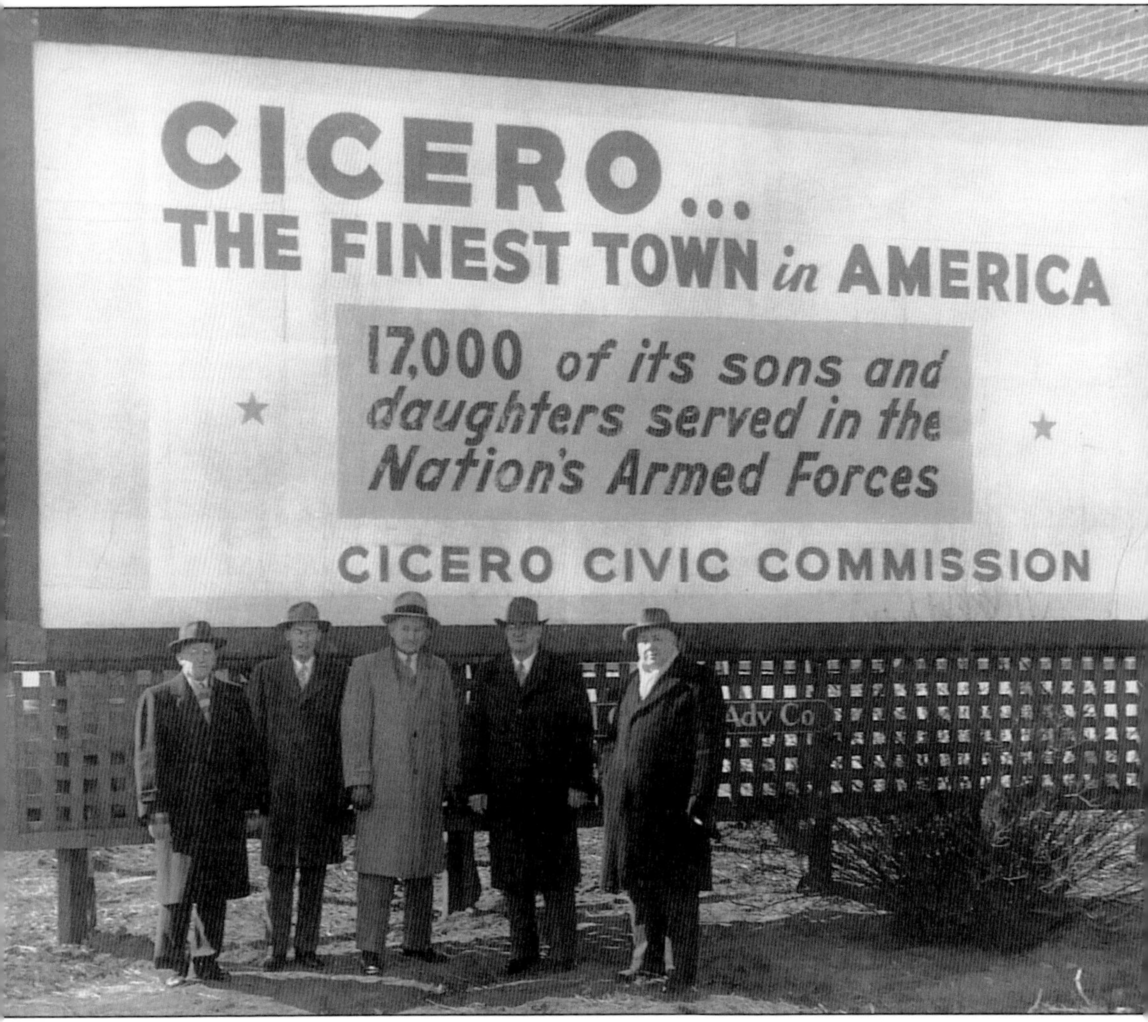

CICERO, THE FINEST TOWN IN AMERICA. The end of WWII saw a burst of civic pride. Proudly hailing the 17,000 sons and daughters who served in the armed forces are some members of the Cicero Civic Commission, standing in front of a huge billboard. (Courtesy Cicero Public Library.)

Eight

Racial Intolerance

By moving into an apartment at 6139 W. Nineteenth Street in 1951, the Harvey Clark family broke the unwritten rule that blacks were welcome in Cicero during the day, but had to be out of town by nightfall. Harvey Clark Jr. was a college graduate and a WWII veteran. He moved his wife and two children into the apartment building owned by Camille de Rose on July 10, 1951. Cicero would prefer to forget the next few days of mean-spirited bigotry, but the world remembers. The family's belongings were thrown onto the lawn outside their windows, and set afire. It is said that a piano was one of the destroyed possessions. Police were at the mercy of a crowd fueled by heat and drink. By the time the National Guard was called in to quell the riot, there wasn't much to save. The family moved elsewhere. No one was ever punished.

Such is the history of Cicero, a town so fearful that it chose violence over kindness. Years passed, and even Martin Luther King Jr.'s march down Cicero Avenue in 1966 didn't change things much. Agreements for fair and open housing didn't seem to make much difference. But time does. Slowly, very slowly, too slowly for most people, Cicero is changing. A small percentage of blacks are living here now, and a black police officer has been hired. The population is now overwhelmingly Hispanic, with a growing Muslim population. And Cicero has not been destroyed. In fact, the changing population has revived the aging town in many healthy ways.

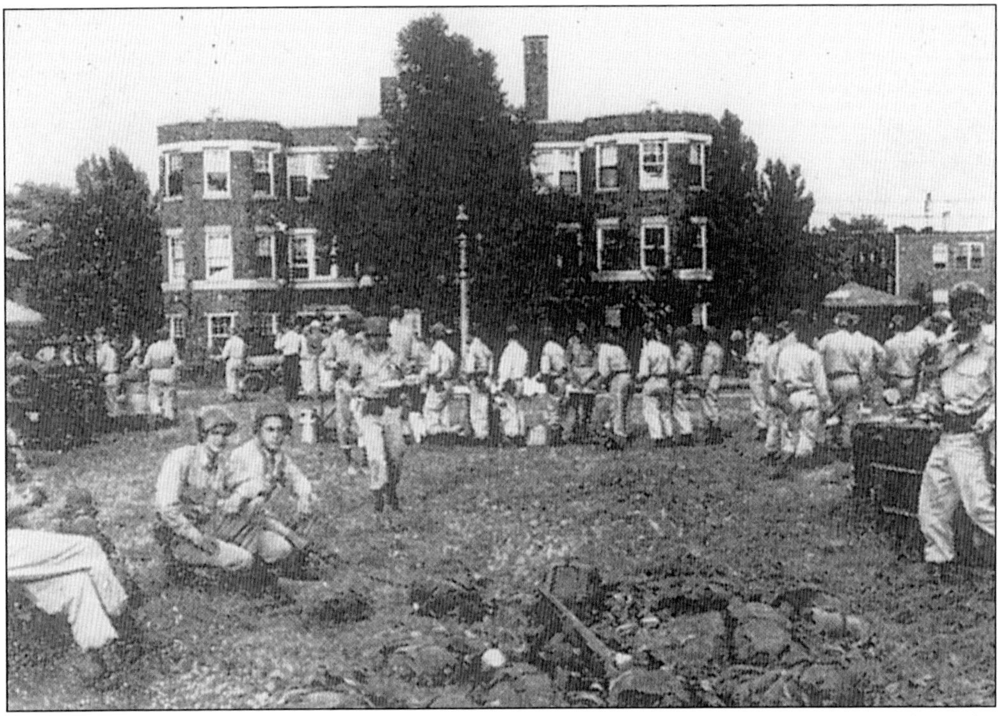

THE APARTMENTS AT 6139 W. NINETEENTH STREET. The National Guard camped on the vacant lot across from the apartment building where the Harvey Clark Jr. family attempted to live. They arrived when the incident was almost over.

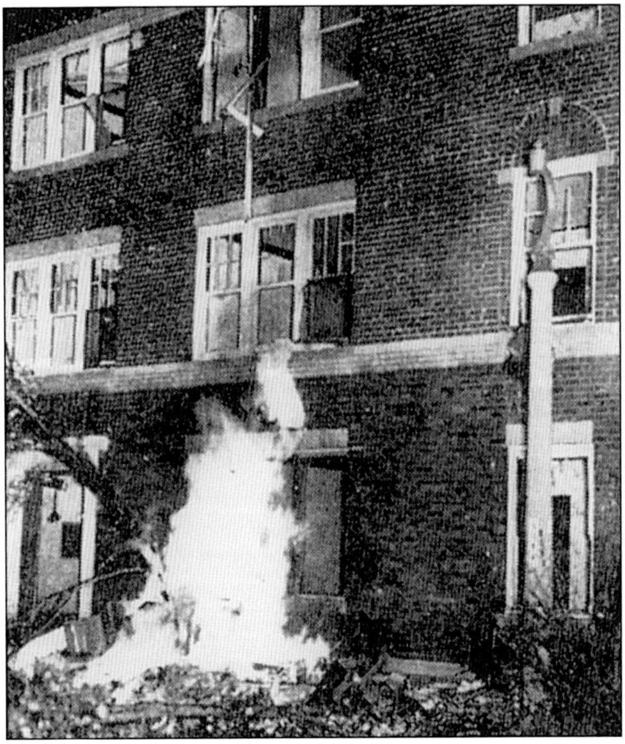

TORCHING THE FAMILY'S POSSESSIONS, 1951. Vandals threw the Clark family's possessions out the window and set them on fire. The family moved away unharmed—physically, at least.

Nine

Then and Now

The Cicero we know now was once fields and farmland, beckoning immigrants to come and prosper. Lois Palmer Huth's grandparents came to be beekeepers, because of all the fields of clover in the area. The Andrew Anderson family came in the 1890s to grow the hay needed by the Chicago breweries to maintain the horses that pulled the wagons of beverages to saloons in Chicago and the outlying area. The Jerry Knipp family came from Holland to a dairy farm in the area where Western Electric later stood.

The first non-farming employer was the Dolese-Shepard Stone Quarry, located where the Bel-Air Drive-In now stands. Then came the era of big factories and immigrants willing to work day in and day out to build new lives outside the confines of old world ghettos. With their traditional foods and clothing styles, they built cozy homes for themselves and the generations to follow. Then they built churches where they could worship in their own languages.

Now, the next millennium has dawned with its changes and challenges. New businesses are slowly replacing the outdated factories with new technology and varied job opportunities. A new population has brought their own food preferences and their own languages to Cicero. This current population is thankful for well-built houses that they can afford. They are thankful for schools, dedicated to teaching their children how to be successful in this new world. And they are thankful for churches that share the Good News in their own languages. If it sounds as if history is repeating itself, it just may be.

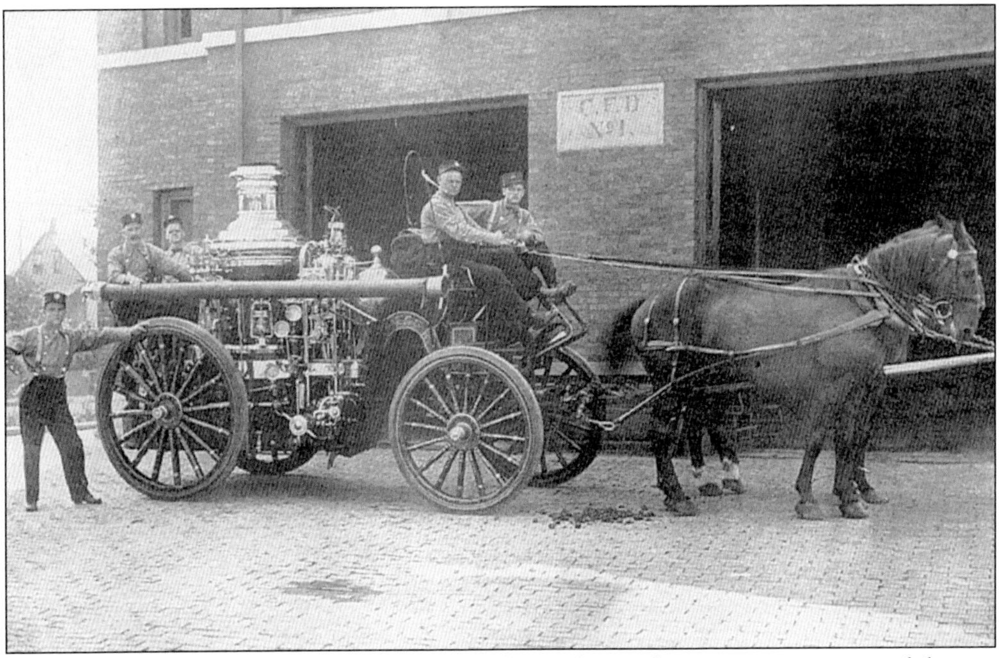

FIRE STATION NO. 1, THEN. In 1913, this horse-drawn fire engine was state-of-the-art. Previously, the volunteer firemen were equipped with a hose cart that the men *pulled* to a blaze. The first motorized equipment was introduced in 1915.

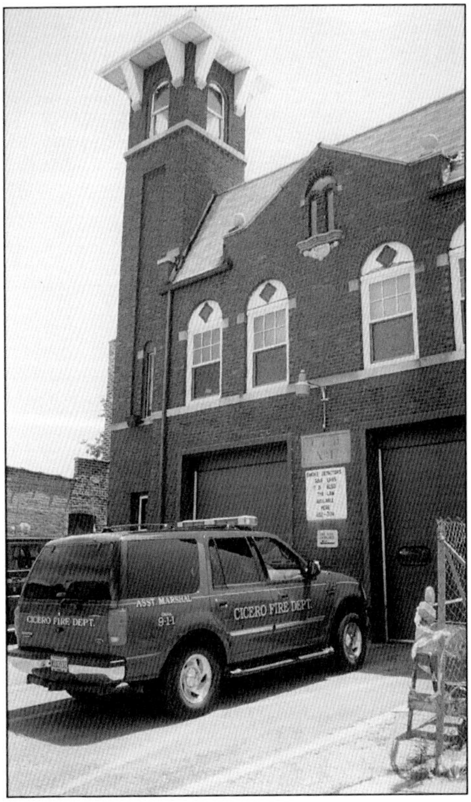

FIRE STATION NO. 1, NOW. Today the fire station is still in the same building on Twenty-Fifth Street. A shiny red assistant marshall's vehicle can be seen ready for action in the driveway.

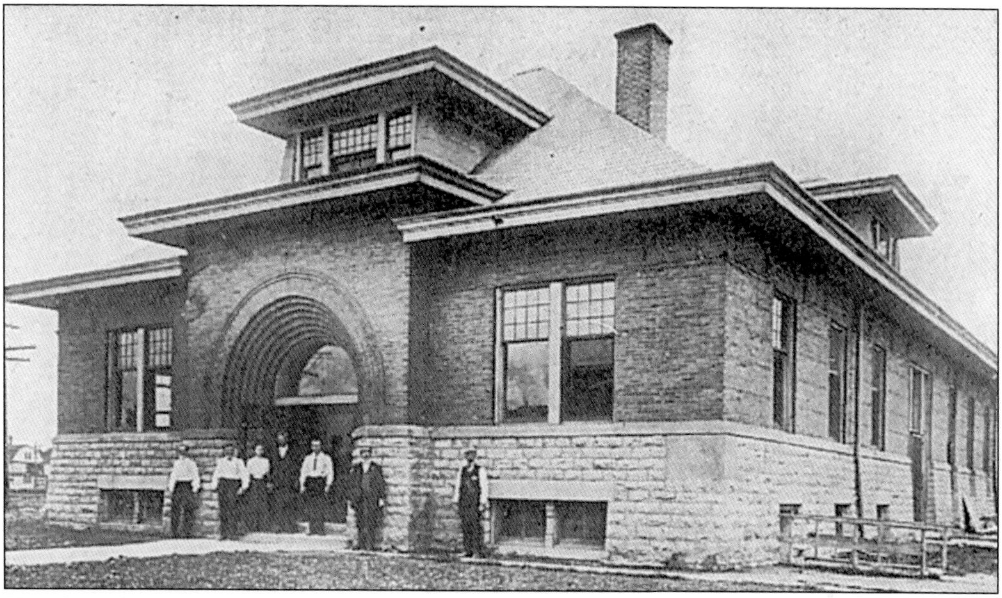

The Old City Hall. The Cicero Town Hall, pictured here in the 1929 *City Directory*, would have been the site of the altercation between Al Capone and Mayor Joseph Z. Klenha, which lead to the cooperation between the two.

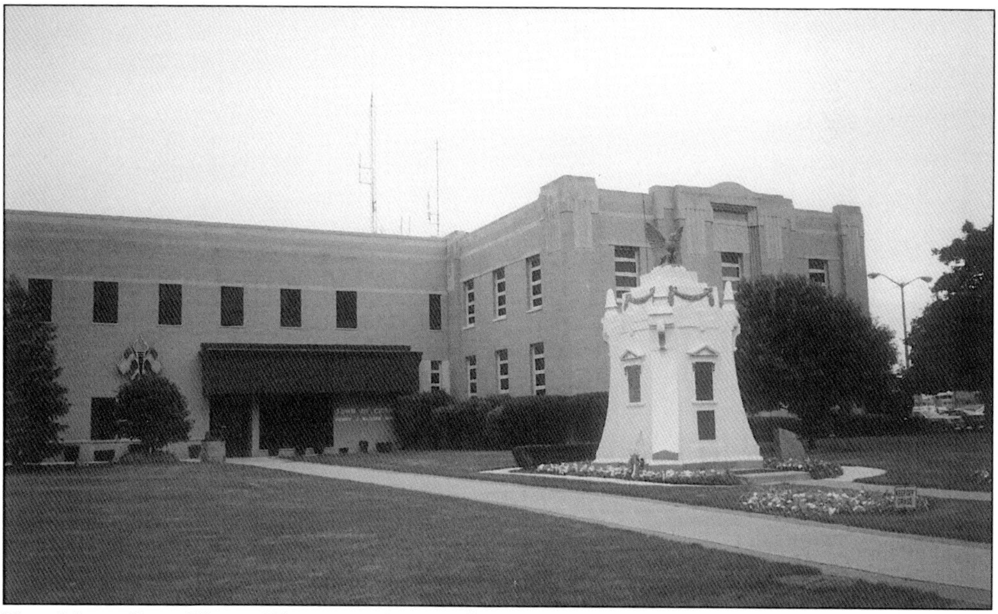

The New City Hall. The new City Hall is at Twenty-Fifth and Laramie Avenue. The monument by James E. Melich to the "boys who dedicated their lives to the cause of democracy in the World War" (WWI) was originally erected at Austin and Ogden Avenue.

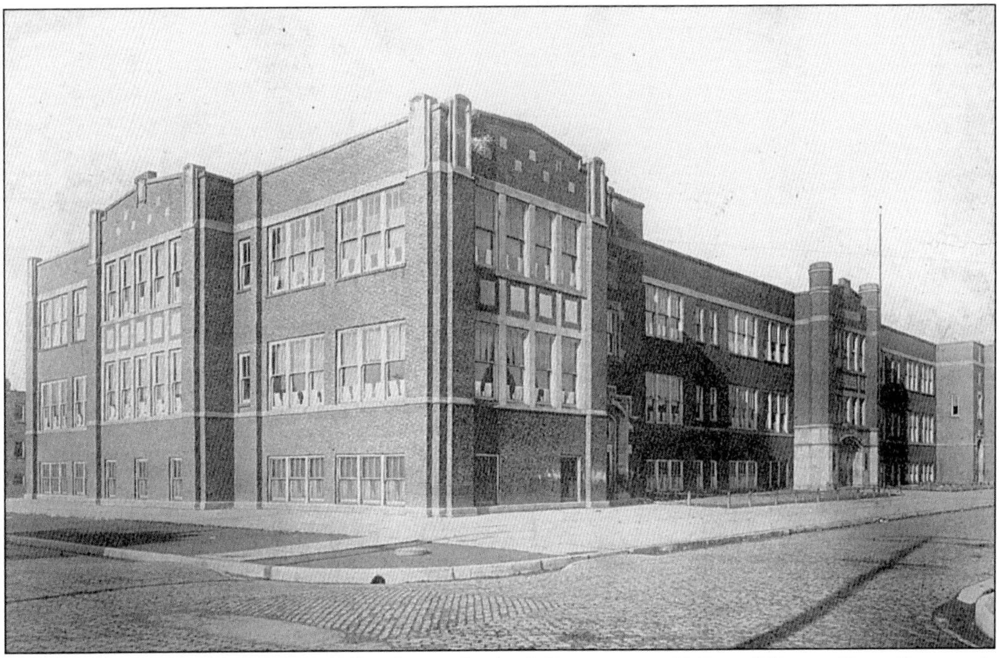

CICERO SCHOOL, THEN. Cicero School, as it looked then, is not all that different from the way it looks today! The old school was built in 1913, had an addition of 12 rooms in 1916, and served the needs of the neighborhood's increasing population at the time of Western Electric's growth. The old building still serves the community at Forty-Ninth and Twenty-Fourth Streets.

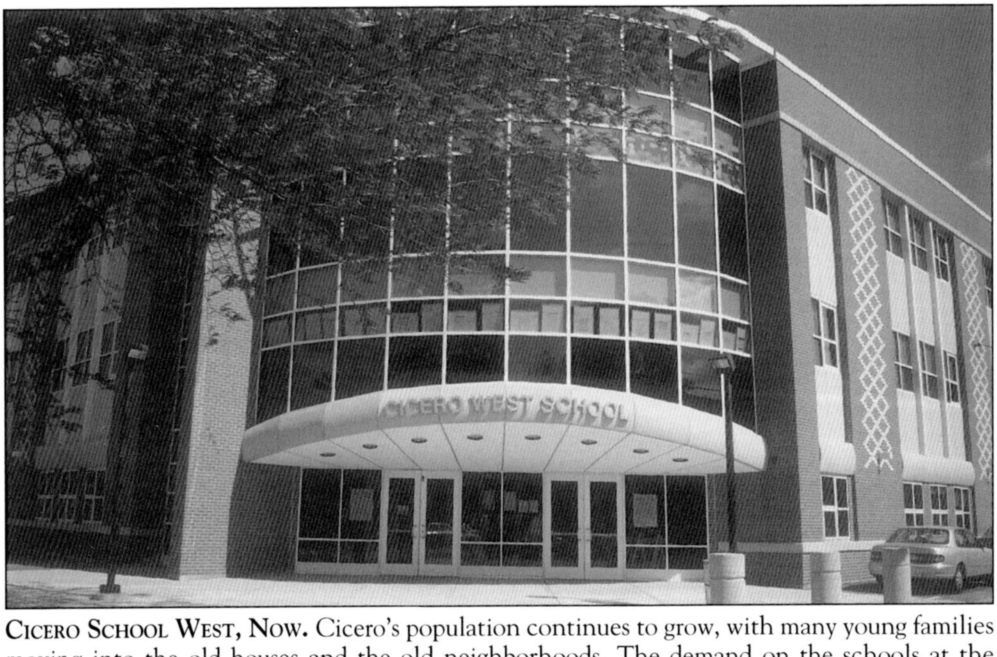

CICERO SCHOOL WEST, NOW. Cicero's population continues to grow, with many young families moving into the old houses and the old neighborhoods. The demand on the schools at the present time is great, and calls for many new classrooms and many new buildings. The handsome Cicero School West occupies the black-topped area that once was a playground.

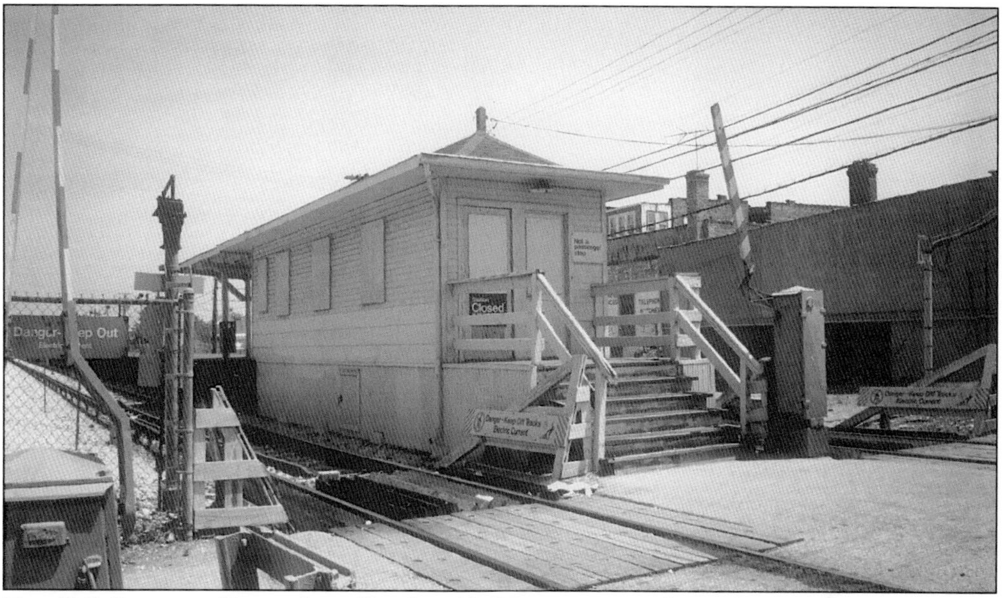

The "L" Station, Then. Actually, the old "L" station is still standing at the Laramie stop, but it is boarded up and no longer used. It looks very small to the eyes that remember it as being very big.

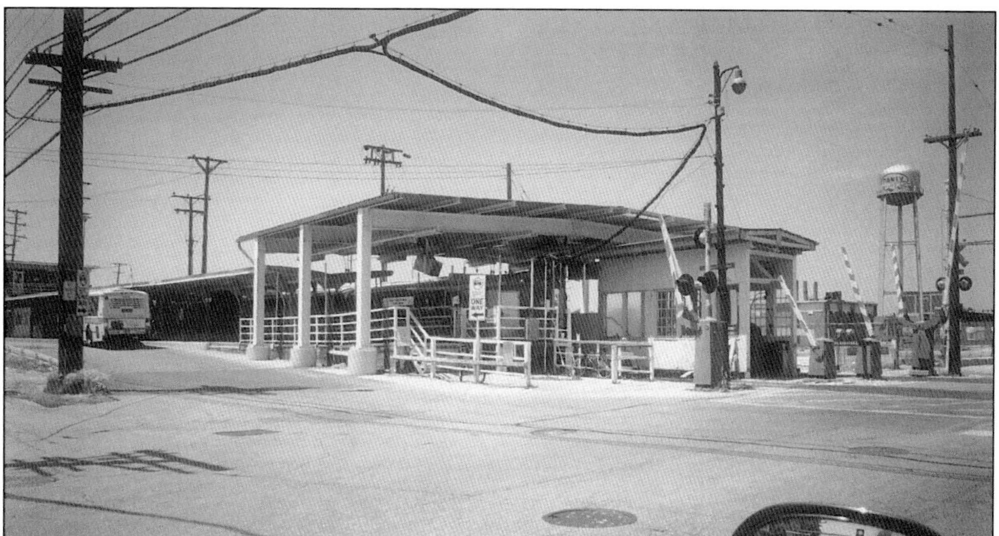

The "L" Station, Now. The "L" ends now at the Fifty-Fourth Street stop. At one time, the "L" ran all the way out to Oak Park Avenue. The old tracks have been paved over and the area now affords ample parking behind the businesses on the north side of Cermak, west of Fifty-Fourth.

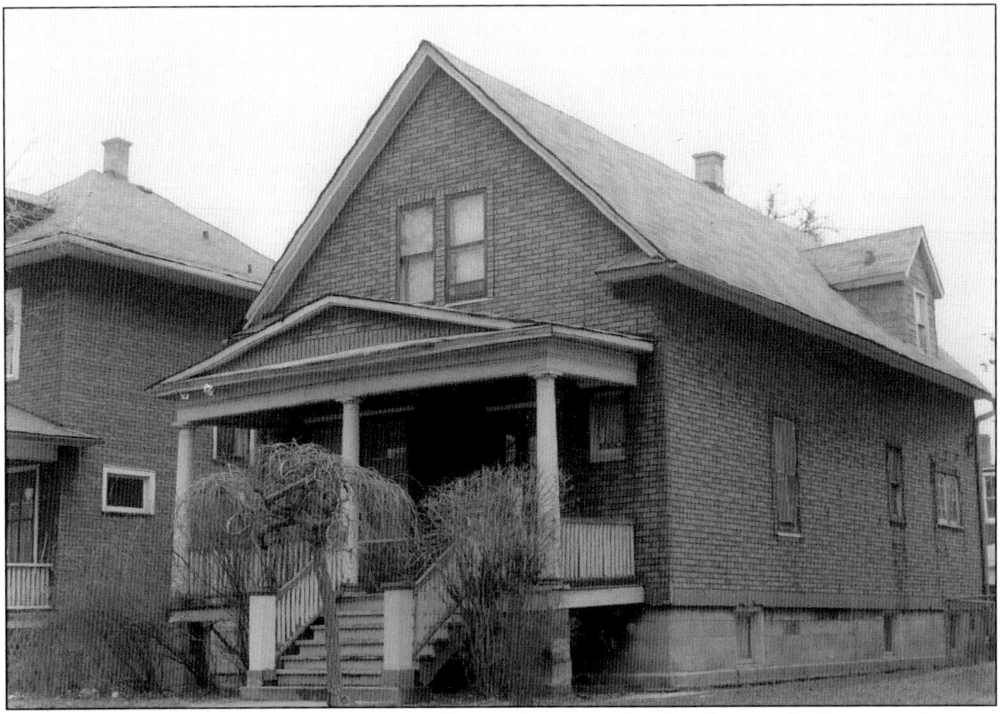

THE HOUSE ON TWENTY-SECOND PLACE, THEN. Imitation brick siding and a large porch were stylish in days past. A friendly family cared for the home, planted bridal wreath in the yard, and slept securely in bedrooms upstairs.

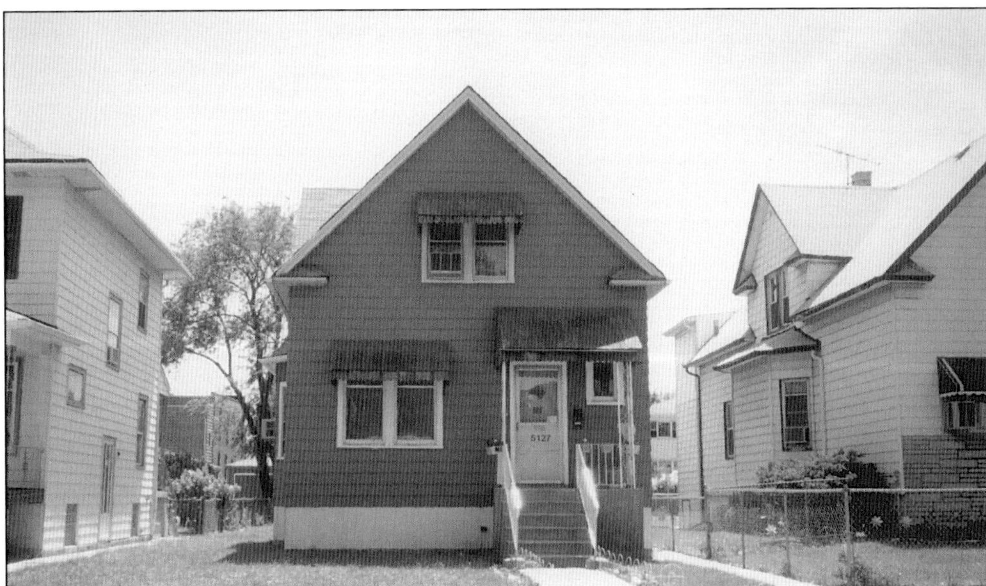

THE HOUSE ON TWENTY-SECOND PLACE, NOW. Today, red aluminum siding and a cement stoop are the style. Another friendly family now cares for the yard with flowers up the walk, and different children sleep securely in bedrooms once filled with other children, now long grown up.

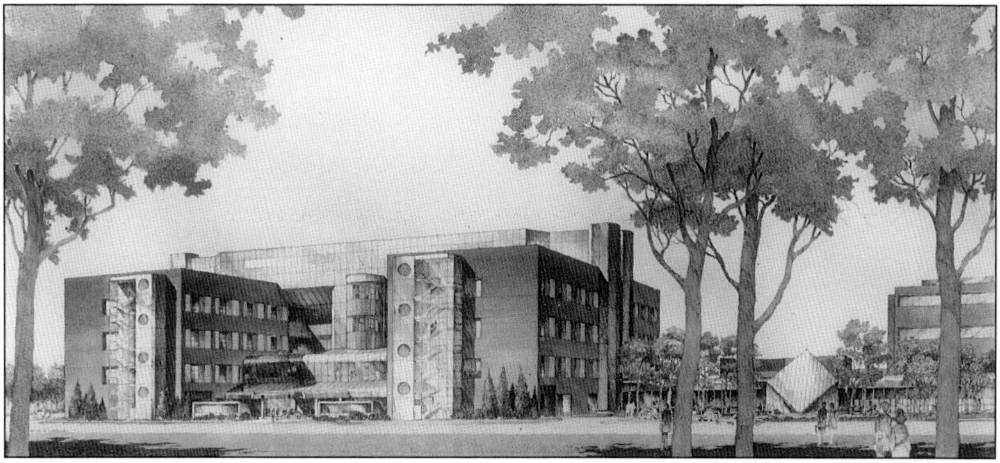

MacNeal Health Care, Then. When the "new" MacNeal Hospital was built, health care was still provided by family physicians in convenient corner offices. There were even times when house calls were made. The hospital served the needs of the Cicero and west suburban areas.

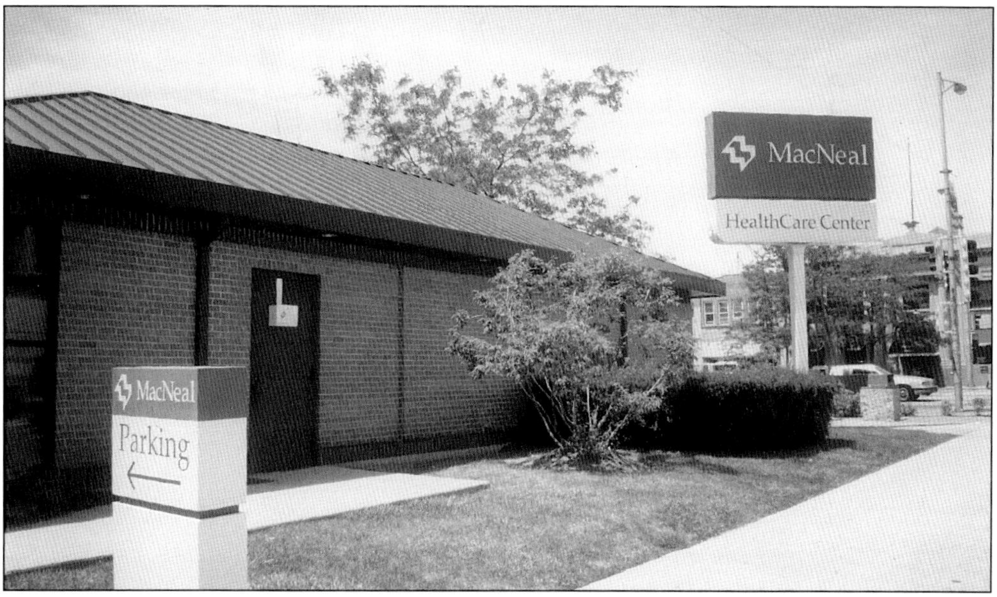

MacNeal Health Care, Now. Healthcare in the year 2000 has seen the decline of corner doctor's offices, and the advent of hospital-owned satellite offices. MacNeal has more than one such office on Cermak Road, offering convenient healthcare to a well-populated area.

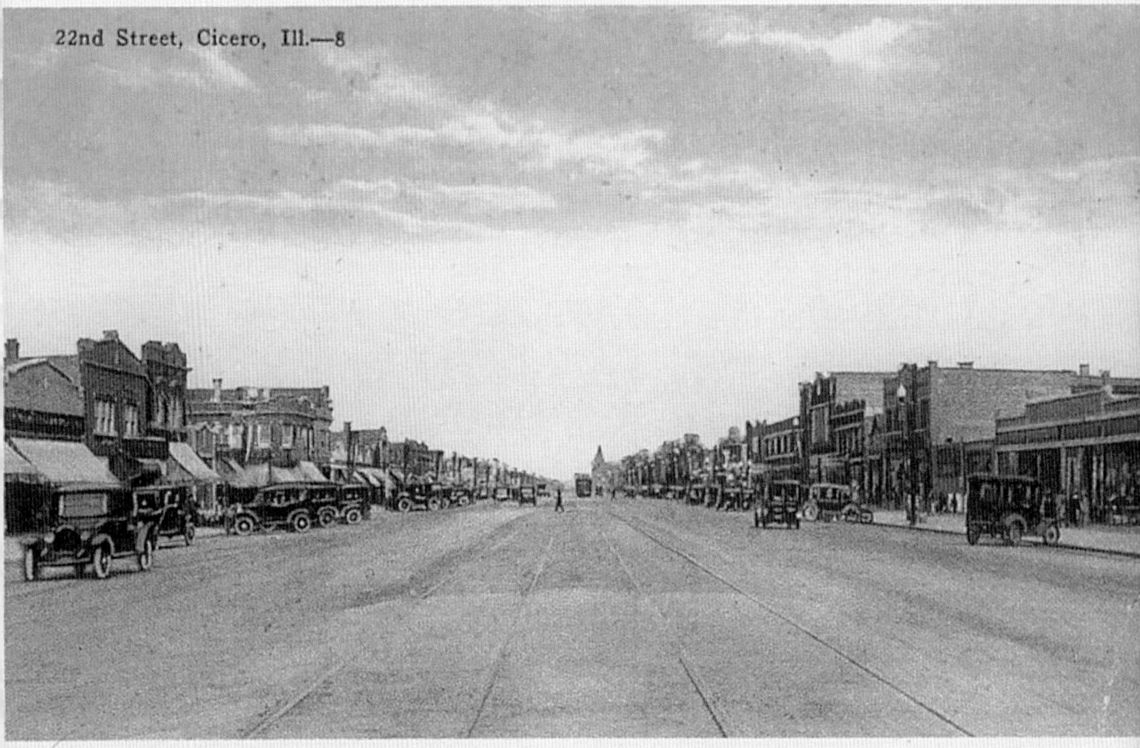

CERMAK ROAD, THEN. This postcard from the 1920s shows the view down Twenty-Second Street from about Austin Boulevard all the way to the Western Electric tower at Cicero Avenue. Streetcar lines march down the center of the street.

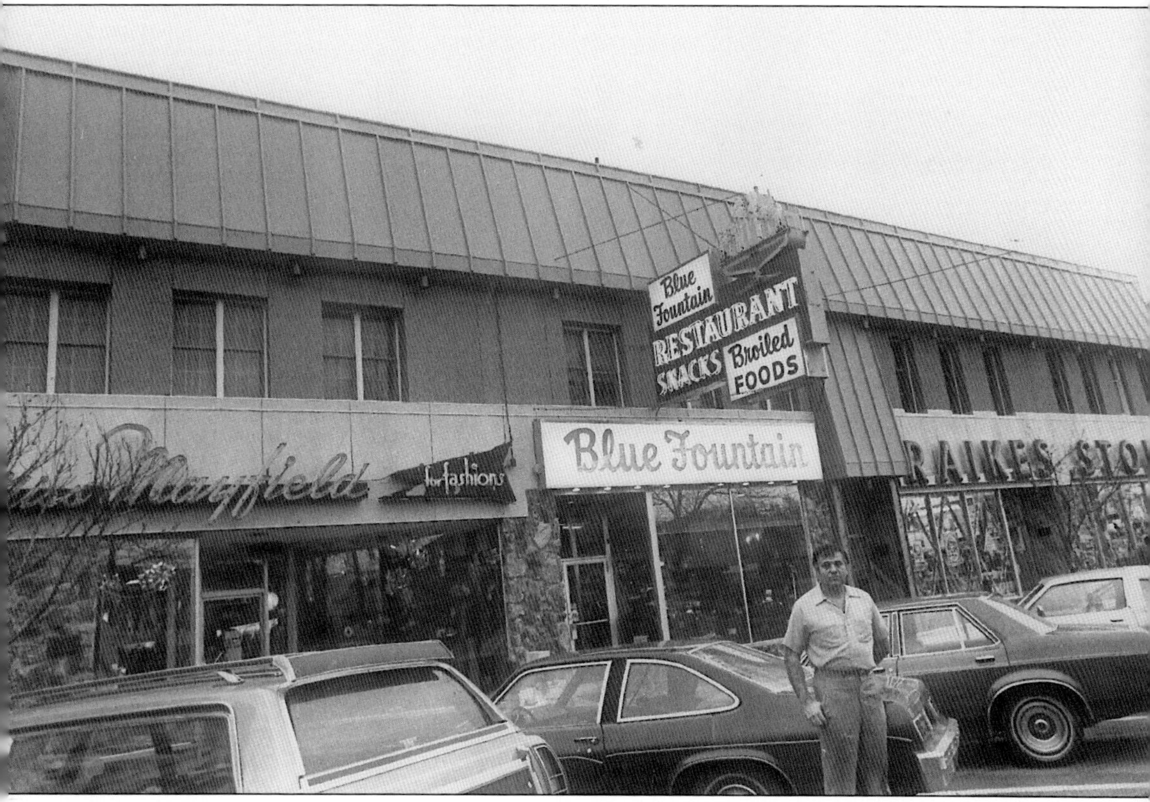

Cermak Road, Now. Today many old buildings have a new facade, and Twenty-Second Street is busier than ever. Diagonal parking has been improved with the widening of the street, and extra parking is available north of Cermak Road where the "L" used to run. (Courtesy *Life* Newspaper.)

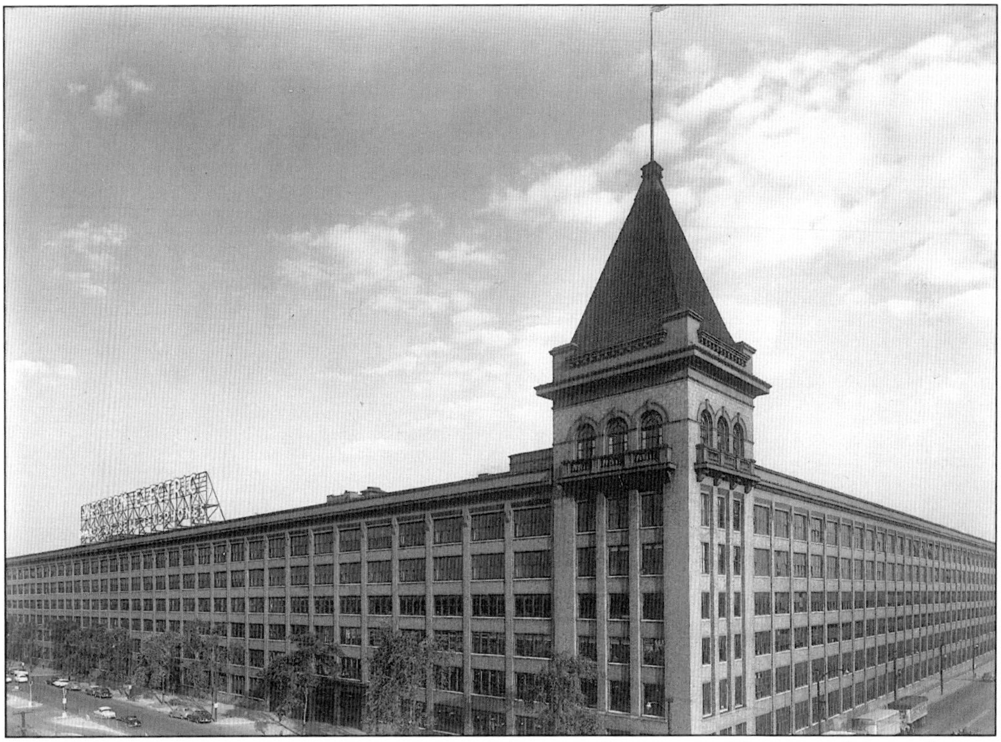

The Corner of Cermak and Cicero, Then. Of course, the corner of Cicero and Cermak once was filled with the proud tower of Western Electric, and beyond the tower were the mighty Hawthorne Works. (Courtesy Harris Erickson Family.)

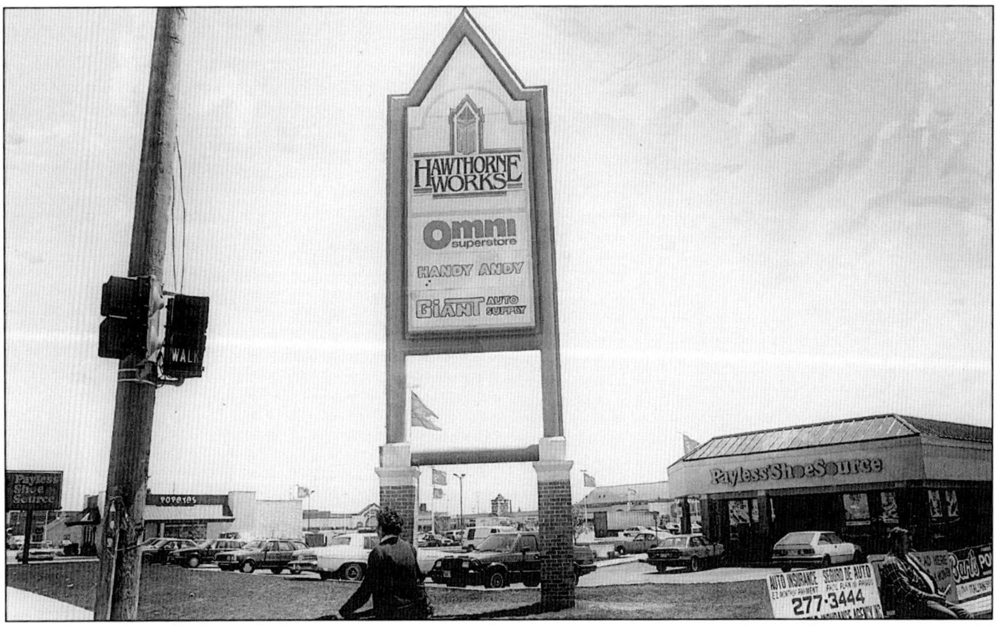

The Corner of Cicero and Cermak, Now. Today, the corner is a busy shopping area still remembering the past in its name, The Hawthorne Center, and in the remaining tower and garages. (Courtesy *Life* Newspaper.)

THE MORTON LIBRARY, THEN. The old library at Morton, across from the Chodl Auditorium on the second floor, is now the Western Electric Museum. The high ceiling with its many arches was quite a magnificent sight in its day. The people of Cicero built the school, the auditorium, and the library for beauty as well as functionality. (Courtesy Morton Archives.)

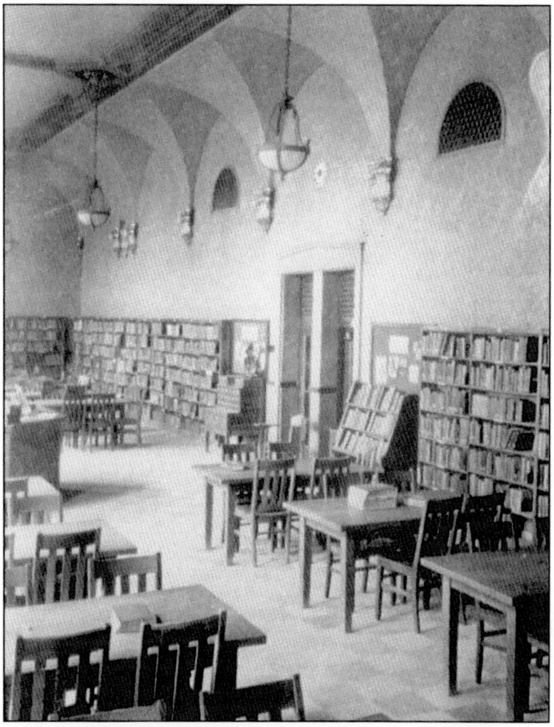

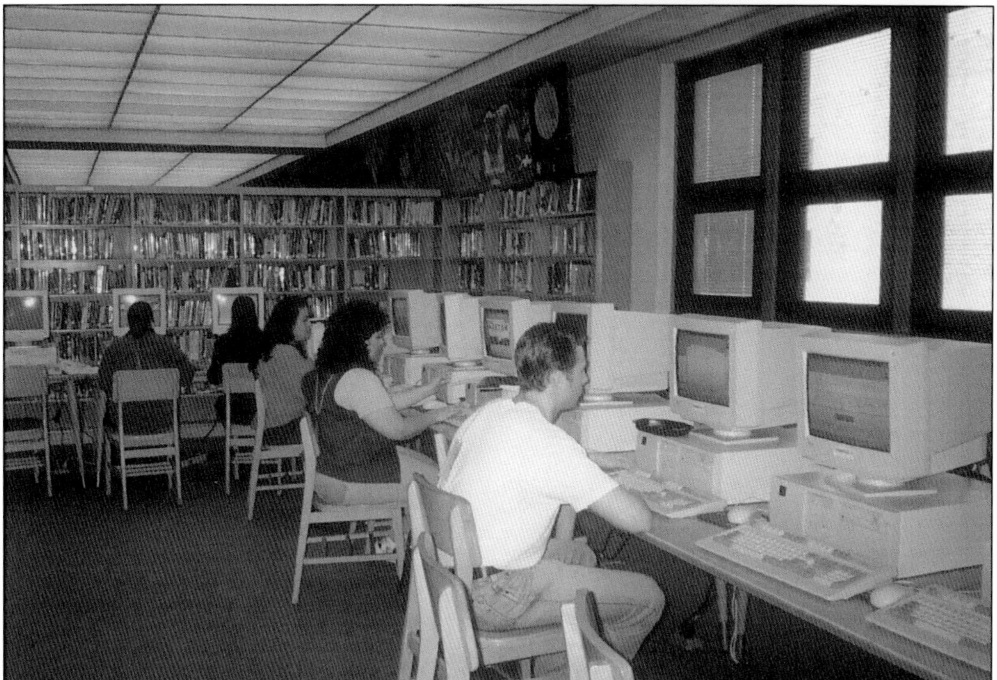

THE MORTON LIBRARY, NOW. Today, the library is housed in what used to be the Administration offices. The first room is filled with heavily used computers. The rear rooms are sometimes used as classrooms or study areas. A serious work atmosphere encourages the students to use their time and their talents well.

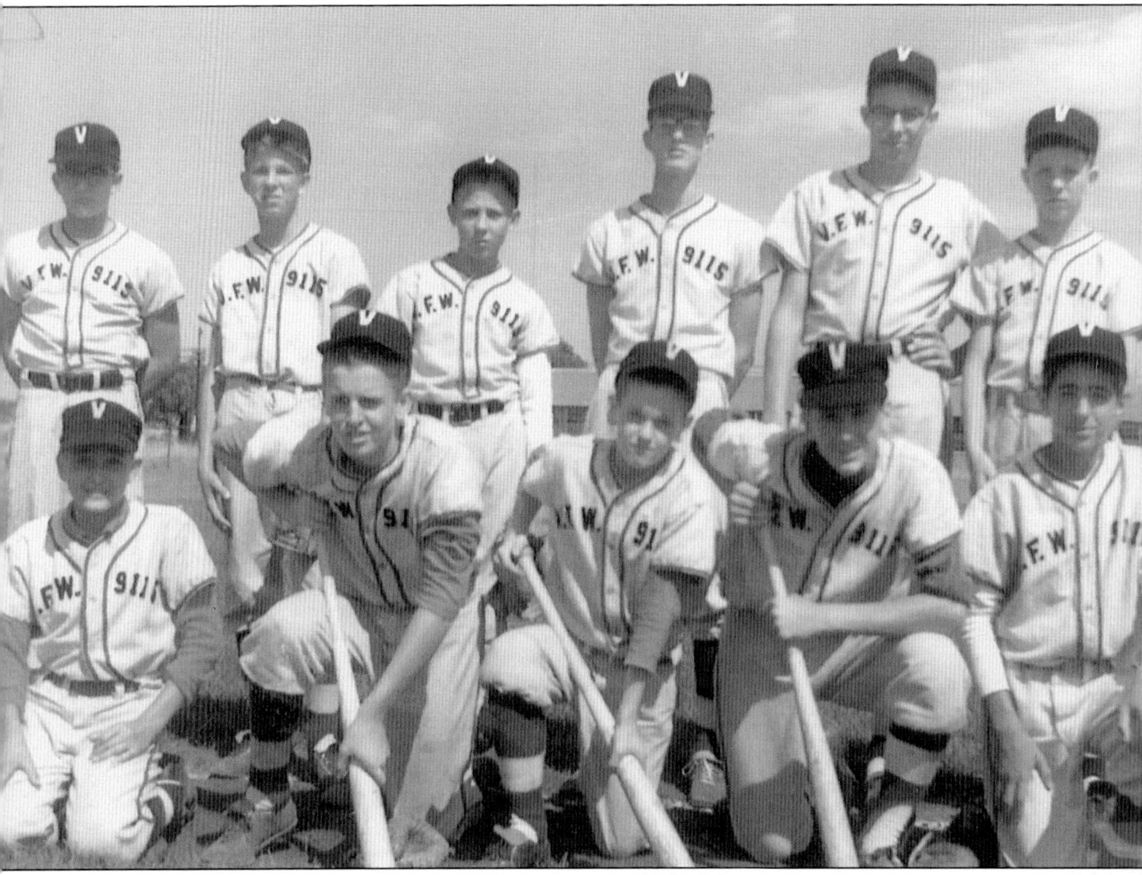

JOE MANTEGNA, THEN. Look carefully and you will find Joe Mantegna as a cute 14-year-old playing on the VFW 9115 team. In the top row, second from right, is Dennis Waldon. Kneeling at the far right is Joe. (Courtesy Dennis Waldon.)

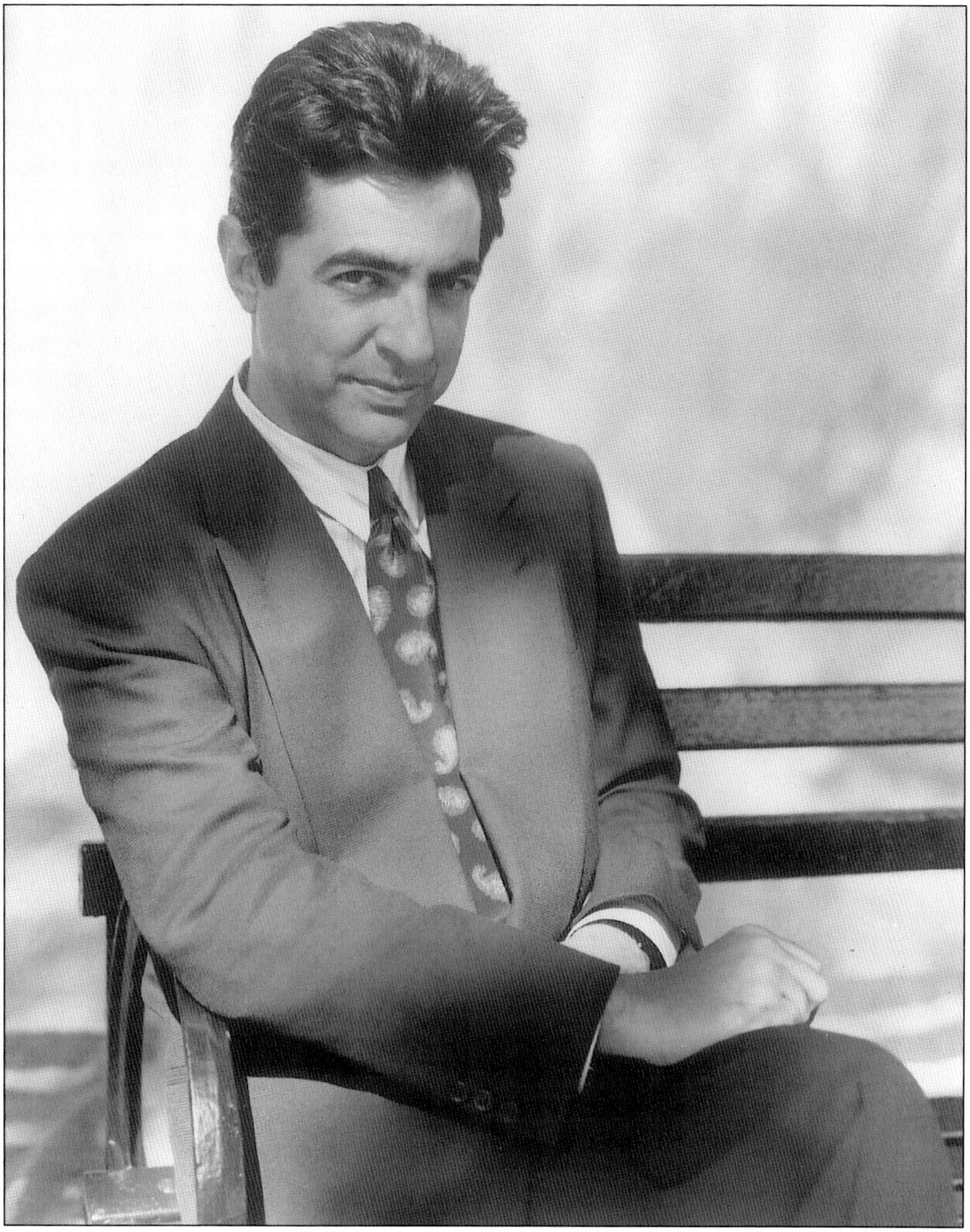

Joe Mantegna, Today. Joe Mantegna was awarded the Tony and Joseph Jefferson Awards for his acclaimed performance as "Richard Roma" in David Mamet's Pulitzer Prize-winning play *Glengarry Glen Ross*. Joe began his career in Chicago at the Organic Theater and the Goodman Theater. He recently completed production on his feature film directorial debut, *Lakeboat*. (Courtesy Joe Mantegna.)

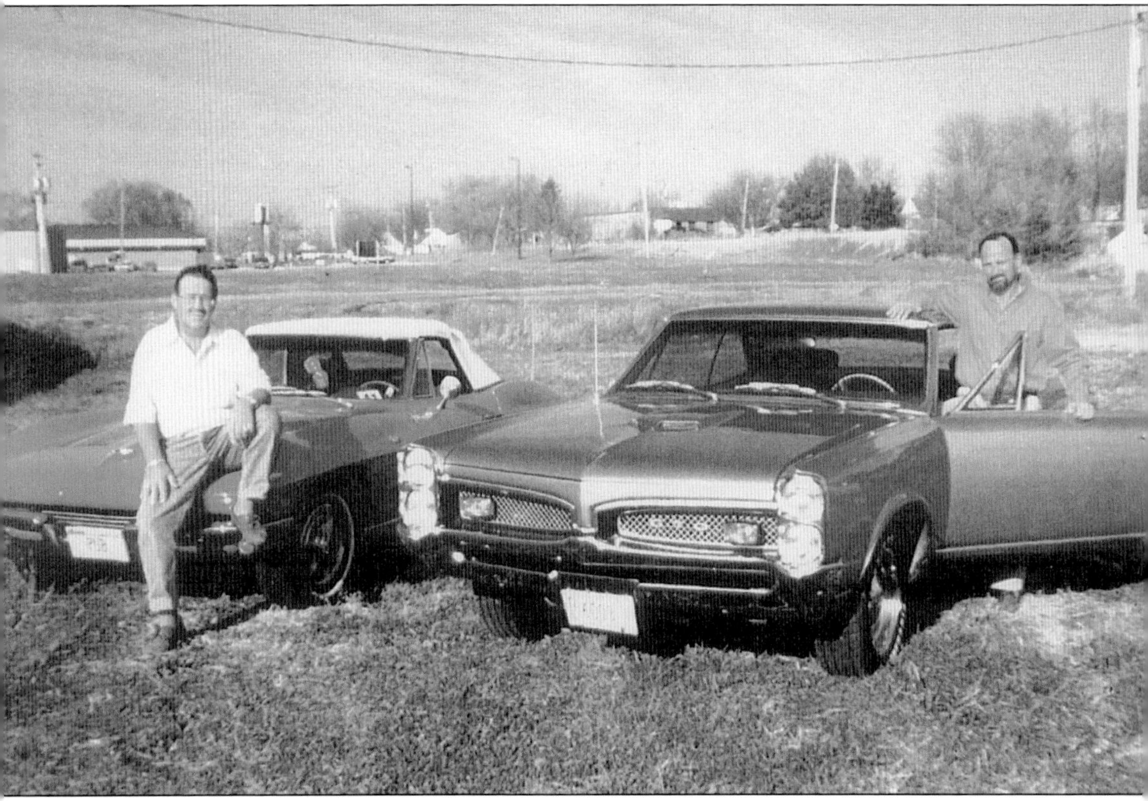

Old Cars Now and Then. John Rokos and Ron Hainrihar pose with cars like the ones they owned in the 1960s. John acquired this '63 Corvette Stingray in the 1980s to mirror the one he owned then, and the '67 Pontiac GTO in the 1990s, to mirror the car Ron owned. When the old friends go riding nowadays, they have plenty of time to recall the cars they drove, the friends they knew, and the Cicero of then and now. (Courtesy John Rokos.)